DATE DUE		
10-1-90		

One Hundred Years of Anthropology

One Hundred Years

EDITED WITH AN INTRODUCTION

1968   Cambridge,   Massachusetts

# of Anthropology

BY J. O. BREW

Harvard University Press

Contents

One Hundred Years of Anthropology

J. O. Brew / Introduction

On Saturday, October 8, 1966, the Peabody Museum of Archaeology and Ethnology at Harvard University had its one hundredth birthday. The event was celebrated the evening before by a party in the Museum and by a dinner in Memorial Hall, where some four hundred and fifty graduates, friends, faculty, and staff were assembled. Portraits of Mr. George Peabody, the founder, and of his great friend, Robert C. Winthrop, Chairman of the Board of Trustees for the first twenty-eight years, gazed down on the affair.

It was a festive occasion, one of the few times in which cocktails have been provided and tobacco freely smoked in the halls of the Museum. During the course of the dinner and subsequent toasts in the most appropriate setting of Memorial Hall, fifteen cases of wine were consumed. The festivities were highly enjoyable and edifying to all concerned; so, too, was the academic side of the celebration, which had begun earlier that same day and lasted through May of 1967.

At four o'clock on October 7, in Lowell Lecture Hall, Gordon Randolph Willey, Bowditch Professor of Mexican and Central American Archaeology and Ethnology, Harvard University, delivered the first of five Peabody Museum Centennial Lectures, "One Hundred Years of American Archaeology."

Some months before, the Curators of the Museum had met in solemn conclave to determine the best way in which to commemorate the impending anniversary. Because the years during which the Museum has been in existence correspond roughly to the period of the development of anthropology as a respected academic and scientific discipline, it was decided that a series of lectures should be given. Each of the lectures would discuss the growth of one of the five major phases of anthropology from 1866 to 1966, without prejudice to, or prohibition against, a salute to earlier manifestations or predictions for the future.

5

Those phases were: American Archaeology, Old World Prehistory, Biological Anthropology, Ethnology and Social Anthropology, and Anthropological Linguistics. The lectures were to be delivered during the course of the academic year.

Leaders in the five fields were selected by the Curators, and the Museum was highly honored by the fact that each of the chosen lecturers accepted the assignment. They were: Gordon Willey of Harvard University; Glyn Daniel of Cambridge University, England; Sherwood Washburn of the University of California at Berkeley; Fred Eggan of the University of Chicago; and Floyd Lounsbury of Yale University. Their lectures were enjoyed by a considerable audience and are presented in this book.

Before proceeding to the lectures themselves, I shall present a brief history of the Museum. Only highlights can be mentioned, since so much has been done in so many different places and in so many different fields. We must start with George Peabody himself. One of many children of an improvident Massachusetts farmer of South Danvers (later named Peabody in his honor), his career transcended those of Horatio Alger's most successful heroes. He became the great innovator of the early and mid-nineteenth century in commerce, international relations, and philanthropy. After apprenticeship to a small shopkeeper in Danvers, and while still in his teens, he inaugurated the dry goods business as a specialty, whereas previously it had been merely a part of the general store. Later, while the American Revolution was still fresh in men's memories, he established the bridge—economic, financial, and intellectual—with Europe. His Fourth of July parties in London were the first to which Englishmen were invited and members of the Royal Family and the Cabinet came (for which he was castigated as a "traitor" by some of our press). He rescued the foundering American Pavilion at the great Crystal Palace Exhibition, his support turning our first "World's Fair" effort into a success. George Peabody and Company, which he founded in London, became the first major commercial and financial agent for American affairs in the Old World. If the wife of the Governor of Maryland wanted two dozen jars of a favorite tooth powder from Paris or if her husband needed $800,000 worth of Sterling to bolster the state finances, George Peabody and Company came through with the goods. When, in the 1850's, Mr. Peabody decided to retire and devote his entire time to his philanthropic program, he looked around his London office for a likely successor to run the business, and picked a young man named Junius Morgan. Eventually, George Peabody and Company became The Morgan Company, which was to continue as the chief European agent of American business and finance for a century.

Mr. Peabody's philanthropies started in London, where he established the Peabody Houses, buying up and knocking down blocks of slums and replacing them with clean, well-equipped, low-rental housing units, the first large-scale application of urban renewal. New blocks of Peabody Houses are still being built under his trust in London. His many charities in England brought about a personal friendship with Queen Victoria (which, again, did not help him with zealous "patriots" at home), and when he died it was proposed that he be buried in Westminster Abbey. His family, however, wanted him home, so he was placed in the Abbey only temporarily, with great ceremony and an overflow crowd standing in the rain outside. A plaque in the floor of the Abbey commemorates his brief interment there. His body was then brought home in Her Majesty's newest man-of-war, *H. M. S. Monarch,* her Captain's saloon transformed to a mourning chamber by Her Majesty's carpenter. There were special trains, with coaches similarly rebuilt, on both sides of the Atlantic and, all in all, the saga of this funeral, which spread over three months, two continents, and the intervening Atlantic Ocean, probably constitutes the most elaborate obsequies of recent times.

Of greatest interest to us here is George Peabody's concept of social service. He was the progenitor of modern philanthropy. His belief was simple, but, in the mid-nineteenth century, revolutionary: namely, that the wealthy people of the world, instead of giving their money exclusively to institutions for the blind, homes for fallen women, and almshouses, should donate a considerable portion of their largesse to organizations whose purpose was to attack social evils at their start, rather than merely to provide care for the irredeemable end results. So, education, slum clearance, community centers, and the like became his aim. He was the first to support such endeavors on an appreciable scale. In fact, the Carnegie, Rockefeller, Ford, and other great educational and scientific foundations in considerable measure owe their existence to the prescience of George Peabody.

Andrew Carnegie, generous in acknowledgment as in other things, wrote that he was indebted to the ideas and example of George Peabody for his own concept of the Carnegie libraries and other philanthropies. Mr. Peabody's largest single gift was the Peabody Foundation for Education in the South. When he realized after the Civil War that the education of youth in the South would be not only a major problem but one to which ordinary resources would not be applied, Mr. Peabody inaugurated the fund that was to become the origin and source of support for many fine institutions of learning in the southern part of our country. This move, also, brought opprobrium upon Mr. Peabody. He was accused of being a "rebel" sympathizer and there was a wide-spread movement to "impeach" him;

but those who espoused this worthy cause could find no way to introduce impeachment proceedings against one who was not a government servant.

We cannot do justice to the man here. On the occasions of Mr. Peabody's visits from his London headquarters to his native land, triumphal arches bridged streets lined with flowers in Baltimore, Washington, and many New England cities and towns; school children paraded, bands played, and orators sang his praises. All these events are now forgotten, which is why some of the main points in his story have been set down here. A definitive biography has been prepared by Professor Franklin Parker, a graduate of Peabody College at the University of Tennessee, and is now being edited by Mrs. Diana Whitehill Laing for publication in connection with the centennial of Peabody's death in 1969.

The Peabody Museum of Archaeology and Ethnology at Harvard was only one of a group of similar institutions which Peabody established or supported in this country. The impetus for this particular benefaction came from a nephew, Othniel Marsh, of the Yale class of 1860. On the occasion of the Museum's twenty-fifth anniversary, he wrote to Professor Putnam as follows: "The first idea of the Peabody Museum at Cambridge occurred to me in October 1865, while digging in an ancient mound near Newark, Ohio, and that evening I wrote to my uncle, Mr. Peabody, at London, urging him to establish such a museum. He had already told me of his intention of making gifts to Harvard and various other institutions and had requested me to look over the ground and give him information on the subject. My own interest in American archaeology was mainly due to Sir Charles Lyell who had just published his 'Antiquity of Man' and, when I saw him in London, he urged me in the strongest terms to take up the subject in America as a new field for exploration . . . When Mr. Peabody came to this country in the following year, I again brought the subject to his attention and at his request consulted with Mr. Winthrop about the matter."

We can do no better at this stage of the narrative than to go to the words of Robert C. Winthrop, long a friend of Mr. Peabody and one of his chief advisers on affairs in New England. Mr. Winthrop's statement has been edited and details not pertinent have been left out. The full text may be seen in the Eleventh Annual Report of the Museum.

On the 1st of June, 1866, I first met Mr. Peabody at the Tremont House in Boston to consult with him on his proposed endowment for Harvard University. Three days afterwards Professor O. C. Marsh of Yale College and Mr. George Peabody Russell, Harvard 1856, both of them nephews of our Founder, called on me at the rooms of the Massachusetts Historical Society. On the 17th of June Mr. Peabody spent an hour with me at Brookline. At this interview he placed in my hands a rough sketch of our Institution, and gave me permission to consult confidentially with one or two of the friends of the University in regard to it.

For this consultation I selected, before all others, President Walker who took the matter into consideration in his calm, wise, commonsense way. He saw, as I did, that in confining his liberality to this one scientific object, Mr. Peabody would disappoint not a few hopes and expectations at Cambridge. [This is a problem not unknown to present university presidents and museum directors.] There were peculiar needs there at that time. The [University] Library was greatly in need. The Museum of

Comparative Zoölogy was not less in need. The general finances of the University were sadly deficient. Meantime, the idea of such an Institution as this had never occurred to anyone, and prehistoric science was too much in its infancy to have enlisted any ardent votaries.

But Dr. Walker soon reached a conclusion, in his own mind, on these and all other points of doubt. I remember how emphatically he said to me: "Mr. Winthrop, I have always been of the opinion that when a generous man, like Mr. Peabody, proposes a great gift, we should accept it on his own terms, not on ours. Even if we could persuade him to change his plans, and endow some other branch of the University, he would never take the same interest in it, or regard it so much as his own. We had better take what he offers, and take it on his own terms, and for the object which he evidently has at heart. The object may not impress the College or the community, at first sight, as one of the highest interest or importance. There may be, and will be, as you say, disappointments in some quarters. But the branch of Science, to which this endowment is devoted, is one to which many minds in Europe are now eagerly turning, and with which not a few of the philosophical inquiries and theories of the hour are intimately associated. It will grow in interest from year to year. This Museum, too, will be the first of its kind in our country, and will have the best chance of securing those relics of our Indian tribes, which are now scattered in so many private collections. It is, moreover, precisely one of those institutions which must necessarily owe its foundation to private liberality. We could never hope to make it the subject of a public subscription or contribution. [This was written before the establishment of the great educational and scientific foundations which George Peabody himself inaugurated, but even so, the Museum is still in considerable part dependent upon the liberality of interested private individuals.] But if Mr. Peabody will make it his own, and endow it handsomely, and if we can get a safe, sound, accomplished person, like Jeffries Wyman, to take charge of it [which they did], there can be no doubt of its ultimate success."

So now we have covered, in brief, the events of the founding of the Peabody Museum. On July 6, 1866, Mr. Winthrop communicated to Mr. Peabody the results of his conversations with President Walker. On September 24, Mr. Winthrop again met with Mr. Peabody and the nephews, Professor Marsh and Mr. Russell, and was instructed to call a meeting of the designated trustees. This meeting was held on September 28, and the Peabody Museum was informally established, to be formalized by the Letter of Gift and Instrument of Trust of October 8, 1866.

In the Instrument of Trust three funds were set up. The income of $45,000 was to be devoted to the acquisition and preservation of objects, including books; $45,000 was assigned to the establishment and maintenance of a Professorship of American Archaeology and Ethnology in Harvard University; and $60,000 was designated as a building fund to be invested and accumulated until it amounted to at least $100,000, at which time it could be used "in the erection of a suitable fire-proof museum building, upon land to be given for that purpose, free of cost or rental, by the President and Fellows of Harvard College." Subsequently we shall see how extraordinarily well the trustees carried out the third provision in this gift.

The letter of gift addressed to the Trustees of the Peabody Museum, dated October 8, 1866, included the following paragraphs:

I have for some years had the purpose of contributing, as I might find opportunity, to extend the usefulness of the honored and ancient University of our Commonwealth; and I trust that in view of the importance and national character of the proposed department, and its interesting relations to kindred investigations in other countries, the means I have chosen may prove acceptable.

Aside from the provisions of the instrument of gift, I leave in your hands the details and management of the trust; only suggesting, that, in view of the gradual obliteration or destruction of the works and remains of the ancient races of this continent, the labor of exploration and collection be commenced at as early a day as practicable; and also, that, in the event of the discovery in America of human remains or implements of an earlier geological period than the present, especial attention be given to their study, and their comparison with those found in other countries.

(signed) George Peabody

The Museum was immediately established with Professor Jeffries Wyman, an eminent natural scientist with a deep interest in the prehistoric American Indian, as Curator. The first exhibit was installed in a case in Boylston Hall, and local people responded liberally to an appeal for specimens. It is interesting to note that of the 36 donors of collections during the first year, 15 were residents of Newburyport and surrounding Essex County towns. Thus, the Museum began with a fine collection of prehistoric Indian artifacts from the Merrimac Valley.

The first purchase of objects by the Museum, arranged during its first year, was of 264 specimens from Northern Europe. This was followed, in the second year, by three other outstanding acquisitions from Europe: the private archaeological collection of Gabriel de Mortillet, the so-called father of prehistoric archaeology in France; the Wilmot J. Rose collection of 1059 archaeological specimens from Denmark and the Duchies of Schleswig and Holstein; and the Clement collection of 865 specimens from the Swiss Lake Dwellings. These were the first extensive collections of prehistoric European archaeological materials to be available for scholars in the New World. Their acquisition established at the outset the Museum's pre-eminence in that field. These efforts culminated in the twentieth century with the research and excavations in Europe, North Africa, and the Middle East of Vladimir Fewkes, Robert Ehrich, Hugh Hencken, Hallam L. Movius, Lauriston Ward, Bruce Howe, Lloyd Cabot Briggs, Marija Gimbutas, and C. C. Lamberg-Karlovsky, and the eventual merger with the American School of Prehistoric Research (founded by the late George Grant MacCurdy), which is now, under the direction of Dr. Hencken, the Department of Old World Prehistory in the Museum.

During the early years, the emphasis of the Museum's acquisitions was on the eastern part of the United States. Extensive collections were accumulated from the New England states, Florida, the middle Atlantic region, Tennessee and the Ohio Valley, Michigan, and Missouri. Then, as the country expanded, the Museum's activities extended to the American Southwest, the Northwest Coast and Alaska, and, during the 1880's, into Middle America, which became one of the major fields of specialization. Much of this had been foreshadowed in the first ten years of the Museum's life, when extensive collections were obtained from Nicaragua, Peru, the Northwest Coast, Alaska, the Aleutian Islands, Brazil, and Oceania. These various collections cannot be listed here, but by the time the first museum building was erected in 1877 there were on hand more than enough specimens to fill it.

One of the most important sources of the earlier collections, and one which clearly demonstrated the need for the Museum, was the gifts received from other scientific societies. Many learned societies throughout Massachusetts possessed collections of anthropological materials which were not germane to their major purposes. Important collections were presented to the Museum by the Boston Athenaeum, the Massachusetts Historical Society, the Boston Marine Society, the Archaeological Institute of America, the American Antiquarian Society, the Boston Museum, the American Academy of Arts and Sciences, the American Philosophical Society, the Peabody Academy of Science, and the Peabody Museum of Salem. There was also, from the beginning, an active exchange of specimens and publications with the Smithsonian Institution and, after they were established, with the American Museum of Natural History in New York, the Pennsylvania Museum, and the R. S. Peabody Foundation for Archaeology in Andover, Massachusetts. In 1871 the Museum of Comparative Zoology presented to the Museum its archaeological and ethnological collections, including a great deal of material accumulated by Professor Louis Agassiz on his various expeditions, and the first objects from Bushman and Ovambo tribes in South Africa to be brought to this country. Thus by the turn of the century the Museum had acquired an enviable collection of materials from all continents and, the Department of Anthropology in the Faculty of Arts and Sciences having by that time been established, teaching materials of a high order were readily available.

The field work undertaken by the Museum beggars description. For the Harvard Tercentenary celebration in 1936, a map was prepared showing 688 expeditions to all parts of the world in which scholars from the Museum had played the leading roles or important parts. In the thirty years since then well over

200 expeditions have been added. In fact, during the Museum's first year, the Curator, Dr. Jeffries Wyman, conducted excavations in shell heaps along the Atlantic Coast and on the banks of the St. Johns River in Florida. During the same year Dr. H. Berendt was commissioned to conduct explorations in Nicaragua. Shell heaps in Maine and Massachusetts were extensively excavated before the Museum was ten years old, and important operations were undertaken in Kentucky, Tennessee, Michigan, Ohio, and Missouri. This activity inaugurated a program in the study of the prehistory of the eastern United States now being continued by Dr. Philip Phillips and Professor Stephen Williams.

Although archaeology received the lion's share of attention during the early years, ethnology was not neglected, particularly after Professor Putnam became Curator in 1875. By 1882 Miss Alice C. Fletcher had been added to the staff and her work on the Omaha is one of the ethnological milestones of American anthropology. Since then there have been excellent contributions in ethnology and social anthropology by that extraordinary ethnographer and teacher, the late Roland B. Dixon, by Carleton S. Coon, Walter B. Cline, Clyde Kluckhohn, Douglas L. Oliver, Cora Du Bois, Evon Z. Vogt, John W. M. Whiting, David H. P. Maybury-Lewis, and others.

Physical anthropology, or somatology as it was then called, also received early attention. Two of the collections recorded in the First Annual Report were a group of 75 crania from Peru, presented by Mr. E. George Squier, and 21 skulls obtained by Mr. Sanford Dole on the Island of Kauai in what were then the Sandwich Islands. Further collections of skeletal material were added annually. In 1882, a physical anthropologist, Miss Cordelia A. Studley, was added to the staff, and in 1896 the first doctorate in physical anthropology was awarded to Frank Russell. He conducted research and taught physical anthropology until his death in 1905, after which the courses were continued by William C. Farabee, who specialized in genetics and first demonstrated Mendelian heredity in man. These scholars set the scene for our brilliant and beloved teacher, Earnest A. Hooton, who came to Harvard in 1913 and who, to quote one of his students, Dr. Edward E. Hunt, Jr., "not only trained most of the best living American physical anthropologists, but stimulated a far larger group of cultural anthropologists to maintain a life-long interest in the biology of man." Upon his death, Hooton was succeeded by Professor William W. Howells, who now gives our courses in physical anthropology, assisted by Drs. Albert Damon, Irven DeVore, and Eugene Giles.

One of the Museum's special areas, as mentioned earlier, was then, and still is, the Middle American field. Although collections and various explorations had been made previously, concerted research effort began in 1888, initiated and financed by Mr. Charles Pickering Bowditch. By 1891 the program was well under way and in July of that year the government of Honduras gave to the Museum, by a special edict, the charge of the antiquities of that country for a term of ten years, with the exclusive right of exploration and with the privilege of bringing to the Museum one half of the collection obtained. Under this concession our great excavation program at the site of Copan was undertaken, the results of which are to be seen in our reports and in the exhibitions on the third floor. With Mrs. Zelia Nuttall continuing her research on Mexican prehistory, Mr. E. H. Thompson working in Yucatan, and Mr. G. A. Dorsey conducting explorations in Ecuador, Peru, and Bolivia, the foundation had been laid for our Latin American studies. These studies have continued ever since, with Professor Alfred

M. Tozzer taking charge in the new century. Dr. Tozzer was an inspired teacher who encouraged and directed two generations of Middle American scholars. The Latin American program continues today, even at an accelerated pace, under the direction of our Bowditch Professor of Mexican and Central American Archaeology and Ethnology, Gordon R. Willey; Curators Harry E. D. Pollock, A. Ledyard Smith, William R. Bullard, Jr., and Thomas Patterson; Research Associates John Ladd, Doris Stone, and Robert Smith; and various graduate students. Again, although archaeology has received the bulk of our attention, ethnology has not been neglected, and a major study is now being made of the vigorous surviving Maya population of Chiapas by Professor Evon Z. Vogt, Curator of Middle American Ethnology, under the joint auspices of the Laboratory of Social Relations and the Museum.

The Ninth Annual Report describes the excavations of Dr. C. C. Parry in southern Utah; during the following five years active excavation was conducted by Dr. Edward Palmer in the American Southwest. The program of studies in that region, so ably carried out by Alfred V. Kidder, Samuel J. Guernsey, Donald Scott, and their successors, did not begin earlier because that field was being actively tilled by another local institution— The Hemenway Southwestern Archaeological Expedition. This was a private research organization founded and financed by Mrs. Mary Hemenway. Its first director was Frank Hamilton Cushing, who was succeeded in 1890 by Jesse Walter Fewkes. Since the husband of the founder, Augustus Hemenway, and Dr. Fewkes were both members of the Museum's Visiting Committee, there was obviously a close connection between the Expedition and the Museum. Dr. Fewkes was also the editor of the Expedition which published *A Journal of American Ethnology and Archaeology* in five volumes. Extensive excavations were conducted by the Expedition in Arizona and New Mexico, and excellent ethnological collections were made from the Hopi and Zuni Pueblo Indians. Upon Mrs. Hemenway's death the entire holdings of the Expedition came to the Museum.

Mr. Peabody directed, in his letter of gift to the trustees on October 8, 1866, that ". . . in the event of the discovery in America of human remains or implements of an earlier geological period than the present, especial attention be given to their study, and their comparison with those found in other countries." The Museum's work in comparative studies in the Palaeolithic in the Old World is outstanding and has been mentioned above. In the New World, early man studies have, for the most part, occurred only within the last 25 years. Professor Putnam was one of the few scholars in the nineteenth century who believed in the antiquity of man in the New World. Assiduously, throughout his forty years as head of the Museum, he encouraged and supported the search for evidence, beginning in 1875 with the examination of the Trenton gravels in New Jersey. This was followed by work in peats and gravels in Pennsylvania, Ohio, and Indiana and in the auriferous gravels of Calaveras and Tuolumne counties in California. In the twentieth century, excavations were conducted in deep deposits of southwestern Texas and southeastern Colorado. During the past decade expeditions from the Museum have made outstanding discoveries in New Mexico, Colorado, Wyoming, Idaho, Mexico, and Peru. Occupation sites dated as early as the twelfth millennium, B.C., and probably earlier, have been found; house remains antedating 8000 B.C., some five thousand years earlier than any previously dated structures in the New World, have been uncovered at Hell Gap, Wyoming; the earliest Indian corn, from the fourth millennium B.C., was encountered at Bat Cave in the Plains of San Águstin in New Mexico; and many finds are constantly filling the gap between the days of the very early hunters and the civilized tribes which occupied so much of the United States at the beginning of the Christian era.

The Peabody Museum Library, now pre-eminent in the world of anthropology, with over 90,000 titles, did not begin so impressively as did the collections and the research program. This is understandable in a new field which, in 1866, was not even established as a respectable academic subject. There were few books in anthropology, and the people who were to write them were busily at work in the field or, for the most part, still unborn. There were no "professional" anthropologists and no courses of study in the universities. The Peabody Museum and Professor Putnam were to lay the ground work, and it would be three decades before the results would appear in college catalogues and on library shelves.

The First Annual Report lists the gift of only four titles and one of these was the Catalogue of the Ward Series of Fossils. The first book presented to the library is, however, of unusual interest. It is, in fact, an ethnological specimen as well as a bibliographic curiosity. It bears a date of 1859 and was presented at Gotthavn in Greenland by Governor Rink to P. A. Chadbourne of Williams College, who gave it to the Museum. The following inscription occurs in the first volume: "The first book ever printed in Greenland. Written, printed and bound by Esquimaux. Dr. Rink imported a small screw printing press and gave them such instruction in regard to printing and engraving as he could." The text is in both Eskimo and Danish and the title is *Kaladlit Okalluktualliait* or *Gronlandsk Folkesagn.*

When Professor Putnam was appointed Curator in 1875 he realized the absolute necessity of a good library. In the Tenth

Annual Report he wrote: "During the year there have been a few additions to the limited library of the Museum, and we may hope that as it becomes known that the formation of a library is one of the objects of the trust, authors will send copies of their papers on anthropological subjects, either as donations or in exchange for the publications of the Museum."

The results of Mr. Putnam's suggestion were immediately evident. During the succeeding year, the holdings of the library were doubled, and gifts came in from 21 authors. At the same time, Mr. Putnam began urging the Trustees to approve the publication of a special series of papers by the Museum. Up to this time, and for a number of years to come, scientific reports were included as appendices to the Annual Reports. The Curator pointed out that one of the advantages of a separate series would be the possibility of exchange with other learned bodies and with individual authors, which in turn would aid in augmenting the holdings of the library. Approval of this policy bore ample fruit, and by the time of the hundredth anniversary the Museum publication list presented five series of monographs: The Papers of the Peabody Museum with 57 volumes, including 119 individual monographs to date; the Memoirs, restricted to Middle American Archaeology, a quarto series in 13 volumes; the Harvard African Studies in 10 volumes; 21 Bulletins of the American School of Prehistoric Research, of which 5 have been issued since the School became part of the Museum; and 7 numbers of the Russian Translation Series. There have also been several special publications, including two albums of primitive music and two ethnographic sound films.

It will be remembered that Mr. Peabody's Instrument of Trust set up a building fund of $60,000 to be left to accumulate until it reached $100,000. The fund prospered, as would be expected of any fund in the hands of Massachusetts trustees. The goal was reached on January 15, 1876, the actual figure being $103,836.19. Thereupon a building committee composed of Robert C. Winthrop, Stephen Salisbury, and Asa Gray recommended that "the work should be undertaken at once." The committee was "moved to come to this conclusion, *primarily,* by the great and growing want of accommodation for the collections of the Museum. We cannot do justice to the treasures which have been gathered from so many sources . . . without much larger space than our present temporary rooms . . . Meantime [we] cannot but remember that it is a peculiar and favorable moment for entering upon such a work, and that contracts for its execution may now be made to great pecuniary advantage."

Not only did the Building Fund show a steady increase during the crippling financial panic of 1873 and its long aftermath, but the Trustees wasted no time in getting to work to take advantage of the depressed state of trade. It is interesting to note, also, that the first segment of the building is the most soundly constructed.

Some mention of the basic relationship between the Museum and Harvard University is needed here. The Museum was built on University land. When constructed, the first two sections of the building became by mutual agreement the property of the University. The Museum was intended by Mr. Peabody to be a part of the University and was designed and built in conformity with Professor Louis Agassiz's over-all plan for the science museum building complex. (This far-sighted plan was actually completed by the final addition to the Peabody Museum in 1914 and exists today as Agassiz conceived it except for the great dome over the central section on Oxford Street

Years of American Archaeology

THE PAST HUNDRED YEARS—the lifetime of Harvard's Peabody Museum—span almost the entire growth of American archaeology as a scientific and an academic discipline. To summarize the history of this discipline is no small task, especially if one assumes that archaeology is at once the substance of prehistory and the methods and theories whereby this substance has been assembled and interpreted. What I can offer in the compass of a brief paper is, at best, a sketch of highlights and of main trends.

To set forth these highlights and trends I have devised an historical scheme of four periods.[1] The earliest of these periods was a pioneer or preparatory era, which actually antedates our past hundred years; however, it is important to a proper perspective of the subject. It begins with the European discoveries of the New World and lasts up until the middle of the nineteenth century. It will be called the "Speculative Period," a designation which captures the prevailing archaeological spirit of those times.

The second period is termed the "Descriptive Period." It saw the beginning of systematic and descriptive archaeology. Starting in the mid-nineteenth century, it lasted until the early twentieth. The Peabody Museum, which we celebrate, was founded early in this period.

The third period, the "Descriptive-Historic," followed after the second decade of the twentieth century. It was the time of the "stratigraphic revolution" in American archaeology and of a concerted attack upon problems of chronology. This period continued up until about 1950.[2]

From 1950 to the present we have been witnessing new trends which, I believe, will culminate in a fourth period. These new trends are concerned with natural environmental, social, and

NOTE: Gordon Randolph Willey is Bowditch Professor of Mexican and Central American Archaeology and Ethnology at Harvard University.

cultural contexts; but they also go beyond the reconstruction of contexts to comparative considerations of structure and function in past societies and cultures, and aim toward an understanding of causality in human events. I shall call the trends, or the period, the "Comparative-Historic."[3]

THE SPECULATIVE PERIOD
(EUROPEAN DISCOVERY TO MID-NINETEENTH CENTURY)

Wonder and curiosity are the precursors of knowledge, and, when directed to phenomena not easily susceptible of explanation, speculation is the result. In the early sixteenth century, the unknown New World and its inhabitants were a source of infinite wonder. Who were these people of the Americas? From where had they come? And when? What was the history of the civilizations seen on this side of the Atlantic, so tantalizingly similar to those of the Old World and yet so oddly different? These are some of the main questions of American archaeology—certainly not fully answered even today. At the time of Columbus they gave rise to a spate of speculation, which continued and mounted in the ensuing centuries. Much of the speculation was bizarre and fantastic. It was indulged in by explorers, soldiers, priests, travelers, historians, and, in later years, by persons whose principal avocation was archaeology. In judging it, one must keep in mind that, in the sixteenth and seventeenth centuries, geographical knowledge of the world was hazy, and history was a pastiche of the biblical and classical. Later, geography was better understood, but historical perspective remained limited by theological considerations. The nature of much of the speculation about the American Indian can be attributed to these circumscribing factors, but sheer exuberant imagination was a factor too.

One of the earliest theories about the American natives came from Peter Martyr, a well-known historian of the period of the conquest. Martyr held that they were Ethiopians who had found their way to Yucatan. Lopez de Gomara was equally convinced that the American Indians were Canaanites. A Dutch professor named Horn saw a much more complex set of origins and voyages, involving Norwegians, Celts, Carthaginians, and Chinese.[4] Another favorite hypothesis—and certainly one with a high survival value down through the years—considered the Indians as descendants of the "Ten Lost Tribes of Israel," who, in customs, language, and racial appearance, were said to be strikingly similar to Peruvians or Aztecs. This is but the merest sampling. Welsh, Hindus, Scythians, Tartars, Phoenicians, Huns, Greeks, miscellaneous "Mahometans," and the men of "Lost Atlantis" also were advanced to play the part of ancestors of the American Indian. By the late eighteenth century so many changes had been rung on the identity and homeland of the ancient immigrants to the New World that there was little room for originality. So distinguished a person as the president of Yale, in an address in 1783, simply contented himself with "the Canaanites of the expulsion of Joshua"—Lopez de Gomara's old choice—to explain the presence of the American natives.[5]

More strictly archaeological activity—including expeditions into the field, archival research, and museum study—tended to replace speculation in the early half of the nineteenth century, but the transition was certainly not a sudden one. Moreover, in many instances, some of the most distinguished archaeological scholars also sailed the wilder shores of romantic fancy. Kingsborough brought out his celebrated *Antiquities of Mexico* in 1831.[6] In many ways a contribution to scholarship, with its hundreds of illustrations of codices and specimens, it was, at the same time, a labor devoted to the demonstration of the "Lost Tribes of Israel" hypothesis. In France, that impressive student of Americana, the Abbé Brasseur de Bourbourg, who, among other works, had translated the *Popol Vuh*, spent his declining years in the pursuit of "Lost Atlantis."[7] And, in North America, Caleb Atwater, the closest thing to a professional field archaeologist of his time, and the author of a carefully compiled study of Ohio mounds and earthworks, was unshaken in his opinion that the cultivated builders of these mounds were wanderers from far-off "Hindostan," and quite separate and distinct from the later and inferior American Indians.[8] Nor were similar ideas to pass from the scene after American archaeology had assumed a more dignified and scientific bearing. As we know, they still crop up. Nevertheless, a new attitude was in the making in the middle of the nineteenth century.

This attitude had earlier roots. These go back to the factual discoveries and descriptions of some of the first Conquistadores—to men such as Bernal Diaz or Cieza de Leon.[9] Later, there were descriptions of ruins, often commissioned by the Spanish Crown or governmental authorities, such as those of Garcia de Palacio on Copan or Del Rio on Palenque.[10] These reports, and others like them, date all the way from the sixteenth to the nineteenth century. For the Maya area of Central America, they were climaxed by the vivid descriptions and excellent drawings of John Lloyd Stephens and Frederick Catherwood, published in 1841–1843.[11] In America north of Mexico, the Bartrams described Indian mounds in Georgia and Florida in the eighteenth century. Their accounts were straightforward; they did not speculate beyond saying that they were unconvinced that these works in any way related to the Old World.[12] Thomas Jefferson scored a "first" by excavating an Indian mound in Virginia and keeping careful notes of the excavations. His few speculations about the American Indians strike a very conservative note. He saw physical and linguistic resemblances to certain northeast Asiatics, but was hesitant to declare for either an Asia-to-America or an America-to-Asia route of migration via the Bering Strait.[13] Atwater's mound explorations in the Ohio Valley have been mentioned; but in North America the nearest counterpart to the work of Stephens and Catherwood was that of Squier and Davis who surveyed and excavated mounds in the Ohio and Mississippi Valleys and published a notable volume on these activities in 1848.[14]

By the 1850's the purely speculative in American archaeology was beginning to be rejected, at least in what might be called the "scientific establishment" of the United States. In fact, there was such an establishment, the newly founded Smithsonian Institution—which had published the Squier and Davis survey and, a few years later, brought out a long summary essay on the status of American prehistory. This latter was a most interesting work. Written by a man named Samuel F. Haven, and entitled *Archaeology of the United States,* it was published in 1856.[15] It bears the approval of the first Secretary of the Smithsonian, Joseph Henry—at that time clearly recognized as the leading scientist of the country. The Haven essay is the first synthesis of North American archaeology. The style is lucid, the tone magisterial. It is as though Haven had set himself the task—or, perhaps, the task had been set for him by Secretary Henry—of passing a fair, but stern, judgment on all that had been written previously on the topic of North American prehistory and ethnology. He opens with fifty pages which review, with polite, but cold, skepticism, all of those speculations on the origins, affiliations, voyages, and migrations of the Precolumbian Americans. Twenty pages are devoted to linguistics and their importance in historical reconstruction, with special commendation for the work of Albert Gallatin. In thirty-three pages he agrees with the leading physical anthropologists of that day that the American Indians constituted a distinct race, but one with "Mongolian" affinities. Only thirty pages are devoted to the antiquities themselves, and even these reveal how very little was then known, especially north of Mexico. Finally, he concludes with twenty pages of opinion which can be read as a base-line statement of what was known and not known about American archaeology a little over one hundred years ago.

In these conclusions, Haven first repudiated, almost without exception, the speculations of three-and-a-half centuries. He saw archaeology as factual and descriptive; he was a spokesman for the new era. In the speculation he does allow, he opts for a Bering Strait or an Aleutian route of migration from Asia to the New World. The people he designates as northeastern Asiatics, otherwise unidentified. He is cautious of making any estimates as to age. What Haven wanted was sufficient time for the physical and linguistic diversity of the American Indian to have taken place without—if possible—violating generally accepted (presumably theological) estimates of man's time on the globe. While not rejecting all ancient transoceanic voyages from the Old World to the New, he concludes that if such voyages occurred, their racial, linguistic, or cultural impress on the Americas was nil. Haven made few comments concerning internal diffusions within the New World, but he had little real distributional information at hand. At that time, the archaeology of the United States was largely that of the mounds and earthworks of the east. He observed that the artifacts found within the mounds were of kinds and numbers possessed by the historic American Indian groups and that in the southern states the early Spanish explorers saw no discrepancy between the social conditions of the natives and their works of art and literature. In a word, he rejected the separation of Indian and "Mound Builder"—a dispute that was to carry over, however, for several decades after 1856. Finally, Haven contrasted North American antiquities with those of Mexico and Peru, noting the developmental differences but making no statements about possible relationships.

THE DESCRIPTIVE PERIOD
(MID-NINETEENTH TO EARLY TWENTIETH CENTURY)

The factual tone and the emphasis on the descriptive as opposed to the speculative that are seen in Haven's account reflect the rise of the scientific attitude in the mid-nineteenth century. This was an age of philosophical rationalism that was to nurture Darwin, and an age that Darwin, in turn, did so much to promulgate. Specifically, for archaeology, a systematic trend had its beginnings in Europe, in the 1830's, with the classificatory studies of the Danish prehistorian Thomsen.[16] Lyell's demonstration of the vast reaches of geologic time and Boucher de Perthes's discoveries of Paleolithic artifacts in Pleistocene strata gave added impetus to the trend; and these were capped in 1859 by Darwin's theory of evolution.[17] The influences of these events were seen in America shortly afterward.[18] In fact, the founding of the Peabody Museum at Harvard, in 1866, was very definitely related to them. Lyell interested Professor O. C. Marsh in the study of archaeology, urging him to pursue it in America. Marsh, in turn, urged his uncle, George Peabody, to establish the museum at Cambridge. Further, it is of special interest to note that the archaeological researches of Jeffries Wyman, the first director or curator of the museum, were in Florida shell heaps not unlike the Danish kitchen middens explored by the followers of Thomsen.[19]

A scientific attack upon the problem of man's origins—or, at least, his antiquity—in the New World was stimulated by European geological and Paleolithic archaeological studies. For much of the latter half of the nineteenth century overoptimism and incautious enthusiasm prevailed; none of the examples adduced to demonstrate early man in the Americas was able to stand up to critical scrutiny.[20] Eventually, the case for Pleistocene man would be won, but this takes us ahead of the story. For the time, it was an advance in attitude, if nothing else: a specific problem could be investigated by field work. The same attitude was to prove more fruitful in other directions. The old argument of the Ohio Valley "Mound Builders" as a mysterious and gifted race who built the fabulous earthworks but were then driven out by the uncouth American Indian was scuttled by a linking of ethnography, ethnohistory, and archaeology. Cyrus Thomas demonstrated what Haven had believed earlier—a cultural continuity between the peoples who had made the mounds and their Indian descendants of the historic period.[21] This same procedure—a working back from the ethnographic present to the archaeological past (later dignified by the name "direct-historical approach")—was followed by Cushing who led the Hemenway expedition in the southwestern United States, seeking the prehistoric ancestors of the Zuni tribe.[22] Through all of these new developments there ran the thread of professionalization, of improving standards of archaeological work. The leading figure in this in the United States was another director of the Peabody Museum, F. W. Putnam, who, in addition to building up this institution and founding other museums and departments of anthropology, found time to indoctrinate a new generation of students with modernized excavation and field recording techniques.[23]

In many ways the archaeology of late nineteenth century Mexico and Central America was ahead of that of the United States. For one thing, there was simply a greater richness to its content, and this gave greater and more interesting descriptive substance to the writings about it. Contrast, for example, Stephens and Catherwood with Squier and Davis. Also, in

Mexico and the Maya area there had been a native literature, and this offered problems of epigraphy and documentary study that attracted outstanding European scholars—for the most part of a humanistic rather than a natural science bent. Brasseur de Bourbourg translated native manuscripts; Ernst Forstemann deciphered parts of the Dresden Codex; and the erudite Eduard Seler began his researches of codices and iconography.[24] North Americans also participated in such studies. The Peabody Museum's Charles P. Bowditch became an authority on Maya astronomy, and it was also through his interests that a long-time program of field and library investigations was launched in Maya archaeology.[25] Among his other important contributions, Bowditch was responsible for bringing Harvard's great teacher, Alfred Tozzer, into Middle American studies.[26]

Peru—an area rich in archaeological monuments and iconography, but lacking in native documents—had the good fortune to receive the early attentions of that indefatigable field worker, Max Uhle. Already knowledgeable in Peruvian and Bolivian antiquities from his work in the Berlin museum, Uhle explored the central Andes and the Peruvian coast at the close of the nineteenth and into the early twentieth century. His greatest contribution was the establishment of a four-period, area-wide archaeological chronology based on stylistic seriations of pottery from graves. Working back from the historic horizon, he recognized an Incaic, an immediately pre-Incaic, a Tiahuanaco, and a pre-Tiahuanaco period. In 1900 this was the only archaeological area chronology in the New World, and it has stood the test of all subsequent research.[27]

Curiously, archaeological chronology, and stratigraphy as a means to such chronology, remained in their infancy throughout the Descriptive Period. Frequent gross observations were made on superposition in refuse strata, in structures, or in graves; and, on occasion, differences in pottery or other artifacts were correlated with these observations, but, for some reason, this did not seem to lead on to the establishment of local, regional, or areal culture sequences.[28] The Uhle sequence, just mentioned, was derived from stylistic seriation rather than stratigraphy. I would surmise that the reason for this delay in adopting the stratigraphic method in American archaeology had something to do with the kind of analogy that was then drawn between the geological and chronological uses of stratigraphy. In Europe, stratigraphy was a discovery of the geologists, and, as far as archaeology was concerned, it was first employed most successfully and spectacularly in Paleolithic deposits.[29] These deposits involved great spans of time and, frequently, interpositions of Pleistocene geological and archaeological strata. In the New World, as we have noted, the early attempts to demonstrate man's great antiquity under similar circumstances were not successful. It is very likely that this tended to discredit stratigraphic methods in the eyes of many American archaeologists; and the close association, in their minds, of stratigraphy and geological strata left them disinclined to apply the method to the study of time change in later prehistoric deposits where geological strata were not involved. In any event, the stratigraphic method did not become truly viable in American archaeology until after 1920.

We may take a retrospective glance at the achievements of the Descriptive Period in American archaeology by contrasting the chapter on the Americas in Kroeber's first edition of *Anthropology* with Haven's earlier summary.[30] Kroeber's résumé was published in 1923, and, although successful stratigraphic studies had been conducted in Mexico and the North American Southwest a few years before this, it may be taken as a statement pertaining largely to the pre-stratigraphic era.

On the question of man's origin in the New World, Kroeber does not differ significantly from Haven. In brief, New World peoples are Mongoloids who entered the western hemisphere from Asia by way of the Bering Strait. As to chronology for this event, Kroeber surmised that the first migrations took place at about 8000 B.C. He had no hard evidence upon which to base this; instead, he reasoned, as had Haven, that an appreciable span of time had been necessary for the physical and linguistic differentiation of New World man. In addition, he was aided by increased knowledge of Old World Paleolithic archaeology and dating estimates there. If, as he believed, the New World was not settled until the close of the Paleolithic, 8000 B.C. was a reasonable estimate. Kroeber was puzzled by the "gap" between the arrival of the earliest Americans and the beginnings of the much later agricultural societies. It was his feeling that little of "wide significance" happened during that long time. He saw maize cultivation as probably beginning in southern Mesoamerica, and he thought that pottery probably had a "substantially contemporaneous" origin in the same geographical center. He followed Spinden in placing these beginnings at about 3000 B.C.[31] For the southwestern United States, Kroeber reports a culture sequence of pit-houses preceding above-ground pueblos, but few other details of this sequence had been synthesized for him to draw upon. A year later he would have had Kidder's "Introduction" as a source.[32] A page on the Peruvian area is clearly grounded in Uhle's chronology. Statements about Mexico and Central America indicate some awareness of time depth for the area—derived largely from native calendars or quasihistorical sources—but little more. Joyce's volumes on Mexico and Central America, published a short while before, would have been representative of the amount and kind of detail then known for Mesoamerica.[33] For the eastern United States a number of Ohio Valley cultures had been defined, but their chronological positions were uncertain.

In spite of the lack of chronological information, Kroeber's outlook was, nevertheless, resolutely historical and evolutionary. In this his summary differs from Haven's. He felt that the Mexican and Peruvian societies had evolved from simple village life, through political states, and on to empires. The lesser achievements of peoples in areas marginal to Mesoamerica and Peru were viewed in the perspective of diffusion and culture lag. There was in his thinking an ever-present time-scale against which he considered the actual—and the hypothetical—events of New World culture history. He referred to the probable several millennia of the "gap," between the earliest Americans and the rise of settled farmers, if only to indicate that our knowledge of this time span was woefully inadequate. It did not matter that there was then no reliable means to date these millennia. The important thing was the necessity for considering the data of American archaeology in a framework of time. In this he was ahead of most of his contemporaries, and he fore-shadowed the major emphasis of the next period of American archaeological history.

THE DECRIPTIVE-HISTORIC PERIOD
(EARLY TWENTIETH CENTURY TO 1950)

Shortly before the first world war, Gamio and Boas demonstrated a three-period stratigraphic culture sequence in the Valley of Mexico—based on refuse layers containing potsherds and figurine fragments.[34] Then, in 1914, N. C. Nelson led the way to the "stratigraphic revolution" in the southwestern United States with potsherd stratigraphy; and Kidder drove the point home, a few years later, with his large-scale digging in a deep rubbish mound at the Pecos pueblo.[35] From that time forward, American archaeology was fully committed to chronology. Our name for this new period, Descriptive-Historic, is intended to emphasize a continuity of objectives with the preceding period, but with the added new concern of the vital dimension of history—time.

The early man front was reopened with the discoveries of distinctive projectile point types in association with Pleistocene fauna at Folsom, New Mexico, in 1927.[36] In the next few years comparable discoveries were made in other locations in New Mexico, Colorado, and Texas.[37] In 1938, associations of man and extinct fauna were reported from the bottom layer of a deep stratigraphic column at the Strait of Magellan, in far-southern South America.[38] Now ancient man was established for the geographical range of the Americas. The route by which he had entered from Asia was given closer attention by archaeologists and geologists, and some attempts were made to relate the early American chipped stone industries to those of Siberia and the Old World. These attempts were hampered, however, by the vagueness of geological and glacial dating and by lack of knowledge of Asian archaeology.[39] Kroeber, in his second edition of *Anthropology,* in 1948, sums up the dating estimates on early man in the Americas as ranging from his earlier guess date of 8000 B.C. back to 25,000 years ago.[40] He also expresses the generally held opinion of the time that no specific Old World derivations for Folsom, Clovis, and related industries were known.

The great chronological "gap" between early man and the later prehistoric cultures, which had bothered Kroeber in 1923, was still there in 1948.[41] By this time the western Desert cultures and the Archaic cultures of eastern North America were known, but not fully appreciated as to time range.[42] In looking back, we now see that this "gap" was, to a very great extent, an artifact of the lag in applying stratigraphic procedures in American archaeology. Remains were thought of either as dating from remote Pleistocene times or as being the residue of the more or less immediate ancestors of the historic Indians.

The stratigraphic sequences of the Descriptive-Historic Period had begun to correct this, but the "gap" would not be closed until after the advent of radiocarbon dating. Progress was rapid in the chronological organization of later cultures. The North American Southwest boomed—and Peabody Museum archaeologists had a large part in the boom. Systematic survey and digging led to a number of regional chronologies; tree rings provided absolute dating for some of these. The four major sub-areal divisions of Anasazi, Hohokam, Mogollon, and Patayan were blocked out.[43] In the eastern United States stratigraphic-based culture sequences sprang up in the wake of the numerous Federal Relief-supported archaeological programs. By the 1940's, syntheses appeared that set a chronological framework for the area.[44] It had become apparent that, following a long Archaic period, there were two mound constructional and ceremonial climaxes, an earlier "Burial Mound" and a later "Temple Mound." The latter, associated with Mississippian tradition cultures, was clearly Mesoamerican-influenced; the other, seen in a setting of the Woodland cultural tradition, was much less certainly so. On the Great Plains, archaeology became firmly hooked to a "direct-historical" approach, and the ancestors of many of the colorful horse nomads of the nineteenth century were seen to be riverine farmers whose traditions stemmed from the East.[45] In the Arctic, a long prehistoric continuum led directly into modern Eskimo communities; but one of the biggest surprises from this area was the discovery of the extraordinary Ipiutak culture of the Arctic Ocean, with its Scytho-Siberian derived ivory art.[46]

In Mesoamerica, G. C. Vaillant went on from the earlier pre-Toltec-Toltec-Aztec chronology of Gamio to detail a finely calibrated sequence for the Valley of Mexico.[47] Caso outlined a chronology for Monte Alban; and in the Maya Lowlands the traditional studies of architecture, art, and hieroglyphic dating were at last related to stratigraphic sequences of ceramics and artifacts by Carnegie Institution archaeologists.[48] The major Olmec art style first attracted wide attention, although its chronological position remained undecided.[49] Maya civilization of the highlands, as well as the lowlands, finally received proper attention; and archaeologists began to appreciate the horizontal force and significance of Teotihuacan.[50] In Peru, the Chavín horizon was revealed, preceding the four-period sequence of the Uhle chronology; and beneath Chavín were the still earlier levels of the preceramic coastal cultures.[51] In the West Indies, Rouse was well under way with his highly systematic spatial-temporal organization of the prehistory of those islands.[52]

In contrast to the intensive effort on areal chronologies, extra-areal or inter-areal studies were relatively rare. This seems a logical situation; it was first necessary to establish culture sequence reference points before wider relationships could be studied. The few writings addressed to problems of inter-areal connections were rather tentative.[53] It was beginning to be evident that stylistic patterns rarely overran culture area boundaries, with the result that diffusional connections had to be traced by criteria of a less specific nature than those of style. This raised questions of time-lag which could not be settled without means of absolute dating.

On the possibility of transoceanic contacts between the Old World and the Americas, it is interesting to note that Kroeber, in 1948, maintained the same position held by Haven in 1856. In a word, such contacts may have occurred, but, if so, they were insignificant in the development of New World culture history.

Kroeber's 1948 summary shows progress with culture chronology in a few places other than those mentioned, principally in California, but vast territories were still known only descriptively and in a most limited way. Among these were the northern Andes, the tropical and temperate lowlands of South America, and much of western North America. The job of chronological ordering had begun, but was by no means finished.

Although chronology was the principal theme of the Descriptive-Historic Period, there were other concerns, and some of these point the way to the developments of the next period. A well-known example would be Spinden's hypothesis about the rise of New World civilizations. It was his opinion, as early as 1917, that the high cultures of Peru and Mexico, as well as many of the simpler cultures of areas peripheral to these centers, rested upon a platform of village farming—a sort of American "Neolithic" base which had its origins in the Valley of Mexico.[54] In fact, the idea was born in the revelation of the Valley of Mexico stratigraphic sequence which had such a culture as its basal member. First known as the "Archaic hypothesis," it was hotly contested for thirty years; since then it has been refurbished as the "formative hypothesis" and is still debated.[55] Its pertinence to the question of how civilizations developed is obvious. It has chronological implications, to be sure, but it is also an opening inquiry into culture process. Other examples may be taken from Peru, an area where the establishment of a culture chronology was closely related to the phenomena of "horizon styles" and where the examination of regional chronologies led to the concept of "pottery traditions."[56] Originally conceived of as devices for cross-dating or demonstrating cultural continuity, they are, in another sense, statements about the workings of culture.

COMPARATIVE-HISTORIC PERIOD (1950 TO THE PRESENT)

In the last few years there have been signs that American archaeology is entering another phase. There have been a dissatisfaction and restlessness with the somewhat limited objectives of spatial-temporal ordering. It has not been enough to ask where and when; we must also ask how and why. The very successes achieved in chronology, particularly with the advent of radiocarbon dating after 1950, have turned the attentions of archaeologists to analyses that will translate the data of prehistory more meaningfully as human activity.[57] The beginnings of these trends go back, of course, earlier than 1950. European archaeology, again, has been influential. Gordon Childe and Grahame Clark began moving in these directions some time ago, although perhaps less self-consciously than has been the case on this side of the Atlantic.[58] Certainly cultural ecology in American archaeology antedates 1950 and so do interpretations of architecture and settlement as to social and cultural functions. Still, it is only recently that these approaches have had a real vogue, and it is only in the last few years that American archaeologists have attempted to analyze, critically and systematically, the processes of culture change that they were observing in their data and to compare these processes.[59] In this, I think it very important to point out that in America, and especially the United States, archaeologists have been, as it were, raised up in the "house of anthropology," and that cultural and social anthropological theory has had strong influence on archaeology. This has probably been salutary. Certainly it has resulted in stimulation, if not always in clarity of presentation. The association began in the latter part of the nineteenth century and has, I think, increased steadily.

But before discussing new trends, it is important to point out that archaeological results have poured in at a tremendous rate since 1950. Field work, supported by River Basin salvage programs and National Science Foundation grants, has proceeded as never before.[60] The number of active professionals has doubled or tripled. The volume of research publication has been greater. For the most part, these results can be considered primarily in the Descriptive-Historic tradition. They have changed the picture from the way Kroeber saw it in 1948.

In early man studies we now have, through radiocarbon, substantial datings on Clovis hunters that cluster between 10,000 and 9000 B.C.—not far off from some of the guess dates of a good many years ago. A chronology, replete with additional carbon dates, has been developed for the High Plains, tracing a history of these early hunters from the tenth to the fifth millennium B.C.[61] The presence of fluted points is well established throughout eastern North America, and they are followed by later and derived forms.[62] In the far northwestern United States, an Old Cordilleran hunting tradition is characterized by leaf-shaped projectile points.[63] So far, no fully comparable stone artifact complexes have been found in the Arctic, or in Siberia, that would provide the link of migration and the original hearth for these early American industries—although there are some suggestive indications on both scores.[64] I think now that the weight of evidence favors a spread of hunting cultures and a bifacial-flaked blade technology from northeast Asia to America sometime between 15,000 and 20,000 years ago, although this is still beyond clear proof. There are also some New World finds— from all parts of the hemisphere—which have been interpreted as evidence for still earlier peoples.[65] The technology of these is crude; projectile points are lacking; but convincing radiocarbon dates, geological contexts, and stratigraphy are also lacking. As of 1966, pre-Clovis man in the Americas is a possibility, not a demonstrated fact.

The "gap" which Kroeber commented upon, the time span between Pleistocene man and the later prehistoric cultures, has been closed. In eastern North America, Archaic hunters and fishers appear to have evolved from the earlier hunting populations between 8000 and 5000 B.C.[66] In the West, the seed-gathering Desert cultures have been shown to have existed from 8000 B.C. up to the historic horizon.[67] A related cultural tradition in highland Mexico was the matrix of the slow development of plant cultivation which eventually led into full-fledged Mesoamerican village farming.[68] The "gap" has also closed along the Peruvian and Chilean coasts and in northwestern Argentina.[69] In each area, these cultures of the "middle" millennia show distinct adaptations to local environmental conditions. All are essentially hunting, fishing, or collecting adjustments, although in some cases there are clues to incipient cultivation. The general picture seems to have been one of small, early population groups developing new technologies and cultural patterns at the close of the Pleistocene. Apparently, the process went on in virtually all parts of the Americas, although for some areas the archaeological record is incomplete or unknown. One area where the story may have been significantly different is the Arctic. Here, there are indications that, as early as 4000 B.C., if not well before, new migrations or diffusions from Siberia brought cultures of an Asiatic Mesolithic heritage; and these, later, developed into prehistoric and historic Eskimo.[70]

Areas which, heretofore, had no archaeological chronologies received attention. Long sequences have been demonstrated for Ecuador, northern Colombia, Lower Central America, and the Amazon Basin.[71] A number of surprises emerged from this work. One is that the earliest New World pottery, by a thousand years or so, comes from the Ecuador-Colombian area, where ceramic levels have been dated back to 3000 B.C.[72] Another is that manioc or root-crop cultivation has a long history. Just how long is uncertain, but by 1000 B.C. sedentary communities were dependent upon it in Venezuela, Colombia, and the upper Amazon.[73] In Colombia it appears to have antedated maize. In North America, Northwest Coast and Interior Plateau archaeology have been opened up with sequences running back to about 1000 B.C. Before this date there are also indications of human occupation, although here the "gap" between early man and later cultures remains somewhat obscure.

Inter-areal relationship problems have been carried a little nearer solution, although not as near as one would like. Excavation in northern Mexico has now very definitely established Mesoamerican-southwestern links; many details remain to be worked out.[74] Mesoamerican-southeastern United States ties are still perceived in rather general terms, and for the "Burial Mound" cultures and their Mesoamerican relationships there is still no agreement even in general outline, although a few recent discoveries hint at contacts between southern Mexico and the southeastern United States on this time level.[75] Prehistoric Eskimoan–Northwest Coast relationships are still hotly argued; and the idea that early North American polished stonework is the result of a "Boreal zone" diffusion from Asiatic Mesolithic sources, while having an appeal as a way of explaining a lot of puzzling similarities from New England to British Columbia, is still far from being demonstrated.[76] Some very specific and complex similarities have been shown for ceramics and figurines between southern Mesoamerica and Ecuador; and these, I think, indicate contact between the two areas.[77] However, this is undoubtedly only one tantalizing glimpse into the intricate relationships that must have existed within the nuclear American sphere.[78]

A number of things have been said about trans-Pacific relationships in the last sixteen years. The most important, in my opinion, are the parallels noted between certain Japanese, Chinese, and Korean manufactures and items found in archaeological sites on the Ecuadorian Coast.[79] The earliest contact argued for is one which is believed to have resulted in the introduction of pottery—a rather simply incised and plastically decorated ware—from the Middle Jomon cultures of Japan to Ecuador at about 3000 B.C. According to this argument, this is the explanation for the early occurrences of ceramics in north-western South America. The parallels and resemblances that have been pointed out are highly intriguing, as is the consistency in the radiocarbon dating from both sides of the Pacific. Opinion is divided on the matter.

Much has been written since 1950 on the rise of New World agriculture and New World civilization. This, it will be remembered, was the theme with which Spinden dealt; however, since then, a good many archaeological facts have come in which show us that the story was by no means as simple as Spinden had supposed. No one area, not even one as important as Mesoamerica, was the source of all New World farming and settled life. Recent excavations by MacNeish have shown us that maize began to be cultivated in the highlands of southern Mexico as far back as the fifth millennium B.C., and it is highly likely that this is an original habitat for the plant and close to its primary center of domestication; but, more or less contemporaneously, other food plants were beginning to be cultivated in far-off Peru and, most probably, in the South American tropical lowlands.[80] These different lines of agricultural development eventually converged, in varying ways, but no one of them can be singled out as the most important in the rise of New World sedentary life. Similarly, even within the area of Mesoamerica, no single region can be pointed to as the *fons et origo* of the sedentary agricultural condition. This applies not only to Spinden's choice, the Valley of Mexico, but to the Tehuacan Valley, to the south, where MacNeish has found the record of a long, slow evolution of plant domestication. The evidence in the Tehuacan Valley shows that, for a very long time after the domestication of maize, communities still relied heavily upon hunting and collecting for subsistence and were seminomadic rather than sedentary. Full-fledged sedentary farming, rather than emerging in a single-line cultural evolution in the Tehuacan Valley, probably resulted from the diffusion of the highland maize plant to a Mesoamerican coastal setting where it was assimilated by populations who were nonagricultural, but sedentary, fishers. This fusion of a sedentary tradition with maize cultivation, and probably with a maize plant that had enjoyed a sudden improvement by the change of natural environmental habitat, then spread back to the highlands.[81] This is an hypothesis, but its sophistication reflects the complexity of the data and the ways in which American archaeologists are now considering them. It is representative of recent trends which, as I have said, are concerned with process. MacNeish, Coe, and Flannery, all of whom have contributed to this hypothesis, approached their data in the contexts of ecological, or micro-ecological, settings.[82] The Tehuacan Valley was contrasted with an archaeological site on the Pacific Coast of Guatemala. The micro-environmental zones which the peoples of each site could have exploited for foods were defined; food remains of all sorts from the refuse of the two sites were subjected to detailed quantitative analyses; weapons or tools related to the food quest were similarly treated; and all of these results were correlated to offer the reconstruction of past events given in the hypothesis. Although the authors of this particular study do not go on to do so, the way is clearly open for comparative examinations of the processes involved in the rise of settled farming communities in other, and unrelated, parts of the world.[83] Through such comparisons I think we can look forward to an elucidation of at least some regularities in culture growth.

A very recent study takes such a comparative outlook as its organizing theme. This is Adams' *The Evolution of Urban Society*, which is a comparison of the "dirt" and documentary archaeological records of Mesopotamia and Mesoamerica.[84] The focus of the problem is the development of cities, subsequent to village agriculture. The author treats of subsistence, settlement, and public works, and, on a higher level of inference, of the class structure and political and religious institutions implied in the evidence. From all this, in spite of significant and interesting differences, he emerges with a convincing similarity of process in the evolution of civilization and urban society. The comparative consideration of civilization is, of course, not new. Philosophers of history have been at it for a long time; but Adams' study shows that archaeology, with its extended time perspective, may provide a better vantage point for this kind of inquiry than conventional history.

These discussions of an archaeological concern with culture process, which are so closely related to new substantive findings in Mesoamerican prehistory, carry us ahead of our history of American archaeology. To go back a bit, the first strong statement of the new trends that we are considering under the rubric of the "Comparative-Historic Period" was Walter Taylor's *A Study of Archaeology*.[85] This was essentially a critique of American archaeology's overriding concern with chronology. Taylor argued that the archaeologist had sacrificed context, the real meat of history or prehistory, for bleak chronicles of pottery-type sequences. In 1948, at the time of publication, there was much to justify this criticism; I would only reply with the extenuation that some semblance of a spatial-temporal framework was a necessary prerequisite to inquiries of context. Taylor advocated what he called a "conjunctive approach," a shifting of the primary emphasis from sequence and wide-scale distributions to a close-up study of the individual site, stratum, house-floor, or hearth. By "conjunctive," he meant a bringing together of all possible lines of examination—technological, stylistic, social, and ecological—on any given archaeological find. The influence of Taylor's ideas was slow to take hold. In part, this was due to immediate reactions against a new and controversial statement; in part, it was the result of the presentation of ideas in the abstract. He offered some examples, but these did not have the effect of a site or regional monograph that came to grips with a segment of culture history.

Still, one new departure of the early 1950's was, at least indirectly, stimulated by Taylor's work. This was a concern with prehistoric settlement pattern.[86] An aspect of archaeology that had been neglected in the New World, its potential for cultural-environmental and social inferences was obvious. It is true that settlement is only one aspect of cultural context, but it is a basic aspect which serves as a convenient point for a convergence, or a "conjunction," of inquiry into other aspects. This, I believe, is seen in a number of studies of the 1960's, wherein settlement—usually the micro-pattern of the single site or community with its various house and building arrangements—has been skillfully combined with fine-grained analyses of pottery and artifact types to give us information on kinship and other aspects of social organization.[87] So far, the only monograph of this kind is one by Deetz on prehistoric and protohistoric Plains settlement, pottery styles, and kinship.[88] It should be noted that the statistical operations involved in this study were of a large order and were handled by computer procedures.

The most articulate and programmatic spokesman of the new trends is L. R. Binford, who, in a series of articles dating in the 1960's, has outlined a "systemic" and "multivariate" approach to archaeology.[89] In a degree, this follows Taylor's "conjunctive" approach in that a functioning culture is recreated through a study of the interrelationships of the various kinds of remains; but Binford also goes beyond this in arguing that a comprehension of process and causality will only result from a study of the covariations of subsystems within a culture, or, in other terms, from an analysis of the interrelated evolutionary changes which occur among the technological, social, and ideological aspects of that culture. Assuming my brief paraphrase of his position to be correct, I would agree. Change in culture can only be measured or appraised in comparison with culture. Archaeologists have long operated along these lines in examining change through time within certain cultural categories—water jars, for instance, or projectile points. They have not, however, as Binford insists, given much attention to the way change in one category may correlate, or covary, with change in another. Here I believe Binford is correct in saying that this is the key to an understanding of process; however, with the outlook of one who grasps the tangible example more readily than the abstract theoretical statement, I await with interest some large-scale demonstrations of these principles with the data of New World prehistory.

American archaeology, in a little over one hundred years, has come from the most uncontrolled speculation about the past, through an era of collecting and classifying, through another of chronological ordering, and now is attempting to explain and understand the past. It may be my optimistic or conciliatory nature, but I think these steps have been logical. Given human fallibility, I am not sure we could have planned it better. Now, in a sense, things have come full circle. The old spirit of speculation, held in checkrein, to be sure, by professional discipline, is once again with us. We are ready to wonder, speculate, and ask questions once more. This time they should be better questions: at least, we hope so.

Glyn Daniel/One Hundred

Years of Old World Prehistory

IN THE FIRST PAPER OF THIS SERIES, Gordon R. Willey set out a scheme dividing the history of American archaeology into four periods: first, the pioneer or preparatory era, the "Speculative Period"; second, the "Descriptive Period," from the mid-nineteenth century until the second decade of the twentieth century —the period which saw the beginning of systematic and descriptive archaeology; third, the "Descriptive-Historic Period," following what he calls the stratigraphic revolution in American archaeology, from the second decade of the twentieth century to 1950; and, fourth, the "Comparative-Historic Period," from 1950 onward.[1]

Old World archaeology can be similarly divided into four periods. The first period—the pioneer, preparatory, or "Speculative Period"—extended from the medieval antiquaries with their guesses, from men such as Geoffrey of Monmouth, whose *Historia Regum Britanniae* was written about 1135,[2] to students of the material remains of the past of the late eighteenth and early nineteenth centuries, who, not satisfied with Dr. Johnson's dictum that all that could be known about the ancient past was derived from early writers, were trying to find facts by observing field monuments and by digging. After years of excavation, Richard Colt Hoare had to confess that, though his aim was "to ascertain to which of the successive inhabitants of this island (*he was writing about Britain*) they (*that is, the prehistoric antiquities*) are to be ascribed, or whether in fact they are the work of more than one people," after ten years' work, he was forced to confess "total ignorance as to the authors of these sepulchral memorials."[3] Rasmus Nyerup in Denmark wrote despairingly that "everything which has come down to us from heathendom is wrapped in a thick fog: it belongs to

NOTE: Glyn Daniel is a Fellow of St. John's College, Cambridge University, and Editor of *Antiquity*.

a space of time we cannot measure. We know it is older than Christendom, but whether by a couple of years or a couple of centuries or even by more than a millennium, we can do no more than guess."[4]

The second period of Old World archaeology which, again following Willey, we can call the "Descriptive Period," or, as I would prefer, the formative period, was from 1797 to 1859–1865. I chose the date 1797 because it was in that year that a gentleman farmer from Suffolk, John Frere, sent to the Society of Antiquaries in London a package of what we would now call Acheulian hand-axes. He said that the situation in which they were found—twelve feet below the surface of the ground, in the bottom layer of some undisturbed strata and associated with the bones of extinct animals—rendered them "particularly objects of curiosity"; he described them as "weapons of war, fabricated and used by a people who had not the use of metals," and added "the situation in which these weapons were found may tempt us to refer them to a very remote period indeed; even beyond that of the present world";[5] and by "the present world" he meant the world of six thousand years, the world which began in 4004 B.C., which had been the accepted chronology of Christian historians since the times of Eusebius, Jerome, and Julius Africanus.[6] Between 1797 and 1859 the new uniformitarian geology had been propounded and accepted,[7] and the great antiquity of man, demonstrated by Boucher de Perthes in the Somme gravels, by William Pengelly in south Devon, and by Nyerup's countrymen, C. J. Thomsen and J. J. A. Worsaae, had provided a technological system of three successive ages of Stone, Bronze, and Iron which at last penetrated the fog of which Nyerup had complained.[8] In 1865 John Lubbock was able to write the first of many popular books about archaeology, and, in it, to popularize the word "prehistory," and to introduce, for divisions of the Stone Age, the neo-gre-

cisms, Palaeolithic and Neolithic.[9] I suggest that the publication of *Prehistoric Times* in 1865 and the Paris Exposition of
1867 mark the end of the formative or descriptive stage of Old
World archaeology. Old World archaeology had now come of
age; in 1871 Tylor wrote that: "The history and prehistory of
man take their proper places in the general scheme of knowledge"—albeit he was unduly optimistic.[10]

The third and main stage in the development of Old World
archaeology is from 1865 to 1945: again following Willey, we
can call it the "Descriptive-Historic." The stratigraphic revolution in Old World archaeology dated before this: Frere had
observed stratigraphy at the end of the eighteenth century;
Worsaae had described his stratigraphical observations in the
Danish peat-bogs and the barrows of Jutland; Meadows Taylor
made stratigraphical observations in the megalithic tombs of
Hyderabad in 1851. However, it was not until the last quarter
of the nineteenth century that good stratigraphic practice developed in Old World archaeology.[11] I like to refer to this
period of eighty years as from Lubbock to Libby, because there
is no doubt in my mind that the discovery and development
of radiocarbon dating starts a new period in Old, and, of course,
in New World archaeology. If the second period was characterized by what I have elsewhere described as the geological
and antiquarian revolutions,[12] and the third period by the
statigraphic revolution, the fourth period was brought into
existence and characterized by the Carbon 14 dating revolution.

The first two periods of Old World archaeology are outside
the scope of this paper; our concern is with the third and fourth
periods—with the eighty years of period three and the, so far,
twenty years of period four. The year 1866 which starts out
period three, and which saw the establishment of the Peabody
Museum of Archaeology in the University of Harvard, also saw
the first international meeting of archaeologists and prehistoric

anthropologists. The first international congress—the twenty-first was held in Prague in 1967—was held in Neuchâtel in 1866. The congress had been founded the previous year at a meeting of the Italian Society of Natural Sciences at the instigation of Gabriel de Mortillet; this meeting was at Spezzia and it founded what was at first called the Congrès International Paléoethnologique. The Neuchâtel meeting coincided, as it was planned to do, with the annual meeting of the Societé Helvétique des Sciences Naturelles, and it was full of incident—"collations et soirées avec illuminations et feux d'artifice . . . vin d'honneur à la lumière des flammes de Bengale, dans les souterrains qui doivent approvisionner d'eau de la ville de Neuchâtel; refraichissements offerts dans les bois, sous un gigantesque bloc erratique."[13]

The President of the Congress at Neuchâtel was Desor, author of *Palafittes ou constructions lacustres du lac de Neuchâtel,* and his presidential address referred to the "passé antéhistorique de notre suisse" and to "la période antéhistorique" or "la période qui a immediatement précédé les temps historiques."[14] Lubbock's *Prehistoric Times,* published in 1865, had argued against the use of the word "antehistoric" and recommended "prehistoric," as also launching the words "Palaeolithic" and "Neolithic." These neo-grecisms were not much used in the first 1866 conference in Neuchâtel, but they were used the following year when the second conference was held in Paris, during the time of the Exposition Universelle. At this second conference, Edouard Lartet served as president and de Mortillet as secretary. The conference itself was now called the "Congrès international d'Anthropologie et d'Archéologie Préhistoriques."

Lubbock was not the first to use the terms "prehistory" and "prehistoric." "Prehistoric" had been used by Daniel Wilson in his *Archaeology and the Prehistoric Annals of Scotland* (1851).

Wilson was a remarkable and interesting man—Canada's first anthropologist, as Professor Bruce Trigger has called him.[15] Wilson came to Toronto in 1853 to take up the Chair of History and English Literature at University College, and stayed on to be the second President of the College and the first President of the reorganized University of Toronto. He was one of the great mid-nineteenth century pioneers of archaeology and anthropology: he had quickly realized that Christian Thomsen in Denmark, with his museum ordering of Ages of Stone, Bronze, and Iron, had, by adopting this technological model of the prehistoric past, introduced a new way into our thinking about that past. It is worth quoting what he said in 1851: "A very simple theory sufficed until very recently, for the classification of all British antiquities. Whatever was rude and barbarous . . . was native and Druidical; whatever manifested skill, invention or any progress in the arts was Phoenician, Roman or Danish! Britain was tacitly assumed to have been sunk in the lowest state of barbarism, until humanised by the bloody missionaries of Roman civilisation . . . such ignorant assumption will no longer suffice . . . The name of Dane has in fact for centuries been one of those convenient words which so often take the place of ideas, and save the trouble and inconvenience of reasoning."[16]

Wilson had campaigned for the word "prehistory," although he himself did not invent it. The Frenchman Tournal had used it earlier, although Trigger thinks that Wilson himself did make an independent invention.[17] As we look back over the last hundred years, we should reflect that the words "prehistory," "Palaeolithic," and "Neolithic" were not in common parlance when the Peabody Museum was founded.

The 1867 Paris Conference was a much bigger and more impressive affair than the gathering in Neuchâtel. There were three hundred and sixty-three members present, two hundred and seventeen from France, thirty-one from Italy, eighteen from Great Britain, thirteen from Switzerland, and none from America. This year was truly a great moment in the development of archaeology: the Great Exhibition of London in 1851 had no prehistory: the purpose of that exhibition was to demonstrate the material advances made during the first half of the nineteenth century. Sixteen years later—and it is those sixteen years that saw the acceptance of the great antiquity of man, the publication of Darwin's *The Origin of Species,* and the work of Boucher de Perthes in the Somme gravels and of William Pengelly in Devon—came the Paris Exposition and it had prehistory and archaeology. That this was so showed how Old World archaeology was at last developing. The archaeological collections included material from Aurignac lent by Lartet; material from Laugerie Haute lent by the Marquis de Vibraye; a case of rock-shelter art; material from the flint-mines of Grand Pressigny and from the megalithic tombs of Brittany; material from the Comte Costa de Beauregard's collection found in the lake villages on the shores of the Lac de Bourget. Gabriel de Mortillet was very proud of the archaeology in the Paris Exposition and wrote of it that it was "la première fois que les temps préhistoriques se manifestent d'une manière solennelle et générale. Eh bien, cette première manifestation a été pour eux un triomphe complet."[18]

In response to repeated requests from readers of his new journal, *Matériaux pour l'Histoire positive et philosophique de l'Homme* (founded in 1864), de Mortillet wrote a guide to the archaeological collections in the Exposition: it was called *Promenades préhistoriques à l'exposition Universelle.* It showed, he said, the progress of man: "Impossible," he wrote, "de mettre en doute la grande loi du progrès de l'humanité . . . Pierre taillée à eclats, pierre polie, bronze, fer, sont autant de grandes étapes qu'a traversé l'humanité entière pour arriver à notre civilisation." And, at the end of this guide book, de Mortillet summarized the three main facts which, according to him, had so far emerged from prehistoric scholarship; he printed them in capital letters as follows:

LOI DU PROGRES DE L'HUMANITE
LOI DU DEVELOPPEMENT SIMILAIRE
HAUTE ANTIQUITE DE L'HOMME[19]

Certainly the last of these three propositions was true. The new uniformitarian geology of Lyell and the evolutionary theory of Darwin had banished the "present world" of 4004 B.C.; there was now a long past of man to study and describe.

Old World archaeology did not enter on its Descriptive-Historic, or formative, phase in total ignorance of New World archaeology. Lubbock's *Prehistoric Times* had a chapter, "North American Archaeology," in which he discussed the work of Squier, Davis, Lapham, and Haven, and pointed out that, in a curious and accidental way, the antiquities of Mexico had a special influence on the development of European archaeology and anthropology. The first Professor of Anthropology in Oxford, and, for that matter, in the British Isles, was Edward Burnett Tylor; the first sentence of his first book, *Anahuac* (1861), was as follows: "In the spring of 1856 I met with Mr. Christy accidentally in an omnibus in Havana."[20] Henry Christy was a hat-maker and banker who, among other things, introduced Turkish towels into western Europe. His Turkish towels were exhibited at the Great Exhibition of 1851 and were allowed to be called "Royal Turkish Towels," after Queen Victoria had ordered six dozen for her own use. This exhibition fired Christy with an interest in comparative ethnography and, from 1851 until his death in 1865, his main interest was in traveling and collecting. Hence, his presence in Havana. In 1856 Tylor was a young man of twenty-three who had gone into his father's business of metal-founding: it did not suit him and, on the verge of a nervous breakdown, he had traveled to America. With Christy, he traveled around Mexico, picking up implements of obsidian and visiting temples. The journey over, Tylor returned to England and started on a career which carried him on to be the first professional anthropologist in England. Christy returned to England and soon retired from business to devote himself to archaeology and ethnography. He interested himself in research in the South of France and collaborated with Edouard Lartet, financially supporting his work in the Pyrenees in 1860–61. In 1863 Christy took part in the French excavations himself and in the last five months of that year the major reconnaissance work in the Dordogne (forever associated with the names of Lartet and Christy) took place. Lartet and Christy planned together a large and complete work on what they called "the aborigines of Perigord," but they died before the work was completed. It was brought out posthumously in 1875, under the editorship of Rupert Jones and under the title of *Reliquiae Aquitanicae: Being Contributions to the Archaeology and Palaeontology of Perigord and the Adjoining Provinces of Southern France.* Here, if anywhere, is the beginning of systematic Upper Palaeolithic archaeology.

I must for a moment revert to the Paris Exposition—for an interesting event took place there. On show in the exposition was a collection of ancient Egyptian jewelry sent from the new museum, founded at Boulak, a suburb of Cairo, in 1859. The Empress Eugénie was so delighted by the jewelry that she informed the Khedive Ismail that she would be graciously pleased to receive the whole collection as a present. The Khedive had often wanted to give away exhibits from the Boulak Museum to his friends, and on one occasion had suggested that the whole collection should be given as a present. It was a great moment in the history of archaeology when the Khedive, surprised by the request of the empress—yet anxious to please France, and himself short of money—made his consent conditional on the agreement of a Frenchman, Auguste Mariette, who had been sent out to Egypt in 1850 by the Louvre to collect Coptic manuscripts, but stayed on in the country and, in 1858, was appointed chief of the newly created Egyptian Service of Antiquities. "There is someone at Boulak more powerful than I," the Khedive said to the empress's agent—to the agent's considerable surprise—"and you must address yourself to him."

Mariette firmly refused, and the jewelry came back to his museum at Boulak. Here, surely, was the beginning of what is usually referred to as the archaeological conscience.[21]

But despite his many virtues, Mariette could not be described as a good excavator; he came in the wake of tomb-robbers like Belzoni and Drouetti, and himself excavated over thirty important sites in as many years. Petrie describes how Mariette dug near the Sphinx, blasting away with dynamite the fallen ruins of a temple. In 1883, just after Mariette's death, Petrie wrote of Egyptian excavation that "nothing was done with any uniform plan, work is begun and left unfinished, no regard is paid to future requirements of exploration and no civilized or labour-saving appliances are used. It is sickening to see the rate at which everything is being destroyed, and the little regard paid to preservation."[22]

The first and most obvious change in archaeology between 1865–1866 and now has been in the technique of excavation. Gradually a sense of purpose and discipline was introduced into digging, and this was, in the Old World, due to the development of two traditions of excavation—the first, German-Austrian, and, the second, British. Excavation in the mid-nineteenth century was a quick search for objects suitable for a cabinet of curiosities or a museum. Loftus described his object in excavating as actuated by "a nervous desire to find important large museum pieces at the least possible outlay of time and money."[23] In his *Ruins of Palmyra,* Robert Wood says: "Inscriptions we copied as they fell in our way and carried off the marbles whenever it was possible, for the avarice and superstition of the inhabitants made the task difficult if sometimes impracticable."[24] In 1844 the British Archaeological Association met at Canterbury and excavated eight barrows in one morning: the weather was bad—"The only interruption arose from a heavy shower of rain . . . many, both ladies and gentlemen, raised their umbrellas . . . and stood patiently looking at the operations of the excavations . . . The barrows were less productive than was anticipated. All however contained human remains . . . the party proceeded to Bourne Park . . . where two barrows were excavated . . . after the excavation of these ten barrows the party partook of . . . a plentiful repast."[25] Modern excavators might well be pardoned for saying that anyone who excavated ten barrows in one day deserved good and plentiful food and drink.

In 1866, just a hundred years ago, a party of archaeologists of high international reputation went off to see the excavations at Hallstatt in the Salzkammergut region of Austria. The party included John Evans, Lubbock, Lartet, Morlot and Franks. Evans describes their visit and, in a letter to his wife, gives a picture of Old World archaeology a hundred years ago: "We arranged with the Bergmeister to set some men at work digging and are going up there early tomorrow morning to see the result: it may be that we shall stop all day." And the next day: "We found our diggings too pleasant for us to be able to tear ourselves from them. Lubbock and I breakfasted soon after 6 and about half past 7 were up at the cemetery . . . and found that the men had already discovered a bronze bracelet and a broken fibula. I subsequently found in one of our trenches and dug out with my own hands one of the iron socket celts with a part of the handle remaining in it and having on one part the impression of a fine twilled cloth against which it had lain . . . I hope to be able to arrange in Vienna for our friend the Bergmeister Stapf to carry on some further excavations for us."[26]

Seven years later the Austrian excavations began at Samothrace. The excavation of the Sanctuary of the Great Gods on the island of Samothrace was the scene of the first real excavations in Greek lands, and perhaps one of the first modern excavations anywhere. Alexander Conze was in charge and he dug there from 1873 to 1875. He had two architects working with him and a photographer—and for that matter the Austrian government placed at his disposal a man-of-war. A complete record was published of the Samothrace excavations: it is the first modern excavation report in existence. The plans were beautifully drawn by the architects and the reports were illustrated. This was the first time that photography had been used to illustrate archaeological reports; of course, C. T. Newton— and other excavators—had made extensive use of photography in field work, but they had lithographs made from the photographs for publication.[27]

In 1875 a branch of the German Archaeological Institute was set up at Athens, and for the next six winters Ernst Curtius directed operations at Olympia. £30,000 was spent on this work and the expenses of the 1880 season were borne personally by the Emperor William. The stratigraphy at Olympia was very carefully and completely studied. The architectural work there was carried out for a while by Dorpfeld, who himself became a moving spirit in the practice and dissemination of the new methods of excavation, preservation, and recording.

Dorpfeld joined Heinrich Schliemann in 1822. Schliemann's place in the development of modern excavational technique has been variously evaluated. Michaelis declared that he was "a complete stranger to every scientific method of treatment of his subject and had no idea that a method and a well-defined technique existed."[28] Stanley Casson, on the other hand, claims Schliemann as the founder of modern scientific archaeology, saying that Schliemann laid "the solid foundations of a proper archaeological method which could be followed in any land."[29] Michaelis's judgment is harsh and historically difficult to understand: Schliemann began digging at Hissarlik in 1871, and there was no method or well-defined technique in existence then. Such remained to be forged by Germans, Austrians, and the British in the last quarter of the nineteenth century.

Schliemann's excavation at Hissarlik was, it should be remembered, the first excavation of a tell: as Myres put it, "the first large-scale dissection of a dryland settlement unguided by the remains of great monuments such as simplified the task in Babylon and Nineveh."[30] He cut through the mound and distinguished successive occupation levels. The principles of stratigraphy applied to archaeology had been appreciated by Worsaae in Denmark, Keller and Morlot in Switzerland, and Gastaldi and Strobel in the *terremare* of northern Italy, but it was Schliemann who demonstrated how these principles could be applied to excavating a tell.[31] Certainly when Dorpfeld joined Schliemann in 1882, he brought to the excavations at Troy the new system and efficiency of the Germans at Olympia. He was able to expose the stratigraphy at Troy much more clearly than previously, and may be said to have revolutionized Schliemann's technique, changing it, as Myres said, "from digging to dissection."[32]

The stratigraphic revolution in Old World archaeology had its first development then in Samothrace, Olympia, and Troy in the 1870's and 1880's. The next thirty years saw the development of this tradition of classical excavation—the French at Delos and Delphi, the Greeks themselves in Athens, the Americans under Bacon and Clarke at Assos and Neandreia, and, from 1900 onward, Arthur Evans at Knossos. The second late-nineteenth-century tradition of excavation, which equally firmly established the new technique and the stratigraphic revolution, was the British. This tradition stemmed from two highly contrasted individuals and two very individualistic men—Pitt-Rivers and Flinders Petrie. The first was a professional soldier and an amateur collector of archaeological and ethnographical objects. He was born Augustus Lane-Fox, but when he inherited the Rivers estates in Cranborne Chase, changed his name to Pitt-Rivers and began a brilliant career as a field archaeologist. Between 1880 and 1900 he dug camps, villages, cemeteries, barrows, and linear earthworks. In place of the technique of the mid-century treasure hunt—a matter of digging a hole quickly in the middle of a barrow to find the primary interment and its associated grave-goods—he substituted the total excavation of sites, stressing the importance of stratigraphical observation and of the necessity of recording the positions of everything found. He was fortunately unlimited by considerations of finance, time, or labor, and he made his excavations a model of scientific work. He believed in the prompt and complete publication of all his excavations, and practiced this belief—at his own expense—by privately printing between 1887 and 1898 four sumptuous volumes, under the title *Excavations in Cranborne Chase;* he set and achieved the very highest standard of archaeological publication.[33]

Flinders Petrie began his career as an archaeologist working in Britain. His first book was *Stonehenge* (1880). He transferred his attention to Egypt the following year, and it was in Egypt and Palestine that he made his name as a field worker and excavator. He got no training or criticism from anyone, and in 1885 he was writing that his work was "in fact a case of breaking new ground in archaeology." He adumbrated the four following principles: first, the care of the monuments being excavated and respect for future visitors and excavators; second, meticulous care in excavation and the collection and description of everything found; third, the accurate planning of all monuments and excavations; and, fourth, the full publication of all excavations as soon as possible. In 1904 he set all this out in his manual, *Methods and Aims in Archaeology*. Pitt-Rivers had died four years before. Petrie went on to live until 1940, and published his autobiography under the arresting title of *Seventy Years in Archaeology*.[34] These two dissimilar Englishmen had much in common; they were the leaders of the revolution in Old World archaeology which led archaeology away from the contemplation of works of art to the contemplation of all objects, and particularly of the ordinary artifact.

However, it must not be assumed that the new traditions of careful and scientific excavation set up in classical lands, in Britain, and in Egypt, were universally accepted. Indeed, as late as the twenties, Sir John Marshall, then Director General of Archaeology in India, and his assistant, E. J. Mackay, were excavating Mohenjodaro and Harappa with no concern for the realities of stratigraphy—they were busy recording the exact find-spots of everything they excavated in relation to the mean sea-level at Karachi.[35] Leonard Woolley has described his first experience of excavation, at Corbridge in Northumberland: "I know only too well that the work there would have scandalised, and rightly scandalised, any British archaeologist of today."[36] A committee was engaged on writing *The Northumberland County History* and proposed a small-scale dig at Corbridge. "The Committee naturally appealed to Professor Haverfield as the leading authority on Roman Britain, and he, as he had intended to take a holiday on the Roman Wall, agreed to supervise the excavations . . . Haverfield arranged . . . that I should go to Corbridge. In point of fact I had never so much as seen an excavation, I had never studied archaeological methods even from books (there were none at the time dealing with the subject), and I had not any idea of how to make a survey or a ground-plan; apart from being used to handling antiquities in a museum, and that only for a few months, I had no qualifications at all. I was very anxious to learn and it was a disappointment to me that Haverfield only looked in at the excavations one day in the week and then was concerned only to know what had been found—I don't think that he ever criticised or corrected anything." This first season was a short one, but next year Woolley was asked to begin the complete uncovering of the site. "In 1907, therefore" he wrote, "I found myself in charge of a really important dig, being still, of course, quite unfitted for the task."[37]

Woolley describes his experience as typical of a period when field archaeology was in its infancy "and few diggers in this country [Great Britain] thought it necessary to follow the example of that great pioneer, Pitt-Rivers." Wheeler has often drawn attention to the fact that in the first two decades of the twentieth century no one seemed to pay any attention in England to the methods of Pitt-Rivers. "One of his assistants had even proceeded to dig up a lake village," wrote Wheeler, "much as Schliemann had dug up Troy or St. John Hope, Silchester; like potatoes. Not only had the clock not gone on, but it had been set back."[38]

The clock was put forward again by the new postwar generation of archaeologists in the third decade of the twentieth century, a generation that restored and reinvigorated field archaeology and that deliberately turned back to the work and principles of Pitt-Rivers and Petrie. It is only necessary to mention a few names—Cyril Fox and Wheeler in Great Britain, Bersu in Germany, Carter, Caernarvon, and Caton-Thompson in Egypt, Woolley in Iraq; and the flourishing of this new tradition in the thirties before the outbreak of the second world war—under the Germans at Warka, Speiser at Tepe Gawra, Schmidt at Tepe Hissar, Contenau and Ghirshman at Tepe Giyan, Ghirshman at Sialk, Schäfer at Ras Shamra, O'Riordain and Hencken in Ireland. If the stratigraphic revolution in Old World archaeology was really forged in the last quarter of the nineteenth century it was reforged during the twenty years from 1919 to 1939, which means, in British archaeology, from Wheeler at Colchester to the team who, with war clouds around them, hurriedly yet brilliantly excavated at Sutton Hoo in 1939.[39]

Quite apart from the renaissance of field archaeology in the third and fourth decades of the twentieth century has been the discovery and implementation of a wide variety of new techniques. Pitt-Rivers, Petrie, and Dorpfeld would indeed be surprised if they were to visit a modern excavation or read a modern excavation report. Two of the main differences between, say, excavation at Cranborne Chase and excavation in the present day must be mentioned at once. First, the modern archaeologist has developed the art of detecting, recording, and studying not only the tangible and obvious relics of the past, but what may be described as the "ghosts" of the past, such as the wooden postholes of wooden henge monuments,[40] the sleeper trenches and posts of wooden houses in Little Woodbury in England[41] and Bylany in Czechoslovakia[42]; or the strings of Queen Shub-ad's harp from the Royal Graves at Ur.[43] Second, the techniques of preservation have been so improved that objects found by chance or by excavation which might well have disintegrated if found years ago can be preserved and studied. I am thinking here of the tree-coffins and bog-finds of Denmark and north Germany,[44] the tattooed Scythians from Pazirik, and the recent collection of two hundred wooden figures discovered by Roger Martin at the source of the river Seine.[45] And, third, all kinds of archaeological and scientific devices have been developed which cut down the work of the archaeologist and make it more efficient and accurate. The development of air photography has revealed sites invisible to the ground observer. Other forms of archaeological prospecting by proton magnetometers and periscope surveys have been invented, and archaeologists are now prepared to pursue their activities under the waters of lakes and seas with the widest variety of techniques, including the submarine.[46]

Photography from the air was first suggested as a joke in the middle of the nineteenth century, but became a fact when Nadar took photographs of Paris from a balloon in 1858, when King and Black took photographs of Boston from a captive balloon in 1860–1861, and when Negretti, in 1863, photographed a London suburb. The first archaeological air photographs were taken in 1906 by Lieutenant P. H. Sharpe who took an oblique and a vertical photograph of Stonehenge from a military balloon. But it was the 1914–1918 war that showed the potentialities of the recorded air view, and these potentialities were realized by such men as the German Theodor Wiegand in the Dobrudja, Palestine, and Syria; and by the Frenchman Père Antoine Poidebard; but most of all by Englishmen like Hamshaw Thomas and Beazeley in the Near East, and O. G. S. Crawford in the British Isles. The English local archaeologist Williams Freeman once said to Crawford: "One ought to be a bird in order to be a field-archaeologist." Crawford became a bird when he flew in the 1914–1918 war, and, in the years following the war, he developed and encouraged aerial photography. When he founded the quarterly journal *Antiquity* in 1927, he used it as a vehicle for publicizing air photographs as widely as possible. The 1939–1945 war gave a further fillip to the technical development of air photography, and many archaeologists from many nations fought their wars in air photo interpretation and intelligence centers in many parts of the world.

The interests, skills, and resources engendered by the war were not lost. There is now a special air photography department in Rome, a department of air photography in the Sorbonne, and the air photographic library of the Royal Air Force accumulated during the war has recently been acquired by the University of North Staffordshire at Keele. In my own University of Cambridge, England, there is a special Department of Aerial Photography under a Director, J. K. St. Joseph, who himself has made most notable contributions to archaeology by aerial reconnaissance and photography: this department has its own aircraft, a twin-engined Cessna Skymaster which in the last few years has flown many sorties not only in Great Britain, but also in Ireland, France, and Denmark.[47]

Perhaps the greatest technical assistance now given to the modern archaeologist is through the additional information provided by specialists—geologists who analyze rocks; metallurgists who analyze ores and alloys, pollen analysts; and the rest of them. The demonstration by H. H. Thomas in the early twenties that the so-called "foreign stones" of Stonehenge came from the Preseli mountains of southwest Wales was one of the first clear examples of a fact of history being provided for the archaeologist by a nonarchaeologist specialist.[48] It is now a commonplace to talk about science and archaeology and there are already half a dozen books or more describing the various scientific aids to archaeology.[49]

Even the least archaeologically minded members of the general public cannot fail to have heard of the way in which some of these scientific techniques, notably that of fluorine dating, were used, between ten and fifteen years ago, to expose *Eoanthropus dawsonii,* the "First Englishman" as Arthur Keith had unhappily called him, as a fake and a forgery—the result of a talented hoax which for forty years took in most of the scientific world. There can be few more absorbing books about any aspects of Old World archaeology than Weiner's *The Piltdown Forgery*, very properly voted by the Ellery Queen organization when it appeared in 1955 as "the best detective story of the year."[50]

Perhaps no more exciting contribution by science to archaeology exists than the development of geochronology. Although the great antiquity of man had been accepted in the fifties and sixties of the last century, and the "present world," as John Frere called it, of six thousand years had been banished, there seemed for a long while no certain way of dating the barbarian Old World cultures that lay outside the civilized world of Egypt and Sumer, where writing developed around 3000 B.C., and no way of dating the preliterate cultures of Egypt and Sumeria. Attempts were made by cross-dating artifacts from different places; Flinders Petrie was a pioneer in this, as in many another thing, and he developed cross-dating between Egypt and Palestine and between Egypt and Greece, thus suggesting the first dates for the Mycenean civilization.[51] Cross-dating was developed by archaeologists like Montelius and Childe and provided, in the first forty years of the twentieth century, a chronological structure in absolute dates for the Neolithic, Bronze, and Early Iron Ages of Europe.[52] Petrie himself had very little respect for the three-age system and wrote of it: "Such a piecemeal plan is well enough for a beginning, but it is not capable of exact definition: it is cumbersome and does not express the relation of one period to another."[53] He himself devised a system of sequence dates based on the typology of prehistoric pottery worked out at Diospolis Parva, but this scheme, while it gave an objective relative chronology, did not provide absolute dates.[54]

In America the problem of devising an absolute chronology

was even more difficult—since there could be no cross-dating with Old World chronology. Douglass developed the technique of dendrochronology which, in some special cases, took the dates of pre-Columbian archaeology back from the fifteenth century to the first century A.D.[55] Tree-ring dating was the first geochronological technique to be developed, but it was of little or no use in Old World archaeology: the first major geochronological breakthrough in archaeological dating was achieved by the Swede, Gerard de Geer. Since 1878 he had gauged the potentialities of counting the clay varves laid down by the retreating ice sheet, and in 1910 published his famous paper, "A Geochronology of the Last 12,000 Years."[56] The absolute chronology of the postglacial period which de Geer was able to calculate could be used to date the postglacial climatic phases which Blytt and Sernander had proposed and, through pollen analysis, to date the postglacial vegetational history of Europe.[57]

But the major breakthrough in geochronology was at the end of the 1939–1945 war, when Willard F. Libby—the only Nobel prize winner in archaeology—discovered and established the technique of Carbon 14 dating. There are now over seventy radiocarbon laboratories working in the world, and the journal *Radiocarbon*, produced by the American Journal of Science, is surely one of the journals now most important to the Old World as to the New World archaeologist. For, without accurate dates, archaeology can advance no further, and the annual appearance of a volume of *Radiocarbon* is one of the most eagerly awaited events in the archaeologists' year.[58] To Carbon 14 dating have now been added other techniques of absolute geochronological dating (for instance, potassium-argon dating).[59] This technique has confirmed the work on deep-sea cores of Ericson and Wollin, who, from a study of more than three thousand cores obtained by some forty expeditions (material now housed in the Lamont Geological Observatory of Columbia University), were able to suggest that the beginning of the Pleistocene was about one and a half million years ago.[60]

The development of these excavational, reconnaissance, and interpretative techniques and particularly the development of geochronological methods of dating have meant that the archaeologist has been able to move forward into times and areas he never dreamt of before. Palaeolithic studies which were at first confined to western Europe and the Mediterranean have been extended to the eastern Mediterranean and Africa, India, Russia, China, southeast Asia, and Australia. As early as 1863, Bruce Foote was collecting palaeoliths in India and went on doing so for forty-three years, publishing his collection in 1914. In China, Andersson began excavating at Choukoutien, in 1921, and, in various parts of Asia, work went on under Breuil, Teilhard de Chardin, Movius, de Terra, and Patterson. In the eastern Mediterranean, the work of Dorothy Garrod must be mentioned and Palaeolithic studies in Africa extended from the French in North Africa to the British in the South and East, where the site of Olduvai—at which the Leakeys have been working since 1931—has been described as being "in its field the most significant single find known to prehistory."[61] In Czechoslovakia and southern Russia the development of Palaeolithic studies has produced the first evidence of artificial shelters, among which the oval houses of Gagarino in southern Russia and Dolni-Vestonice in Czechoslovakia are the best known.

In the classic areas of early Palaeolithic studies—southern France and northern Spain—the existence of mobiliary art was known of just a hundred years ago and, by 1875, when Lartet and Christy published their *Reliquae Aquitanicae* posthumously, many examples of home art were known, and the Lartet-Christy collections divided between the British Museum and the Musée des Antiquités Nationales at St. Germain-en-Laye (founded by Napoleon III in 1863). But, although Palaeolithic

home art was known and accepted by 1875, the recognition of
Palaeolithic cave art had to wait for another quarter of a century before it was accepted and respectable. It was in 1875 that
de Sautuola began excavating the cave of Altamira near San-
tander in northern Spain and found monochrome paintings on
the walls: four years later his small daughter wandered into the
inner recesses of this now famous site and found the poly-
chrome paintings of bisons and bulls. De Sautuola claimed
that all these cave paintings were Palaeolithic and, in so doing,
precipitated one of the great disputes in Old World archaeology.
De Mortillet accepted their authenticity, saying: "C'est l'enfance
de l'art, ce n'est pas l'art de l'enfant." But, at first, most people
denied the authenticity of Altamira, and the site was not mentioned in the prehistoric congresses until after the meeting of
the French Association pour l'Avancement des Sciences in
Montauban in 1900. After this conference a group of archaeologists went up into Dordogne to see the evidence at the newly
discovered site of La Mouthe, where a cave with paintings
had been found only after the excavation of Palaeolithic levels
completely blocking the entrance. The group contained the
Comte Begouen, Capitan, Peyrony, and the young Abbé
Breuil—all of whom were convinced of the authenticity of the
cave art at La Mouthe. In the following year the spectacular
discoveries of the cave paintings and engravings at Combarelles
and Font-de-Gaume were announced. Emile Cartailhac, Professor of Prehistory at Toulouse, took the young Breuil with him
to see Altamira: they went, they saw, and they were convinced,
and Cartailhac wrote his famous paper "Mea culpa d'un
sceptique."[62] Palaeolithic cave art, one of the strangest and
most surprising things that archaeology has revealed about
man's most ancient past, was now accepted, and subsequently
we have had a string of great discoveries, all of which are now
household names: let us list a few of them—Bernifal in 1902,

Covalanas and Hornos de la Pena in 1903, Gargas in 1905, Niaux in 1906, Portel in 1908, La Pasieaga in 1911, Tuc d'Audoubert in 1912, Les Trois Frères in 1914, Peche-Merle in 1920, Montespan in 1923, and, the greatest discovery of all after Altamira, Lascaux in 1940. Let us not forget that this last discovery was made entirely by chance: a group of schoolboys, who had gone out hunting rabbits, lost their dog; they heard it whining beneath their feet and, in getting down to where it was, found themselves in the magnificently decorated cave whose name, Lascaux, now means so much to so many people. It is a sad fact that, as we write, Lascaux is no longer open to the public, but we hope that in the next decade the technique of preserving the art of Upper Palaeolithic times will be so developed that there will no longer be any threat that these most ancient paintings and mural engravings of man will disappear or not be on view to the public.[63]

The discovery of Upper Palaeolithic cave art was one of the most remarkable and surprising events in the hundred years of Old World archaeology that we now have under review. Another was the bringing to light of civilizations hitherto entirely unknown. Space does not permit a chronicle of all the great archaeological finds of the past century, but the uncovering of the lost civilizations of the Old World is surely one of the most exciting and still breathtaking stories in the history of man's discovery of his own past, and they must be listed here, however briefly. Egypt, of course, was well away on the road to discovery before the hundred years that we are surveying. The team of scientists and draughtsmen which Napoleon took with him to Egypt in 1798 began the organized and scientific study of that ancient civilization: the decipherment of the Rosetta Stone by Champollion in 1822 provided the key to ancient Egypt.

The necessary parallel decipherment, of cuneiform writing, by Rawlinson, took place fifteen years later. Edward Hincks, one of the decipherers, pointed out, with great acumen, that the Semitic-speaking Babylonians could not have been the originators of cuneiform writing, which, he said, must have been borrowed by them from an earlier people. In 1869 Jules Oppert identified these people with the non-Semitic pre-Babylonians, the Sumerians. In 1875 some Arabs informed the new French consul at Basra, Ernest de Sarzec, that stone statuettes of a very interesting kind were being found in a place called Telloh. De Sarzec began digging there in 1877, continuing his work intermittently, under the auspices of the Louvre, until 1900. His finds showed Telloh to be the Sumerian city of Lagash, and his discoveries caused a sensation. As de Genouillac said: "C'est Telloh qui nous a révélé les Sumeriens."[64]

But the Sumerians, the earliest civilized people in the world—old or new—did not become a reality to most people until the joint expedition of the British Museum and the University of Pennsylvania began work at Ur in 1922, under the direction of Leonard Woolley (a long time after his years of initial inexperience at Corbridge). In 1926 Woolley's expedition excavated the great prehistoric cemetery there—the Royal Tombs with their splendid treasures of gold and lapis lazuli, and their remarkable evidence of funerary ritual. It takes rich and sensational discoveries to excite the public, and Egyptian archaeology has never been so exciting as it was in 1923, when Howard Carter, Mace, and Carnarvon discovered and excavated Tutankhamen's Tomb, with its astonishing riches—some of which still lie in this tomb in the Valley of the Kings, while others provide an unbelievable sensation for any visitor to the National Museum in Cairo.

The Bronze Age civilizations of the eastern Mediterranean—the lost civilizations that lay behind classical Greece—were discovered by two archaeologists we have already mentioned, Heinrich Schliemann and Arthur Evans. Schliemann began excavating at Hissarlik in 1871 and worked there for four seasons before his death in 1890. Dorpfeld carried on in 1893 and 1894. The work was then restarted in 1932 and carried on every year until 1938 by the archaeological expedition of the University of Cincinnati—under Semple and Blegen. In the intervals of his four seasons work at Troy, Schliemann dug on the mainland of Greece at sites such as Mycenae and Tiryns and Orchomenos. He knew what he had been looking for at Hissarlik—the old Troy, the old Illium of legend and saga. He did not really know what he was looking for on the mainland of Greece and was surprised when he found what he called the Mycenean civilization—the first civilization of the mainland of Europe.[65]

Those who wondered where the Mycenean civilization had come from began to look south to Crete, where seals had been found with curious markings on them. Schliemann himself had ideas of excavating in Crete, but it was left to Arthur Evans, after Schliemann's death, to dig at Knossos, beginning in 1899, and reveal yet another lost civilization which he called the "Minoan."[66] In his work in Crete, Evans found and described three kinds of writing, the first, pictographic, as seen on the Phaestos Disc; the second and third, linear writing which he labelled A and B. Linear B was deciphered by a professional architect, the late Michael Ventris, and by John Chadwick, a professional archaeologist and ancient historian. Ventris gave the first news of this decipherment in a broadcast on the B.B.C.'s Third Programme in 1953.[67]

While Schliemann was working at Troy, another civilization, that of the Hittites, was being discovered further east in Anatolia. When, in 1860, Perrot visited the large ruined city of Boghazkoy he realized he was looking at an entirely new art. In 1906–1908 German and Turkish excavators, under Hugo Winckler, excavated the site found by Perrot and revealed it to be the capital of the Hittites; these excavations brought to light thousands of tablets which were part of the official archives of the Hittite kings. The Czech scholar, Friedrich Hrozny, published his *Die Sprache der Hithiter* in 1917; eight years earlier he had set out the key to this decipherment.[68]

In 1922, the then Director General of Archaeology in India, John Marshall, was complaining that there was little evidence of the prehistory of India before the invasion of that sub-continent by the Aryan-speaking people from the northwest, but, in 1924, he was announcing in *The Illustrated London News* that members of his staff excavating in large mounds in Pakistan— the sites of Mohenjodaro and Harappa—had discovered a prehistoric civilization comparable with that of Sumeria. This Indus or Harappan civilization has taken on a completely new look in the last quarter century due to the comparative researches of Stuart Piggott and the new campaigns of reconnaissance, excavation, and interpretation undertaken by Mortimer Wheeler.[69]

During the last few decades of the nineteenth century, farmers tilling their fields in the little village of Anyang in the north of China came across curious pieces of bone, some of which were decorated with characters. The finding of these oracle bones led the Chinese Academy, together with the Smithsonian Institution, to begin excavations in 1928 at Anyang. This work has been carried out since the war by the present Chinese government, and no less than a hundred and twenty-five Anyang-type sites have been found, dating from the second millennium B.C.—sites that can now be safely equated with the Shang dynasty of historical China.[70]

In a hundred years, the hundred years we are here surveying so quickly and in such broad outline, archaeology revealed the existence of at least eight ancient civilizations in the Old World—the civilizations of Egypt, Sumer, Troy, Mycenae, Crete, the Hittites, the Indus, and the Shang people of China's

Yellow River. This alone is a most fantastic and romantic contribution made by prehistoric and protohistoric archaeology to our understanding of the past of man in the Old World. And now, particularly in the last twenty-five years, the archaeologist has made a most notable contribution to our knowledge of the antecedents of these civilizations. Zarzi, Karim Shahir, Jarmo, Hassuna, Jericho, Hacilar, Çatal Hüyük—to mention only a few sites in the ancient Near East—show how the process of incipient agriculture through peasant village economy to the synoecism of the urban civilizations came into existence.[71]

One thing was clear in Old World archaeology a hundred years ago. It was obvious to the writers of 1866–1867 what archaeology was about: it dealt with the Stone Age savages, the Neolithic and Bronze Age barbarians, and with the old known historical civilizations of Greece, Rome, Egypt, Assyria, and Babylon; the sphere of the archaeologist geographically was clear—it was the Old World of Europe and the Near East. And the sphere in time was also clear—it began with the first men in the Somme gravels and ended with Greece and Rome when history and art history took over. By the middle of the twentieth century, Old World archaeology was completely changed from what it was at the time of the Neuchâtel conference, the time when Lubbock wrote his *Prehistoric Times,* the time when the Peabody Museum was opened. It was now worldwide and had no barriers in time or space; it could perform its archaeological surgery of excavation with great skill; and it had a wealth of auxiliary techniques to assist it in reconnaissance, excavation, and interpretation. It had discovered the riches of the culture of Upper Palaeolithic savages, not only in the caves of the Dordogne and Cantabria, but in eastern Europe and southern Russia, and the beginnings of peasant village agriculture in the Near East and elsewhere; and it had found civilizations hitherto unknown in the land of Shinar, in the lands of the Indus and the Yellow River, in Crete, Greece, Anatolia, and Persia; and it had deciphered the early scripts of some of these people.

Old World archaology is now in possession of a vast body of information before which the student quails and indeed before which the professional often boggles. The problem is how to organize and interpret this material meaningfully, a problem from which so many Old World archaeologists turn away, with a sigh of relief, to their own cabbage patch: it is so much easier to arrange your artifacts in pigeonholed compartments than to ask yourself why you are doing it and what it contributes to human history. Writing in 1950, I said: "Without a sense of history, and of historical problem, archaeology can revert again to mere collection: and there is always the danger of a new antiquarianism."[72] This danger still exists, but in the last fifteen years two things have happened to revitalize Old World archaeology and to give its practitioners a new hope and a new purpose.

Curiously enough, both those things have happened in the New World. The first we have discussed already and it is obvious: it is the fact that, because of Carbon 14 dating, prehistory in the Old World, as in the New, is revolutionized. For guesswork, we have fact; for estimations and relative chronologies, we have a growing structure of absolute dates. The Old World archaeologist, like the New World archaeologist, seeks to write history: "The goal of archaeology," to quote Brønsted, "is the history of culture."[73] There can be no worthwhile chronicle without reliable dates.

The second, less obvious, thing is the revelation of New World archaeology which shows the independent development of what we conceptualize as agriculture in several areas, and the independent development of what we define as civilization in Mexico, among the Mayas, and in Peru. Wauchope, in his fascinating book, *Lost Tribes and Sunken Continents*, has given us a splendid picture of the lunatic fringes of American prehistory; and I am particularly grateful for the sympathetic portrait of Roland B. Dixon, whose *The Building of Cultures* was a masterly critique of the hyperdiffusionistic Egyptocentric theories perpetrated by two former fellows of my own college in Cambridge, namely Grafton Elliot Smith and W. H. Rivers-Rivers, and disseminated by Elliot Smith's pupil and colleague, W. J. Perry.[74]

It seems to me that it is the excesses of these hyperdiffusionists like Elliot Smith and Perry that made for so long so many Old World archaeologists pay no attention to New World archaeology. That great Old World archaeologist, Vere Gordon Childe, who certainly was one of the finest scholars and synthetists archaeology has ever produced, and who achieved the almost impossible task of being equally informed on the prehistory of India, the Near East, eastern Europe, and the British Isles and of persuading a generation of colleagues and pupils that Old World archaeology was one subject, had no use for the New World. New World archaeology was, he said, off the main stream. In the book about prehistory which he, with characteristic provocativeness, called *What Happened in History*, he explains why he brushed New World archaeology away. This is what he says: "While in historical times the main stream flows from Mesopotamia and Egypt through Greece and Rome, Byzantium and Islam to Atlantic Europe and America, it has been repeatedly swollen by the diversion into it of currents from Indian, Chinese, Mexican and Peruvian civilizations . . . Chinese and Indian civilizations have indeed not failed to absorb currents from one another and from further west. But on the whole they have hitherto discharged these into placid unchanging backwaters. The civilisations of the Mayas and the Incas on the other hand have ceased to run altogether save in so far as their waters are carried on in the main stream of modern Atlantic civilisation."[75] "We are," Childe went on (and he was speaking for most Old World prehistorians at the time), "frankly concerned primarily with the course of the main stream." And to him the pre-Columbian Americas were a curiosity which had produced turkeys and tomatoes, potatoes and tobacco and afforded a ready field for wild speculation about cultural origins and diffusion by amateurs and, indeed, by otherwise sensible and distinguished anatomists and anthropologists.

Now, I believe that, although, of course, the development of pre-Columbian American civilization is not in the main stream of the development of Old World civilization, yet the theoretical and philosophical implications of the works of the last quarter century in New World archaeology are of fundamental importance and of major significance to students of Old World archaeology and origins. All informed people now think that America was first peopled from Asia across the Bering Straits, as Thomas Jefferson argued long ago; that what we conceptualize as agriculture was discovered in many separate places in Mesoamerica and the north of South America; and that civilization came into existence by a process of synoecism, independently in Mexico, among the Mayas, and in Peru—independent, that is, of the Old World civilizations and of any lost tribes: we do not, of course, deny stray contacts, and we remember Ekholm's wheeled toys, and the Meggers-Evans pottery in Ecuador.[76]

The lesson of New World archaeology to Old World archaeology is simple, and it is this: if, as we all now believe, agriculture and civilization developed independently, and perhaps more than once, in the New World, we have to rethink our basic ideas about Old World archaeology. These ideas, as far as my generation is concerned, and, for that matter, the generation of my pupils, stems mainly from such a synthetist as Gordon

Childe. Between 1925 and his untimely death in 1957—for over thirty years—he preached and instilled into us, and (let us make no mistake) believed in preaching himself, except for his brief experimental excursus into Marxist prehistory,[77] a mild but insidious kind of modified diffusionism. At first, he inclined to the views of Elliot Smith and Perry; then he moved to a much modified diffusionism, but one in which things happened once only, and mainly in some part of the most ancient Near East. As Childe saw it, one of the main tasks of the Old World archaeologist was the tracing of culture traits all over the Old World—tracing faience beads from Egypt through Crete and Mycenean Greece to Germany and the British Isles, and sherds of decorated painted pottery from ancient Mesopotamia to India and China. Childe was seldom explicit in his theoretical basis of his interpretation of prehistory, even in his curious *History,* but implicit in it are two doctrines: unilinear evolution in the Near East, and diffusion from the Near East.[78]

The same might be said of the other British archaeologist who produced a synthesis comparable to *The Dawn of European Civilisation.* In his *The Prehistoric Foundations of European Society,* Christopher Hawkes wrote from the same standpoint of unilinear evolution from the most ancient East, although, in all fairness to him, it must be said that his book was about the prehistory of Europe.[79] Childe's work was not confined to Europe: his was an interpretation of the history of man, and his first major essay in this interpretation was called *Man Makes Himself.* What he did not consider then, and indeed what few people knew then for certain, was that man also made himself in America independently of the Old World. I am not saying these things because I am speaking to an American audience: they are directed to an English-reading public in the Old World.[80]

What New World archaeology has taught us is that man did

make himself independently in America; that there is at least one other center, other than Childe's main stream, of agricultural and urban origins; that synoecism happened not only in Sumeria, but quite independently in Middle America and Peru. Once we have learned this lesson, and, by saying "we," I here mean archaeologists and prehistorians in the Old World, we have moved in our theoretical thinking from unilateral evolution and world diffusion to multilinear and parallel evolution. And, once we have done this, there is clearly no reason in theory or practice to confine our ideas of multilinear evolution to Sumeria and Mesoamerica. The Egyptian, Indus, and Shang Chinese civilizations could have developed quite independently of the Sumerians, and the four first Old World civilizations, whose origins we can only know of through archaeology, could be an example of multilinear evolution. I myself do not think that it is as simple as all that; I think that, while the synoecism of the Sumerians and of the Shang Chinese were independent of each other, as most Sumerologists and Sinologists now agree, what happened in Egypt and the Indus valley was that a nascent civilization was catalyzed into synoecism by contacts—stimulus diffusion if you like—with the Sumerians.[81] And, again, I think that what we conceptualize as the origins of agriculture in the Old World could have happened not only in the ancient Near East, but also in southwest Asia and in the western Sudan—in a word, that Murdock and Sauer may be right.[82]

These are some of the exciting new problems which Old World Archaeology is now facing—with all the new techniques we have hinted at, and, at long last, with a certain way of getting absolute dates. That there will be more and exciting new techniques developed in the next fifty years or so I have no doubt. Periscope prospection, proton magnetometers, and archaeological submarines already suggest that archaeology has moved into the realms of space fiction—but, in a way, it has been there since the advent of the air camera and radiocarbon dating. Now that pyramids are being bombarded with X-rays to find hidden chambers, it would seem that anything is possible, and it would not be surprising if techniques were developed which made actual excavation unnecessary.

We Old World archaeologists keep saying that the aim of the archaeologists is to write the history of man, but for so long the writing of that history seemed difficult and uncertain, and it seemed easier and more profitable to concentrate on artifacts and sites. To describe sites and types, to list cultures and objects, seemed what we ought to do, and we were forgetful of Mortimer Wheeler's clarion call: to study not things, but men. We are now moving into a new stage in the development of prehistoric archaeology which I call the "Comparative-Historical Period." This is surely what W. W. Taylor said we should do when he urged the "conjunctive approach" to archaeology—the study of the totality of the culture of a period of prehistoric time.[83] A complete chronicle of the remote past is what we now aim at, and the interpretation of that chronicle by comparative studies.

To do this, we need new orientations and studies that cut across traditional arrangements of facts. One of these was Grahame Clark's *Prehistoric Europe: The Economic Basis* (1952): this is indeed about men and how they lived, and not about things. It will be much more difficult for someone to write a book on the noneconomic basis of prehistoric Europe, the Mediterranean, and the ancient Near East because of archaeology's limitations in illuminating the social, political, and cultural development of preliterate man—limitations which were well set out and argued by Gordon Childe in his *Social Evolution*. But we must try, at long last, to write prehistory rather than to describe artifacts, cultures, and sites.

To do this demands something we still lack in Old World archaeology, namely, an objective, impartial terminology for the main stages of our early socio-cultural development. Our major terminology in the Old World grew up in a haphazard way, and for long—too long—everything has been related to subdivisions of the three-age system of Thomsen and the four-age system of Lubbock. We have, for too many years, been referring to types, cultures, time, and the major stages of man's cultural development by one terminology; and you will still find the less reputable textbooks full of Neolithic types of ax head, Neolithic cultures, the Neolithic period, the Neolithic stage of culture, and the Neolithic revolution. When Lubbock invented this neo-grecism a hundred years ago, he could not have thought it would be so hardly used and abused. As we go forward in archaeology in the Old World, we must have different terms for the different aspects of our study we are talking about. There is, since Libby, no excuse for any denomination of time save in calendar years. Let us call our types and cultures by names, and here I think New World archaeology is ahead of the archaeologists of the Old World. I know that I have been preaching this since, thirty years ago, I wrote the first draft of a small book on the evolution of the three-age idea: so has Robert Braidwood and he is right in demanding a trinomial system of nomenclature in all archaeology. The difficulty is to get an accepted nomenclature and, for long, it has seemed easier not to think about this problem and to make do with divisions of the Neolithic, and with a Chalcolithic, a Leptolithic, and the rest of it. It is interesting that Petrie in Egypt and Arthur Evans in Crete rejected the use of divisions of the three-age system, but Evans himself devised the threefold (or rather ninefold) division of his Minoan civilization. This Early, Middle and Late concept has spread from the Minoan to many other aspects of archaeological nomenclature, but it has never been clear to me what magic or, indeed, cogency, there was in the tripartite division.[84]

New World archaeology has also rejected the subdivisions and elaborations of the three- or four-age system as a basis for nomenclature: but it seems to me unlikely that Old World archaeology will adopt some entirely new scheme of names like the Archaic, Lithic, Formative, Classic, and post-Classic of American archaeology. At present in Old World prehistory we talk about incipient agriculture, the first peasant-village farmers, and so on; and this is a fumbling toward a new terminology— one that is clearer than the neo-grecisms. The change will take time: it took years to get words like "Neolithic" and "Chalcolithic" into our museums and it will take more years to get them out.[85]

But this must be done and this will be one of the features of what I am calling the "Comparative-Historic Period" of Old World archaeology in which we are living and have lived since the chronological revolution of Libby. This phase will see a prehistory free of the older terminologies, a prehistory that can describe cultures and societies fully, can study their economic and noneconomic content and can engage in a comparative study of cultural evolution. As an example, and a very good example indeed, of the new prehistory of this Comparative-Historic Period, I cite one book, *Ancient Europe from the Beginnings of Agriculture to Classical Antiquity*, by Stuart Piggott. It was published in 1965—twenty years after Libby announced the discovery of Carbon 14 dating, forty years after the first edition of the *Dawn of European Civilisation*, eighty years after Montelius wrote *Sur la chronologie de l'Age du Bronze*, a hundred years after the publication of Lubbock's *Prehistoric Times* and the founding of the Congress at Spezzia. The historian of archaeology who looks back at the growth of his subject in fifty to a hundred years time will, I think, use Piggott's book as a landmark in the development of the new prehistory.[86]

Christopher Hawkes said recently: "Purely material studies naturally vital for archaeology in every period, are for proto-historic Europe not enough. Always, of course, we should seek from them not the economic basis only but all we can of the social structure of life."[87] Now we may not be able for a long time—perhaps never—to describe with anything approaching certainty the social evolution of prehistoric man in the Old World, but we can do one thing now better than we have done it before: we can study one aspect of early man's noneconomic development. We can study the evolution of his art; we can describe and discuss the art that survives from prehistoric times. There has been for too long a divorce between art historians and archaeologists: I am not suggesting that there ought to be art prehistorians, but I hope that, increasingly, Old World archaeology will turn to the cultural content of early societies, and art is one of the most important of these contents, as T. G. E. Powell has recently shown.[88] Let us go on digging and photographing and making reconnaissances and classifying our flints and sherds and safety pins and dating our finds ac-curately. All such work is essential and there would be no prehistory without it. But let us sit back sometimes and enjoy the past. And, enjoyment apart, I wonder whether—by looking at the bulls and horses from Lascaux, the carvings in the Mal-tese temples, the sculptures of the early Egyptian pharaohs and scribes, the dancing girl from Mohenjodaro, the Shang bronzes—we may not sometimes get nearer to the men of the past than we would in any other way.

I am not propounding a new heresy of subjective archaeology. I am merely saying that, in our concern, and our very proper concern, in Old World archaeology for building up a structure of cultures and dates—the essential references in the three-dimensional structure of the past that we chronicle—we may have neglected the artistic achievement and endeavor of our forefathers. This was brought most forcibly to my attention again when a few weeks ago I visited in the Hague the remarkable exhibition of Russian art and archaeology from Chellean times to the sixteenth century. Now, when Libby and the Carbon 14 laboratories have taken over our problem of time, and the economic basis and geographical limits of the early societies we call prehistoric cultures are becoming well known in detail, we can begin to think of the neglected aspects of the culture of our forefathers. Perhaps in the end the Comparative-Historic Period of archaeology will lead into a cultural-analytic phase, and perhaps then the discipline of prehistoric Old World archaeology will take its proper place in the study of mankind.

S. L. Washburn / One Hundred

Years of Biological Anthropology

Dedicated to the memory of
EARNEST ALBERT HOOTON

ONE HUNDRED YEARS take us back into the heart of the Darwinian era.[1] The _Origin of Species was published in 1859_, Huxley's _Man's Place in Nature_, and _Lyell's Age of Man_ in 1863. Darwin's _Descent of Man appeared in 1871_, and we may well start this review with Darwin's view of human evolution. Darwin's object in writing the _Descent of Man_ was to consider "whether man, like every other species, is descended from some pre-existing form."[2] The work of the forerunners of Darwin,[3] Darwin's contributions, and the history of the era have been extensively reviewed in numerous symposia and books, many of them celebrating the hundredth anniversary of the _Origin_. Here we are concerned only with Darwin's view of the nature of man and the problem of deriving man from some kind of pre-existing ape. Since very few fossils were known at the time Darwin wrote, the evidences he used were largely indirect and based on still existing forms of life. But _Darwin saw the problem of origin in terms of behavior and of the modification of correlated behavior and structure through time._ For example, Darwin attributed the reduction of the canine teeth of the male ape and the origin of erect posture to the importance of tools. Further, in the comparison of the mental powers of man and animals, Darwin considered emotion, curiosity, memory, and imagination. He considered language, beauty, and religion, and he pondered on the way natural selection had produced social, moral, intellectual human beings. This breadth of vision tended to be lost and the recent books on human evolution are more limited and tend to be concerned with interpreting the record and the process of evolution. The

NOTE: S. L. Washburn is Professor of Anthropology at the University of California at Berkeley.

comparison of the behavior of man and apes was confused both by the state of social science and the lack of reliable accounts of the behavior of nonhuman primates. Today, we can reopen the problem of human nature, of understanding the differences between man and ape, with more effective social science, new evolutionary theory, and major field studies on the behavior of the contemporary monkeys and apes.

The problem of the origin of man is the whole problem of the evolution of human nature. Fossil evidence is essential in charting the course of our evolution, and without genetics there can be no understanding of the process of evolution. But because natural selection operates only through successful behaviors, it is the study of the evolution of behavior that is central to an understanding of the problem of man's origin. In spite of oversimplification, misuse for racist purposes, and misunderstanding, Darwin's view was essentially correct, and the scientific interest in the evolution of behavior has recently revived.[4]

If we accept that the goal of biological anthropology is the understanding of human nature in all its complexity and richness, then we must stress at once that this nature only exists and expresses itself in a social system. Just as the role of the actor is meaningless without the play, so human biology has no meaning without society. For a particular problem in the short run, either biological or social facts may be stressed, but the evolution of man can only be understood as a biosocial problem. Murdock (1945) stressed this in his paper on "The Common Denominator of Cultures."[5] He pointed out that a great deal of culture is universal and the explanation of the universal pattern links all known cultures "simple and complex, ancient and modern."[6] And its explanation can be sought only "in the fundamental biological and psychological nature of man and in the universal conditions of human existence."[7]

More recently, Goldschmidt (1966) in his call for a comparative functionalism has restated the interrelations of biology and society,[8] and Hamburg (1963) has evaluated the emotions of man in the perspective of human evolution.[9] The problems that Darwin raised are being put into modern form, and in this paper I want to consider some of the implications of this transformation.

THEORY

One hundred years ago scientists were trying to convince people that evolution had taken place and that the general principle applied even to man. Darwin's great contribution was demonstrating a mechanism that could be responsible for the transitions of one form into another. But, in addition, Darwin clearly recognized the need for some theory of genetics, some theory to account for the way the phenotypes of one generation become the phenotypes of the next.[10] Although Mendel's laws were rediscovered in 1900, the full implications of genetics for evolutionary theory developed slowly, and it was not until the 1930's that it became apparent that much of the evolutionary thinking was not compatible with population genetics. The history of the origin of the modern or synthetic theory of evolution has been fully told elsewhere,[11] but for present purposes its origin may be dated by Huxley's book *Evolution, the Modern Synthesis,* which first appeared in 1942. In this country the need for bringing together genetics, paleontology, and systematics was recognized in the 1930's, and a Committee on Common Problems of Genetics, Paleontology, and Systematics was formed, held meetings, and started a journal. This committee's work finally resulted in a symposium which was published under the title *Genetics, Paleontology, and Evolution.*[12] Simpson's *Meaning of Evolution* (1949)[13] made the new synthesis available in simplified form. The new synthesis which was forming in the 1920's and 1930's took shape in the 1940's and became accessible to all by 1950.[14]

Since in anthropology there had been extreme reliance on typological thinking, orthogenesis, irreversibility, and the importance of nonadaptive characters, the synthetic theory devastated most of the structure of traditional anthropological thought. This can be seen most clearly in the study of human races.[15] The majority of physical anthropologists had been busy dividing populations into types, and then manipulating the types in order to reconstitute racial history. Types similar to the existing ones were postulated to have existed hundreds of thousands of years ago; this notion of the fixity of the types of modern man goes along with the theory that modern man is ancient and almost all the fossils represent collateral lines which became extinct. Substitution of the variable Mendelian population for the type (composed of phenotypically similar individuals) simply destroyed the theoretical basis for the vast majority of anthropological thought. Many anthropologists believed in orthogenesis, that evolution proceeds from an internal momentum. The synthetic theory showed that no such process exists, and that trends are due to selection. Also the idea was common that evolution should be traced by nonadaptive characters. This point of view is seen in extreme form in the writings of Wood Jones,[16] who, after giving an excellent comprehensive review of primate anatomy, attempted to determine evolutionary relationships on the basis of a few minor variations in the patterns of sutures. According to the synthetic theory, selection is even more important than Darwin thought, and the explanation of characters should be sought in the understanding of their functions. These theoretical problems were by no means unique to anthropology, but the confusion of typological, pregenetic thinking was extreme in anthropology because of the emphasis on racial types, and the attempt to recreate history without regard to the fossil record.

In summary, the last hundred years may be divided, very approximately, into three major sections. In the first, which lasted to approximately 1900, scientists were primarily interested in proving that evolution had taken place and that the theory applied to man. There were few known fossils and the evidences for evolution of man were primarily indirect from the embryology and comparative anatomy of the living primates. In the second stage[17]—again very approximately 1900 to 1940—attempts were made to reconstruct human evolution in considerable detail. Although some fossils were known, elaborate phylogenetic trees were constructed, still primarily on the basis of indirect evidence. This was an era of extreme typological thinking, and scientists believed many conflicting theories of evolution. By 1940 the implications of genetics had become clear and the synthesis of genetics and paleontology was taking place.

THE FOSSIL RECORD

In the nineteenth century not enough fossils had been discovered to compel any particular point of view on human evolution. Discoveries of Neanderthal, Java man, and an ape (*Dryopithecus*) were important in helping to prove that man had evolved from some other form of primate, but the main proofs of human evolution came from indirect evidence, the anatomy of the contemporary forms. This evidence is useful in considering the general nature of human evolution, but it gives no information on the precise course of evolution or on the detail of anatomy of the ancestral forms. The idea of a missing link more or less halfway in its structure between ape and man was firmly imbedded in the human mind *before* the fossils were found. For example, Neanderthal man was reconstructed walking in a stooped-over position and with a bent-knee gait, and the characteristics of the Neanderthal skeleton were described as apelike, even though in many cases they were ultrahuman! Recent study by Straus and Cave (1957)[18] shows that there is no evidence that the Neanderthals walked differently from the way we do. And now that many fossils are available it is impossible to draw any sharp line of distinction between the Neanderthals and people like ourselves. The populations of ancient men of fifty thousand years ago that were ancestral to us included those which are called Neanderthal (if the term is not restricted to the European forms; if it is, then direct ancestry is still debatable).[19]

The essential point is that, when there are only a few fossils, the climate of opinion may be more important than the fossils in determining how they are regarded. Particularly in the case of human evolution (where feelings are strong and facts are few), it takes repeated discoveries to change the patterns of thought that took form in the period when fossils were few, and when the accepted fossil record included mistakes and even fakes. In the period 1915 to 1940 the most common arrangement of the fossil men of the Middle Pleistocene and later was one which put all the even slightly primitive forms on side lines and which postulated that there had been two separate evolutions in the Pleistocene, one of the ancient forms of man (*Pithecanthropus, Sinanthropus,* Neaderthal, and so forth) and one of the anatomically modern forms (Galley Hill, Piltdown). According to this view, almost all the fossils actually discovered belonged on the side lines and the ancestors were rare indeed. Historically the matter might be put in this way. At the time of the "discovery" of Piltdown man in 1912, there were about as many fossils that appeared to support the early modern man point of view as ones that "proved" that, anatomically, modern man was a latecomer. At present there are fewer fossils that can be made to fit the early modern man theory than there were in 1915 and these are mostly fragments. The other point of view is supported by an ever increasing number of well-preserved skulls and skeletons. As Keith put the matter in 1949, "The tide of discovery turned against me."[20] The statement is even truer today than when Keith wrote it.

The view that the populations of ancient men of the Middle Pleistocene and later belonged to one species, that they were at most racially distinct, that interbreeding occurred between them, arose primarily outside of anthropology, and is closely linked to the rise of population genetics and the synthetic theory of evolution. It is no accident that in this country Dobzhansky (1944), Mayr (1950, 1963), and Simpson (1963)[21] (not anthropologists) have been particularly influential in changing the patterns of thought.

If scientists had problems in regarding fossil men, such as Neanderthal, Peking, or Java, as representative of ancestral populations, even greater difficulties were encountered with the small-brained men of the Lower Pleistocene. The first discovery of Australopithecus was made in 1924 and numerous subsequent discoveries support Dart's (1925)[22] interpretation of the original specimen. Consideration of these fossils by anthropologists was hindered by four very strong convictions: (1) that the size of the brain proved that the creature could not be close to man, (2) that the pelvis was far too human to be part of such a small-brained creature, and (3) that nothing with such a small brain could have made stone tools, and (4) that only one kind of man could have made even the simplest tools. It is probable that all these assumptions are wrong. In the Lower Pleistocene, several kinds of bipedal hominids made simple tools, and the beginnings of tool-making may be found in prebipedal apes. There was an adaptive radiation of early bipedal human forms with the formation of more than one species, and one of these species evolved into the genus *Homo*, the large-brained men of the Middle Pleistocene. At least one species of *Australopithecus* lived on and was for a time a contemporary of the earliest members of the genus *Homo*.

These small-brained bipeds, no matter how they may ultimately be evaluated, give evidence of a stage in human evolution that is quite different from anything previously anticipated. They indicate that the rates of evolution of the different parts of the body were remarkably different, and that the evolution of large brains was very late in human evolution.[23] They conform very well to the pattern suggested by Darwin—that the evolution of both bipedalism and small canine teeth was the result of the new selection pressures that came with tool using. The evidence suggests a very long stage of the use of simple tools, and then an increase in the rate of cultural evolution synchronous with the evolution of the genus *Homo*.

In contrast to the relative abundance of fossils of *Australopithecus*, the remains of apes (Pongidae) are rare. There is only one relatively well-preserved skull of the genus *Dryopithecus* (*Proconsul*), for example, and most of the fossils are limited to teeth and jaws. And most of these are fragmentary. Probably the earliest monkeys and apes occur in the Oligocene, and it is probable that the two families had separated by the beginning of the Miocene.[24] Although there are only a few postcranial remains, none of those that are preserved has the characteristics of the arm bones of the contemporary great apes.[25] When only the teeth of the fossil apes were known, it was expected that the rest of the skeleton, when discovered, would be apelike. For example, when Gregory wrote the paper entitled "Were the Ancestors of Man Primitive Brachiators?"[26] bones of the contemporary apes were used to illustrate the probable conditions in the ancestral apes. Obviously, no scientist expected that the bones would be identical, but the limb bones of the now-known Middle Miocene forms (*Pliopithecus* and *Limnopithecus, Proconsul*) are more like those of quadrupedal monkeys than those of the contemporary apes.[27] The features of the limb bones that man shares with the gibbons and great apes are not present in the known fossils, and, if the similarities between man (Hominidae) and ape (Pongidae) are to be accounted for by common ancestry, then the ancestral common populations must have been late Miocene or early Pliocene. The climbing-feeding adaptation called "brachiation" was not present in the early apes, and the similarities of man are with the late apes and particularly with the genus *Pan* (chimpanzee and gorilla).

The fossil record is so fragmentary that such conclusions would carry little weight if they were not supported by other lines of evidence, but recent studies of the chromosomes[28] indicate a very close similarity between man and the African apes. Immunological tests give the same result.[29] If the recently devised method of converting immunological distance into time in years is correct,[30] then the time of the populations of ancestral *Pan* is on the order of six to ten million years, or middle Pliocene. This fits very well with the evidence of the limb bones, but, according to Simons and Leakey,[31] the dental evidence suggests a much earlier separation. The matter cannot be settled at this time, and it will probably take more fossils and other chemical investigations to bring about any sort of agreement. But whatever may be the ultimate solution to the apparently very contradictory conclusions based on different lines of evidence, all lines support the traditional point of view expressed by Huxley in 1863[32]—of the living primates, man is closer to the apes than the apes are to the quadrupedal monkeys.

In summary, the continued discovery of actual fossils has slowly changed traditional points of view on human evolution. The minority opinion that fossils of the genus *Homo* represent ancestral populations, rather than extinct side lines, has become the majority opinion. A whole new stage of human evolution is now represented by *Australopithecus* of the Lower Pleistocene. The discovery of quadrupedal fossils and the apparent contradiction between the dental evidence and that of the limb bones on the one hand and immunochemistry on the other has raised new problems on the antiquity of the family of man (Hominidae). It is clear from this discussion that fossil evidence is necessary for the appreciation of human evolution and that, in winning the battle for the acceptance of human evolution on the basis of comparing the living forms, scientists created such fixed notions of what the missing links should be like that the acceptance of the actual evidence has always been delayed.

TIME

Much of the background for the theory of organic evolution came from geology. The theory that geological formations had been formed over long periods of time by the same processes that can be observed today laid the background for interpreting the history of the creatures whose remains were found in the rocks. In 1778 Buffon speculated that the earth might have cooled from a molten mass and life evolved in a few thousand years. By the end of the nineteenth century Kelvin had suggested that cooling must have taken some thirty or forty million years. On the basis of the amount of salt in the oceans, Jolly estimated that the earth must be one hundred million years old, but scientists were not ready for estimates of this magnitude and Sollas reduced the estimate.

	Sollas (1905)[33]	Keith (1931)[34]
Pleistocene	350,000	200,000
Pliocene	350,000	250,000
Miocene	460,000	450,000
Oligocene	650,000	600,000
Eocene	1,440,000	600,000

Keith's estimate gave a total of a little over two million years for the age of mammals. This was a short estimate, and it can be seen at once that, if one is operating with such a frame of time and if seemingly little human evolution occurred in the Pleistocene, it does not appear to take a great extrapolation to divide lineages back into the Miocene. The short estimates of time, plus the view that the duration of the named intervals of time were more or less equal, had a profound effect on evolutionary reconstructions.

In 1947 methods were devised for estimating time from the rate of decay of radioactive minerals.[35] The times were startlingly longer than previous estimates, and the entire age of the earth as estimated by Sollas could easily fit within the age of the mammals (some seventy million years). Life is now estimated to be something on the order of three billion years old and possibly much older. This time becomes so vast that it can be appreciated only with the aid of an analogy. For example, if we consider a football field as representing, more or less, the five hundred million years of the history of the chordates (vertebrates, the group to which we belong), then the length of all life would be estimated by five or six football fields. The age of the mammals would be on the last fifteen yards of the five football fields and the duration of the genus Homo would be on the goal line. It simply would not show on a scale of this size. Certainly one of the great scientific revolutions is the new concept of time—also space and size. The universe is now believed to be large beyond the most extravagant scientific speculations, and it is made of units which are smaller than had ever been imagined. And 4004 B.C. has changed to billions of years.

For anthropology, there are now four very different concepts of time. First there is biological time, the immediately appreciated circadian rhythms.[36] With long jet travel, we feel the upset in these deeply rooted biological rhythms, and the importance of the animal's ability to estimate time can be seen in the field studies of the behavior of monkeys and apes. Regardless of weather conditions, the internal rhythms bring the baboons back to the sleeping trees at the appropriate time, and the rhythms continue during sleep with the alternation of deep sleep and dreaming. It is highly adaptive for the essential activities to be patterned, and the meaning of light sleep (dreaming) as vigilance behavior has been discussed by Snyder (1966).[37] The appreciation of biological time is directly related to physiology reinforced by habit.

A second kind of time is social time, the three to five generations which are important to the social system. But even this amount of time is far more than the human organism usually feels important. Evolution has not adapted the organism to feel strongly about distant times, whether in the future or in the past.

History is still a third kind of time, and interest in recorded events of the last few thousand years is usually an acquired taste. Historians themselves debate the meaning of these events, and nations make the same old mistakes with supreme confidence that what they are doing is right.

And the fourth kind of time—geologic time, scientific time, the time of the atom, or whatever one may wish to call it—is again fundamentally different, and so hard for the human organism to grasp that its meaning can be hinted at only by analogy.

But the essential point I want to make is that the appreciation of time is basically a biological problem. Part of the appreciation is immediate physiology reinforced by habit. Then we learn with more and more difficulty to understand longer periods of time. In the short intervals that have been important in the evolution of the species, we learn easily and may feel strongly. In the longest intervals, even appreciation becomes difficult or perhaps impossible. It becomes necessary to resort to analogies to convey meaning.

The problem of appreciating time brings out a very fundamental principle. What has evolved is not a behavior as such but an ability to learn. Hinde and Tinbergen (1958)[38] refer to the evolution of "the propensity to learn," and Hamburg (1963)[39] has called attention to the same problem under the heading of "ease of learning." At the moment, there is no simple designation for this, but the situation can be described as follows. Through evolution, each species is so constituted that it easily learns those behaviors that are essential for its survival. Man learns to be social, learns to walk bipedally, learns language, and he learns these activities easily, almost inevitably, because of his biological evolution. The whole dichotomy between instinctive and learned behavior is an oversimplification, and there is every gradation from behaviors that are almost completely determined by biology to those that can be learned only with the greatest difficulty. The demonstration that a behavior is learned does not remove its biological foundations or limitations.

For example, monkeys normally learn to be social, and Harlow (1966)[40] has described the stages of this learning and the devastating consequences of social isolation. Gibbons also learn to be social,[41] but they learn a very different social system. It is useless to postulate a social instinct, but the relation of biology of a species, the situations, and the behaviors present a series of problems. Monkeys will learn to work for the sight of another monkey. They will make great efforts to stay with their troop.[42] They make clearly observable efforts to sit near preferred individuals[43] or to touch other individuals, and, in addition to mating behavior, many social behaviors appear to be highly rewarding. One aspect, or more correctly, a number of aspects, of the evolution of man's capacity for culture[44] is the evolution of the biological bases for interpersonal relations. The diversity of cultures in no way alters the fact that in every pattern of culture it is biological organisms which learn human ways, are moved by human emotions, and adjust with human limitations.

SPACE AND COMING TO THE GROUND

The effect of rephrasing the traditional problems in terms of behavior may be seen by taking the examples of space and of coming to the ground. Traditionally, the utilization of space was not perceived as a problem at all, and our ancestors' coming to the ground was usually accounted for by desiccation, by the reduction in the forests. However, all the nonhuman primates described so far restrict their activities to areas that are, from the human point of view, tiny, a few square miles at most. Probably the vast majority of monkeys spend their entire lives within three or four square miles. Their vision is excellent and they can certainly see rewards (food, water) beyond their habitual ranges, but they do not move long distances. Man is unique not only in his method of locomotion, but in his treatment of space. Man hunts and gathers over hundreds of square miles, and the evolution of human locomotion (the biology) must be seen as an adaptation to this unique use of space, not just to being upright.[45] In 1963, Napier stressed striding as the crucial factor in the human gait, not just being upright. But the point I wish to stress is that the perception that it is advantageous to go long distances probably has been as important in the evolution of locomotion as any other factor. Or, to put it differently, the whole complex of behaviors involving long distances (gathering more extensively, carrying, hunting, seasonal migration)—*all* these would lead to selection for efficient bipedal locomotion. And all these actions involve habits dependent on the learning capacity of the brain, in addition to the locomotor anatomy.

Coming to the ground also is a behavioral problem, and appears very differently if one starts with the behavior of the contemporary primates as a guide. Both the gorilla[46] and the chimpanzee[47] live primarily on the ground. And there is a considerable adaptation for knuckle walking.[48] Gorillas are primarily ground feeders, and chimpanzees eat mostly fruit, knuckle walking from one area of fruiting trees to another.[49] These data point up problems at once. An ape coming to the ground does not necessarily become bipedal, and, second, the ground living apes are in the forest, not in the savanna. Any reduction of forest would mean a reduction in the number of apes. (This is precisely the reverse conclusion of the desiccation theory.) The larger the forests, the more opportunity for ground living apes. Further, if one argues that the human kind of behavior patterns might have been most likely to evolve on the forest borders, the edge of the forest was much larger when the forests were greater. The Old World forests were much larger and the reduction to the present size took place during the Pliocene, probably due both to the rise of mountains and to the reduction in precipitation. Pilbeam (1967)[50] has shown that, in the early Pliocene and before, forests connected Europe, India, and Africa, and the apes (Pongidae) were widely distributed. There was no necessary separation of the African apes from other forms and *Dryopithecus* (sensu lato, following Simons and Pilbeam) existed all over the area. Similarly, they see *Ramapithecus* as a form similar to *Kenyapithecus*. (The similarity in the dentition is a fact, regardless of whether these forms are ultimately regarded as members of the Pongidae or Hominidae.) The fossils show that the similarity of the African apes to man may be misleading in that the actual ancestral species may have been common to India, the Near East, and Africa. Reduction of the forests led to the separation of Asia and Africa, and to the restriction of our nearest living relatives to Africa. But there is no reason to suppose that the living or extinct African forms are any closer to us than are the extinct ones of India or the Middle East.

In summary, coming to the ground is most likely when forests are extensive and when there are many arboreal species which may make the change. Since the arboreal forms are in the forest, the change is most likely to take place in the forest and along the edges of forests. Knuckle walking is the locomotor adaptation of chimpanzees and gorillas to ground life, and it is probable that our ancestors were knuckle walkers on the forest floor for a long time prior to the emergence of efficient, long-distance bipedalism. The behavior of the living primates shows that merely coming to the ground does not explain human locomotion. The essential question is the nature of the adaptation to ground life, and this may be by quadrupedalism, kunckle walking, or bipedalism.

The problem of coming to the ground illustrates several points in traditional thinking. Origins tended to be considered as due to single causes in relatively restricted times and places. So desiccation might account for ground-living or for domestication around a remaining water hole. But the difference between adaptation and extinction probably depended on many factors over long periods of time. For example, one species of contemporary monkey, *Cercopithecus aethiops,* is distributed over an area some eight thousand miles long. This distance is as great as the distance that separates locations where the fossils of *Ramapithecus* and *Kenyapithecus* have been found. When forests were more extensive, there was no reason why a single species of ape might not have such a distribution. Contemporary chimpanzees have a distribution some three thousand miles long, and the limits appear to be entirely geographical. The transition from ape to man (Pongidae to Hominidae) may have taken place in a highly variable species over some millions of years. The implication of genetics is that there is no "origin" in the typological sense, but hundreds of origins over millions of years. As long as ancestral populations remained part of one species, origin is only localized by the extent of the whole species.

A further aspect of the traditional thinking was to come to conclusions which were stated in a very definite form, rather than as a probability. For example, some stated that man "could not" have been descended from an ape and others that he "must be" descended from an ape. Since the fossil record is extremely fragmentary, the chances of error are great. It is easy to avoid this kind of statement and the controversies that have stemmed from it. Conclusions can be put in terms of probability. For example, I think that our ancestors of some millions of years ago were knuckle-walking apes, but the evidence is scanty and I think that the betting odds on this might be something like two to one. In other words, I would not be surprised if the conclusion is wrong. I think it is probable that at a still earlier stage our ancestors were apes who had the climbing-feeding complex called "brachiation." The evidence for this point of view is much stronger. I would place the odds in favor at a hundred to one. In other words, I would be very surprised if the conclusion is wrong, but there is a chance that that may be the case. I suspect that many futile controversies might have been avoided if it had been clear that the differing interpretations of human evolution were matters of probability, if the scientists had indicated the degree of certainty with which they held their beliefs.

CONCLUSIONS

However this may be, the controversies are primarily over the course of evolution, its precise route. There is no debate on the principal ways in which man varies from the other primates and these differences were clear to Darwin and his contemporaries. Man differs in his pattern of locomotion, and this adaptation is more than 2 million years old. Man differs in the size and form of his teeth, and this adaptation shares a comparable antiquity. Both these adaptations may be a consequence of new selection pressures concomitant with the use of tools.

Man differs in the size and structure of his brain, and this (complex of adaptations) came long after the others. The human brain makes the human way of life possible and the brain evolved along with the changing way of life. As we compare the human way to that of the nonhuman primates, as we view the tremendous adaptive success of man's technical and social life, language appears to be the most fundamental adaptive difference. And the later evolution of the brain may have been in a feedback relation with all the complex social patterns which language makes possible.[51]

If this is true, there can be no biological anthropology, in the sense of an independent science, as in the first half of this century. The physical anthropologist can no longer construct an evolutionary history by manipulating types. Nonadaptive characters no longer provide an escape from the study of history and adaptation. Orthogenesis no longer offers a refuge from the study of the actual setting of the evolutionary process. The central evolutionary problem is behavior and, in the case of man, the principal adaptive mechanisms are social and are dependent on the brain and the behaviors that it makes possible, on language, tradition, complex skills, and social change. Clearly, the physical anthropologist cannot deal with all these subject matters. The vision of evolutionary understanding that comes from the synthetic theory, from the union of genetics and paleontology, requires a synthesis of the efforts of many traditional departments. Or, to put the matter differently, the theory that shows why so much of the traditional evolutionary thinking was wrong also shows why the organization of the university is profoundly wrong.[52] The understanding of human behavior is too complicated and too important to be hindered by departmental structures whose origin lies in the nineteenth century. If there is any lesson from a hundred years of biological anthropology, it is that knowledge cannot usefully be divided along the traditional lines and that, perhaps even more than a synthetic theory of evolution, we need a synthetic theory of education. In our universities it should be possible for a student to gain an understanding of man without having to go to a dozen different departments. To understand human evolution we need more fossils, more studies of behavior, more genetics. The technical specialties should be developed. But, beyond these, new academic institutions are needed which are organized around problems and which will share the results of technical specialization with the student. Biological anthropology is concerned with understanding the dimensions of life, the times, places, and conditions under which our ancestors lived; the processes which produced change; the ecological-psychological problems of territory, diet, home base, defense, dentition, and digestion; the social-psychological problems of the group, mother-child, play, the peer group, dominance and order, intelligence, exploration, and religion. However abundant they may be in the fossil record, man did not live by teeth alone, and those who would analyze the fossils must understand the behavior of those who left the bones.

Fred Eggan / One Hundred Years

of Ethnology and Social Anthropology

WHEN THE PEABODY MUSEUM OF AMERICAN ARCHAEOLOGY AND
ETHNOLOGY was founded a century ago, it was not at all clear
that the nascent science of anthropology would survive and
prosper as an integral discipline.[1] Its chief rival, ethnology,
which was primarily concerned with the history of peoples and
their customs, was well established in the 1860's; and archaeology, linguistics, and physical anthropology were in varying
stages of development—as is shown by other papers from the
centennial celebration. Social anthropology, on the other hand,
as the comparative study of social and cultural systems, was
just getting under way and would not be clearly formulated
for another half century.

During the past hundred years ethnology and social anthropology have developed in interaction with their sister disciplines, and with related disciplines in the social sciences and
humanities, in a continuing process which will shape their
future. On the continent, ethnology has continued as the central
discipline concerned with the history of man's culture, and
anthropology is synonymous with physical anthropology. In the
English-speaking world, ethnology has been largely merged
with archaeology in the larger field of cultural anthropology,
or cultural history, and social anthropology has emerged as a
central discipline, particularly in England. My colleague, Sol
Tax, in noting the diversity of interests represented in the early
integration of anthropology in the 1840's, has emphasized the
common concern of the founders for an understanding and
explanation of "the nature and origin of man and his works in
all their rich variety."[2] But this is a task we share with both
the social sciences and the humanities. The development of

NOTE: Fred Eggan is Professor of Anthropology at the University of
Chicago.

these latter disciplines provides the field within which we can examine the tensions between ethnology and social anthropology and their partial resolution, which is the major theme of the present lecture.

The problem of establishing meaningful units for the development of ethnology and social anthropology is a difficult one. The histories of anthropology generally utilize chronological periods, but the progress of the different subfields varies, both in different countries and in relation to one another, so that chronology is at best a rough guide.[3] An organization in terms of Kroeber's "configurations of culture growth,"[4] in which particular patterns originate, develop their potentialities, and are then abandoned or reshaped, might be more relevant and will be utilized to some extent. Of greater potential significance is Thomas Kuhn's conception of "paradigms,"[5] but Kuhn is primarily concerned with the natural sciences and is not sure whether any one of the social sciences has as yet developed that far. Paradigms are based on scientific discoveries or achievements which attract adherents and provide a model or frame of reference for collecting and organizing data to solve the new problems which emerge. Evolutionism, diffusionism, and modern structural-functionalism approximate such a model or frame of reference in certain respects. We shall utilize chronological periods for convenience, but try to develop more meaningful units within them.

Melville Herskovits has recently suggested a framework for the study of "the sequence of ideas that have marked the development of ethnology,"[6] which I have found very useful. In broader perspective, these ideas need to be put in the framework of intellectual history as a whole, since the developments in anthropology reflect in part the changes in society. But the great majority of all anthropologists are still active and a

consideration of the sociology of anthropological knowledge is premature. The availability of a number of standard accounts of the history of anthropology[7] makes possible a more selective and interpretative approach in this paper. The recent interest of historians in anthropology and the new archival resources now available suggest that our amateur efforts will soon be superseded by more professional accounts of our development.[8]

THE PERIOD 1860–1900

Anthropology had its beginnings in the observations and speculations of the Greeks, but the intervening centuries are no less interesting, as Slotkin has recently demonstrated in his *Readings in Early Anthropology* (1965). Here we see the static Christian world view applied to man and society, and its gradual modification through the rediscovery of the classical heritage and the confrontation with the New World. Most of the questions we ask today have been raised time and again. Slotkin's summary is chastening: "I would say that all fields of anthropology were developed by the end of the eighteenth century. In fact their bases were established in the sixteenth and seventeenth centuries."[9] This conclusion is further documented by Margaret Hodgen in her *Early Anthropology in the Sixteenth and Seventeenth Centuries* (1964), and by A. I. Hallowell in "The Beginnings of Anthropology in America" (1960).[10]

The period from 1860 to 1900 represents the first important stage in the *professionalization* of anthropology. Penniman calls it the "Constructive Period," in which "the great pioneers in the study of Anthropology in all its branches followed Darwinian principles and constructed a Science of Man out of what had hitherto been little better than an inventory of all kinds of

men."[11] But this is too simple an explanation for the developments which actually took place.

At the beginning of the period, ethnology pretty much encompassed the whole study of man, but gradually race, language, and culture were disentangled and treated as separate problems. In this process ethnology came to be associated with the historical study of culture, and ethnologists became primarily concerned with the methods for reconstructing history. The numerous accounts of primitive peoples brought back by travelers and missionaries furnished the raw materials for the early ethnologists. The first ethnologies were mainly compilations, arranged to facilitate comparison, of all that was then known of the various peoples of the world. The major interest was in the history of customs and institutions, but there were no historical techniques for dealing with such materials in the absence of texts and chronology. Hence the ethnologists attempted to find a formula which would explain the historical development of all cultures.

There were two great historical syntheses in the last half of the nineteenth century. The first was the work of the so-called "classical evolutionists," Morgan, Tylor, Spencer, and others, who—under the influence of the idea of "progress"—attempted a universal ordering of ethnographic data in terms of time. They assumed that cultural developments everywhere followed definite laws—unfolding uniformly from the simple to the complex and culminating in the institutions of western Europe. Individual cultures were of interest mainly insofar as they illustrated points along the path of cultural progress; once this path was fully laid out the history of culture would be complete.

The second great synthesis centered around the regional formulation of ethnographic data—their ordering in space—and was primarily the work of Friedrich Ratzel and his associates. Bastian had earlier formulated the conception of "geographical

provinces," based on the local development of his *elementarge-danken*; but Ratzel's geographical training led him to study the spatial distribution of cultural elements and to emphasize the importance of the natural environment in cultural development and the role of diffusion and migration in bringing about cultural similarities.

These two ethnological traditions dominated the last half of the nineteenth century. Each attempted to present a consistent picture of cultural development, but so opposed were their fundamental assumptions that quite different "histories" resulted. Since the evolutionists were largely concerned with social and religious institutions and the anthropogeographers dealt mainly with material culture, the differences were not immediately apparent. It was Franz Boas who attempted to reconcile these two traditions.[12]

Lewis H. Morgan's career illustrates some important aspects of the development of ethnology in the United States. Becoming interested in the Iroquois nations in his native New York, Morgan wrote *The League of the Iroquois* in 1851, the "first scientific account of an Indian tribe."[13] Several years later he discovered the classificatory system of kinship organization and attempted to utilize it to solve a historical problem: the origin of the American Indian, which he believed to be in Asia. In the process he found that the Hawaiian kinship systems were even more "classificatory" than those of the Indians, and he developed an evolutionary explanation for the social institutions he assumed were involved. I have elsewhere appraised Morgan's contributions in his *Systems of Consanguinity and Affinity of the Human Family* (1871)—he was the first scholar to carry out organized field research in terms of particular problems, and his discovery of classificatory kinship systems opened up an area of research that has had an important influence on the development of social anthropology.[14]

In England and the continent, Bachofen, Maine, McLennan, Spencer, and Tylor all made contributions to the development of classical evolution, and Tax groups them—with Morgan—as the "historical evolutionary school" of anthropology.[15] But they often fought among themselves, and their formulations of stages of development differed in important respects. In retrospect, Tylor stands out today for his definition of culture and his judicious handling of ethnographic data, as well as for his later application of statistics to ethnological problems.

None of these scholars was directly influenced by Darwin, though the development of social and cultural evolution grew out of the same intellectual climate that gave rise to *Origin of Species* (1859) and flourished under the stimulus of biological evolution. In the United States the acceptance of Darwinism was slower. Louis Agassiz, the great naturalist and founder of the Museum of Comparative Zoology at Harvard, was a strong opponent of transformation, and his debates with Asa Gray and others stirred controversy on the campus.[16] Morgan accepted Darwinian evolution—except for man. His ultimate codification of social and cultural evolution in *Ancient Society* (1877) stands or falls without reference to Darwin's great contributions.

In addition to a conception of universal history based on progressive development, which had an earlier formulation among the French and Scottish philosophers of the eighteenth century, the classical evolutionists also had a method—the famous "comparative method." Comparison is essential in science and all fields of anthropology utilize comparison in one form or another. But, as Kenneth Bock has pointed out, the use of the comparative method in the nineteenth century involved the "acceptance of some principle on which differences in space could be arranged in a presumably temporal series."[17] By viewing primitive peoples as contemporary ancestors of the more advanced civilizations, comparison became a method for assigning groups to their proper stage of development, or for revealing "survivals" of earlier stages. But when the evolutionary stages were discredited the comparative method was largely abandoned.

The museum whose centennial we are celebrating was the first to be devoted to American archaeology and ethnology, but the restriction to America was tacitly abandoned around 1900. The Smithsonian Institution had been founded in 1846 and the American Museum of Natural History in 1868, but specifically ethnological activities began with the establishment of the Bureau of American Ethnology under J. W. Powell,[18] and with the advent of F. W. Putnam as curator of Peabody, and later as its first professor.[19] Putnam made the Peabody Museum a model which he later applied to the development of the Field Columbian Museum and the American Museum of Natural History, so far as their anthropological collections were concerned. His chief assistant in these latter activities was Franz Boas.

The Bureau of American Ethnology, which had developed out of the various governmental surveys of the West, concentrated its attention on Indian languages and cultures, which were rapidly changing or disappearing under the pressures of expansion and settlement. Frank H. Cushing was probably the first professional ethnologist. Powell sent him to Zuni in 1879, where he learned the language, participated in Zuni life, and made a remarkable series of contributions, which influenced Durkheim and Mauss,[20] among others.

Another important early investigator was A. F. Bandelier, a self-made historian who became a disciple of Morgan in the 1870's and began a revision of Mexican ethnology in a series of monographs on Aztec society which were published in the reports of the Peabody Museum. Later Bandelier was selected, on the recommendation of Morgan, by the newly established

Archaeological Institute of America to initiate historical, ethnological, and archaeological work in the Southwest, and the reports of his researches during the period 1880–1885 provided a foundation for all subsequent work.

Alice Fletcher, the first Peabody ethnologist, joined the museum staff in 1882, and spent most of her active life under its auspices. Putnam had begun to organize the collections in terms of Morgan's famous stages, but Fletcher began with a concern for the welfare of the Indians on their reservations and only later began to record their life and culture. Her monograph on the Omaha tribe, written in collaboration with Francis LaFlesche, the son of an Omaha chief, and her account of the Pawnee Hako ceremony, in which she emphasized the native interpretation and meaning, were remarkable achievements.[21] But interest in American Indian acculturation and welfare, and in the Indians' view of their world, was not to develop until after her death.

In Europe, ethnology also had its primary development in connection with museums during the latter part of the nineteenth century. Bastian was the leading figure in the organization of ethnological studies, first at the Royal Museum in Berlin and later at the Museum für Völkerkunde. In England General Pitt-Rivers organized his museum, which was moved to Oxford in 1884. Here the material culture of various peoples was arranged to show the "succession of ideas and development."[22]

Along with museums, there were established a number of societies for ethnological studies, some as early as the 1840's, which provided forums for discussion and journals for publication. Many of these foundered on the issue of slavery, or on religious questions, but most were reorganized or re-established by the end of the century.

Tylor, whose *Primitive Culture* (1871) defined culture in terms of "habits acquired by man as a member of society"[23] and laid the basis for its modern study, soon became established as the foremost English anthropologist. Appointed a professor at Oxford in 1883, he continued his researches at the Pitt-Rivers Museum, where he devoted his efforts to the development of anthropology. Much of his attention had been devoted to the field of religion where his views were attacked by Andrew Lang, modified by Marett, and elaborated by James Frazer.

In the meantime, the "evolutionary school" was in difficulties. In addition to arguments among its members, Westermarck assembled the data available on *The History of Human Marriage* (1891),[24] which demonstrated the widespread occurrence of monogamy among primitive peoples; and a few years later Boas wrote his devastating criticism of the comparative method.[25] By the turn of the century, new developments were under way which were to revolutionize ethnology and make it the central focus of anthropology for the next three decades. At the same time the developments in French sociology, deriving from Comte and Saint-Simon, resulted in the founding by Durkheim of *L'Année Sociologique*, one of the primary sources for the later development of social anthropology.

THE PERIOD 1900–1930

The turn of the century brought major changes in the direction of ethnology, both in this country and abroad. Anthropology for the first time became associated with the newly established graduate schools in the United States, and the professional training of students was systematically developed. Field research became the hallmark of the ethnologist, and the museums employed the new Ph.D.'s to enlarge and interpret their growing collections. In this country there was a sharp break with the past and the major effort was directed toward the recording of Indian cultures before their disappearance. In England there was greater continuity, but field research got under way with the Torres Straits Expedition of 1898–1900, under the leadership of A. C. Haddon. Diffusion began to be emphasized, and functionalism developed, but no synthesis took place. In Germany the *Kulturkreislehre* attempted a nonevolutionary reconstruction of human history in terms of successive migrations of early cultures from an Asian center into Africa, Oceania, and the New World.

We have already noted that the two great syntheses of the nineteenth century gave contradictory results. Boas was the first scholar to confront the dilemma and seek a way out. Trained in Germany as a physicist and geographer, Boas had gone to Baffin Land in 1882 to study the Eskimo. Finding no permanent position in Germany, he returned to the United States where he ultimately received an appointment in anthropology at Clark University. In the meantime he had made a preliminary ethnological survey of the Northwest Coast which attracted the attention of the British Association for the Advancement of Science, where a committee had been established under Tylor to study the tribes of that region. Boas made four field trips to British Columbia during 1888–1894, under the general supervision of Horatio Hale, who had surveyed the same region forty years earlier with the Wilkes Expedition. In retrospect, it was this field experience which established Boas as an anthropologist and influenced his future activities.[26]

Boas had initially accepted the evolutionist position, but his studies of Northwest Coast mythology and art and his growing data on social organization and religion convinced him of the importance of dissemination and borrowing as a major process in cultural development. He salvaged the evolutionist objective of historical laws, but substituted what he called the "historical method" for the discredited comparative method. His own investigations were turned more and more to working out the actual history of peoples and cultures in limited geographical regions. Only from a comparison of such histories might valid conclusions be drawn as to the influence of the environment and psychological conditions on culture and the relative importance of diffusion and independent invention.[27]

While at Clark University, Boas had trained his first Ph.D., but before long Putnam selected him as his chief assistant for the World Columbian Exposition at Chicago. After the exposition, Boas remained for a year at the newly established Field Columbian Museum and then went to the American Museum of Natural History, where Putnam had just organized a Department of Anthropology.[28] A concurrent lectureship at Columbia grew into a professorial appointment in 1899, and Boas was at last in a position to develop the program of training and research that had been taking shape in his mind.

In the meantime, graduate instruction had begun on a limited scale in Peabody, with George A. Dorsey as the first Ph.D. Dorsey soon became Curator of Anthropology at the Field Museum and later achieved popular fame as the author of *Why We Behave Like Human Beings*. When the Peabody Museum became an official part of Harvard University in 1897, the stage was set for a program of teaching and research which would cover all the fields of anthropology. At the University of Chicago, a promising development of anthropology, connected with sociology, got off to a good start, but failed to develop its potentialities, in part because of frictions with the Field Museum. The pioneer work of Daniel Brinton was likewise not followed up at Pennsylvania, where, for many years, the major interest of the University Museum was in Egypt and Mesopotamia. In Washington the Bureau of American Ethnology, which had done a remarkable job in accumulating and organizing ethnographical and linguistic data on Indian tribes, lost some of its momentum with the death of Powell in 1902.

The period 1900–1930 saw the rise of the "American historical school," which centered at Columbia, but ultimately came to include most American ethnologists. Boas, fresh from the successes of the Jesup North Pacific Expedition, outlined in a letter to Zelia Nuttall his program for comprehensive training in all branches of anthropology as a prerequisite for more adequate field work. He went on to state: "I have the conviction that in certain lines at least I know exactly what is needed for furthering our knowledge of American ethnology, and I believe that the method which I am pursuing is more systematic than that followed by many others. It is only for this reason that I have ventured to concentrate in my hands a considerable part of the ethnological work that is being done on our continent."[29]

During the next two decades a remarkable group of students were trained to carry out this program, utilizing the resources of the American Museum of Natural History and the Bureau of American Ethnology. In the relative absence of documentary data and archaeological results, new techniques had to be developed for historical reconstruction. Cultures came to have an individuality of their own, and the culture-area concept crystallized out of museum organization and the distribution of culture traits. As diffusion came to be reckoned as the major culture process, Wissler and others utilized the "age-area" hypothesis to read chronology from the distributional maps.[30]

One result of these distributional studies was that chronology tended to become an end in itself. Further, culture came to be viewed as a mere aggregation of traits, brought together by the accidents of diffusion, and without any particular relations to one another. The historical results of these studies were also unsatisfactory, not only to historians, but to many ethnologists as well. Some of the latter attempted to remedy the methodological deficiencies in various ways, or abandoned ethnology for the study of other aspects of culture.[31]

In England, Haddon, Rivers, and Seligman all became ethnologists as a result of the Torres Straits Expedition, and Cambridge University and, later, the London School of Economics became centers for research and training. Rivers, who had developed the genealogical method, was much influenced by Morgan's studies of kinship, and utilized his evolutionary ideas in his study of Melanesian society. But he gradually became convinced of the importance of diffusion and migration in the development of Melanesian culture and announced his adherence to the position of Graebner and others. The first world war interrupted Rivers' activities, and he died a few years later, but his studies in kinship and social organization laid some of the foundations for the development of modern social anthropology.[32]

The heliolithic theory, which Elliot Smith formulated as a result of his medical researches in Egypt and Perry popularized in *The Children of the Sun* (1923), assumed that all culture worthy of the name had originated in Egypt and had been disseminated by migration to the rest of the world. This *reductio ad absurdum* of diffusionism helped turn English anthropology in other directions.

In Germany evolutionary formulations were not popular, but the work of the anthropogeographers was soon remodeled into an elaborate theoretical structure designed to explain cultural development everywhere in terms of a series of migrations of cultural complexes. The rules for historical reconstruction were developed by Graebner, a historian by training, who was interested in material culture, but, in the application of these rules, assumptions were often made as to the nature of cultural processes and cultural stability for which there was no warrant. In the hands of Pater Schmidt and his followers in Vienna, the *Kulturkreis* doctrine formed the basis for an elaborate history of culture on a worldwide scale. But even Schmidt's reformulations were not sufficient to maintain the structure in the face of the accumulating ethnographic data.[33]

Returning to the United States, we might now look briefly at the role of Harvard's Peabody with regard to the development of ethnology. In 1901 Roland B. Dixon, who had received his doctorate a year earlier with a thesis on the language of the Maidu, was appointed an instructor, and was joined a few years later by Alfred Tozzer, who had made a comparative study of the Maya and Lacandones. With Hooton, who joined the staff in 1913, this triumvirate ruled Peabody and formed the best-balanced department during the period under consideration. But archaeology remained a central interest; field research in ethnology was a secondary activity. Dixon carried out several seasons of field research in California and traveled widely, but his primary interest came to be in mastering the ethnography of Asia, Oceania, and the New World, and in presenting it in systematic fashion to his students. He sent few students to study the American Indian and those who went abroad generally had other interests.[34]

Dixon's first major publication, *Oceanic Mythology*, was the first important survey of Oceania, and the hypotheses proposed in it as to the sequence of migrations into the Pacific had great influence on the subsequent study of Polynesia. But his most important book was *The Building of Cultures* (1928), in which he brought his knowledge of world ethnography to bear on the problems of diffusion, independent invention, and environmental influence. He criticized the assumptions of Wissler's "law of diffusion" and his utilization of distributional data; he found the *Kulturkreis* formulations not to be in accord with the facts; and he dismissed the heliolithic theory as fantastic. His own view of the processes and factors involved in the building of cultures is balanced and judicious, but by 1928 interest in diffusion theory had run its course and his volume sums up an era rather than setting the stage for new developments.[35] The kind of volume that Dixon might have written, if he had lived longer, is perhaps represented in Ralph Linton's *The Tree of Culture* (1955), which utilizes much of Dixon's framework as presented in his famous area courses.[36]

Looking back on the events of this period, we can see something of the significance of the Boas school. According to Ruth Bunzel: "The first two decades of the 20th century in American anthropology might be called the Age of Boas, so completely did that giant dominate the field."[37] But it was his students who put his program into effect, and their common direction and training gave them a basic unity in spite of their later differences in interests.

While each student focused on his own Indian tribe or problem, they spoke a common language and developed a common conceptual framework. Sapir had early provided a comprehensive methodology for achieving time perspective,[38] Wissler had developed the theory of the culture area, and Kroeber, Lowie, and Spier had developed an objective analytical and distributional approach which could be replicated.[39]

But, although their ethnographic data was gathered in the field, it was largely abstracted from the society in which it was embedded, and it was treated as if it were independent of human motivations and social systems. The search for basic cultural units was unsuccessful, and, indeed, it still goes on today. The emphasis on diffusion seemed warranted, but the mechanical handling of trait complexes and the assumption of uniform rates of diffusion went too far.

By the 1920's the Boas program was in full flower. His students were in control of most of the anthropological centers in the United States. Boas had met defeat in his early attempts to professionalize the American Anthropological Association, which had reprimanded him for his criticisms of anthropological activities during the first world war. But he had maintained a prodigious output and a dominant position in the scientific world.

During much of this period, the view prevailed that ethnographic data could be gathered without theoretical preconceptions, and the assumption was made that, once enough data were available, the answers to theoretical problems would be clear. But Kwakiutl social organization defied easy analysis, and the thousands of pages of texts provided by Boas' assistants only complicated the picture. It was beginning to be apparent that theory was needed, both to interpret the data and to gather it. No longer would the term "ethnographer" be the highest praise.

THE PERIOD 1930–1960

This period, which might be called the "modern period," encompasses a number of variant developments.[40] The decade of the 1930's saw the rise of social anthropology and the apparent decline of ethnology in both Great Britain and the United States, though the proportionate changes were different. The disruption occasioned by the second world war was profound and resulted in new orientations everywhere. The postwar expansion of anthropology in the United States has led to a synthesis of social and cultural anthropology and to new relationships to the social sciences and with history. In England there has been a broadening of social anthropology which is converging toward a similar synthesis. The new developments of social anthropology in France are likewise in the same direction, though with somewhat different overtones. For the first time we are on the verge of a worldwide consensus with regard to anthropology in most of its branches.

The theoretical beginnings of social anthropology go back

to the French and Scottish philosophers of the eighteenth century. We have noted briefly the contributions of Morgan and Rivers, but the modern basis for social anthropology was laid by Durkheim and his French sociological school, beginning in the 1890's. Two anthropologists, Malinowski and Radcliffe-Brown, are primarily responsible for the rise of social anthropology to a dominant position before the war; a third, Lévi-Strauss, has played an important role in the postwar period.

Malinowski, a Polish scientist who had become interested in anthropology through reading Frazer and had studied at the London School of Economics under Hobhouse, Westermarck, and Seligman, was in Australia when the first world war broke out. Technically an enemy alien, he was interned, through the efforts of his friends, in the Trobriands for the duration.[41] Here he learned the language and investigated all aspects of Trobriand life, emerging after the war to write *Argonauts of the Western Pacific* (1922) and a series of other monographs,[42] and to develop a new functional approach to the study of culture. On his appointment to the London School of Economics in 1924, he attracted a remarkable group of graduate students, beginning with Evans-Pritchard and Raymond Firth, who have since dominated anthropology in Great Britain and the Commonwealth.[43]

Radcliffe-Brown was Rivers' and Haddon's first ethnological student at Cambridge and carried out his initial field research in the Andamans in 1906–1908. But, after writing a conventional ethnological thesis, he became acquainted with the new ideas emanating from *L'Année Sociologique* and sought the meaning of Andamanese ritual and myth in the context of their social life.[44] Later, in Australia and Africa, he turned his attention to social organization and its structural aspects, thus adding a new dimension to the functionalism that he shared with Malinowski.[45]

Both the careers and the personalities of these two men were complementary. Radcliffe-Brown had founded departments of social anthropology at Capetown and Sydney before coming to Chicago in 1931. When he accepted the chair at Oxford in 1937, his views had long preceded him, but the onset of the war and his forced retirement soon after restricted his personal influence. In the meantime Malinowski had developed a major program of research on Africa and other regions, the results of which were beginning to appear before the war in Firth's studies of Tikopia, Evans-Pritchard's studies of the Azande and Nuer, and Fortes' and Evans-Pritchard's *African Political Systems* (1940). Malinowski, who had come to this country just prior to the outbreak of the war, remained at Yale until his unexpected death in 1942.

In the United States the 1920's saw the beginnings of a search for more satisfactory approaches to the study of culture. Around the middle of this decade, Boas had decided that diffusion was not the answer,[46] and, as distributional studies reached their climax, some of his students began to explore in new directions. Thus Ruth Benedict shifted from analytical studies to the psychological characterization of cultural wholes; Margaret Mead began her studies of individual development in relation to culture; Radin published his autobiography of a Winnebago Indian; Lowie turned to the study of social organization under the stimulus of Rivers; and Herskovits developed a more dynamic approach through the consideration of the processes of cultural change. A. L. Kroeber, who set out to salvage culture area theory and distributional studies, also turned his attention to the processes of growth in historic civilizations.

Many of these developments were foreshadowed in Boas's "Methods of Ethnology," published in 1920,[47] but a decade later he went much farther: "If we knew the whole biological, geographical and cultural setting of a society completely, and if we understood in detail the ways of reacting of the members of the society and of the society as a whole to these conditions, we should not need historical knowledge of the origin of the society to understand its behavior . . . An error of modern anthropology, as I see it, lies in the overemphasis on historical reconstruction, the importance of which should not be minimized, as against a penetrating study of the individual under the stress of the culture in which he lives."[48]

American anthropologists were not equipped for this type of study in 1930, though some beginnings had been made, notably by Sapir. Malinowski's functionalism, centering on culture and the interrelations of institutions, and oriented toward the needs of the individual, was relatively easy to accept, and some of Boas' students came to believe that "they had known it all the time." But Radcliffe-Brown's emphasis upon society as a central concept and his utilization of organic analogies in defining social function aroused opposition. Both men were critical of "conjectural" history, but Radcliffe-Brown went further in his advocacy of sociological laws and explanations. The newly developing American approaches were emphasizing the individual in relationship to his culture—and explanations in terms of gestalt psychology, psychoanalytical conceptions, and learning theory were becoming important.

The Great Depression also played an important role. The museums which had supported much of ethnological research found their funds greatly curtailed, while the universities expanded their activities. The new departments in anthropology were often associated, in their beginnings, with sociology, which brought about an increasing concern with contemporary problems and a closer association with sociological colleagues. The new developments in archaeology also led to a more complex

picture of the past than had been achieved by historical reconstructions and to a relative decline in ethnology during the
1930's.

The confrontation of the two partly opposing sets of views,
which began with Malinowski's visit to the United States in
1926 and was enhanced when Radcliffe-Brown came to the University of Chicago in 1931, continued throughout the decade.
Debates over functionalism enlivened the scene and there was
much excitement among graduate students. Robert Redfield,
who himself had just completed his study, *Tepoztlán* (1930),
which led to the characterization of the "folk society," and to
his later comparative study, *Folk Culture of Yucatan* (1941),
has well described the impact: "Professor Radcliffe-Brown
brought to this country a method for the study of society, well
defined and different enough from what prevailed here to
require American anthropologists to reconsider the whole matter of method, to scrutinize their objectives, and to attend to
new problems and new ways of looking at problems. He stirred
us up and accelerated intellectual invention and variation
among us."[49] And Ralph Linton's *Study of Man* (1936) reflects
both the debates and the initial integration.

At Columbia there was considerable ambivalence toward
Radcliffe-Brown, as Mead makes clear in her memoir on Ruth
Benedict,[50] but Boas' retirement in 1936 brought about a new
alignment. Instead of continuing the Boas program through
an appointment of one of his distinguished students, Linton,
Steward, and Strong were added, the latter two students of
Kroeber, which created a strong department, but one without
much conceptual unity.

At Harvard, Lloyd Warner, who had been a student of
Lowie at California and had then spent three years among the
Murngin under the direction of Radcliffe-Brown, set out to

make his now famous studies of the social systems of New England and the South, even before he had completed his thesis.[51] He was supported by Elton Mayo, and he attracted a devoted group of students, but these new directions were apparently too radical, despite the results which were achieved, and Warner came to Chicago in 1935. Taking his place was Clyde Kluckhohn, who was just completing a thesis, "Some Aspects of Contemporary Theory in Cultural Anthropology" (1936), notably those relating to the *Kulturkreislehre* and to psychoanalysis, both of which he had investigated while a Rhodes Scholar at Oxford. In the next few years Kluckhohn emphasized the importance of theory in anthropological studies —including both archaeology and ethnology—a topic which most of his predecessors had avoided.[52] He had earlier begun a long-term study of the Navaho Indians, which he utilized as a testing ground for cultural theories throughout his career. The death of Roland B. Dixon in 1934 had paved the way for change, but anthropology at Harvard was not altogether ready for a large-scale injection of theory.

During the 1930's the development of acculturation studies took place under the stimulus of a memorandum prepared by Redfield, Linton, and Herskovits, each of whom went on to make important contributions to the study of culture change.[53] But acculturation was not widely accepted until after the war, when westernization and modernization became a central focus of studies of new nations as well as of marginal groups.[54]

In England the ethnological activities begun by Haddon, Seligman, and Rivers continued, but with diminished vigor, during the 1930's, as the functionalist movement developed and gradually supplanted historically oriented inquiries. Fortes refers to British anthropology of this period as "a bundle of interests held together by the evolutionary frame of thought."

By the 1930's the bundle had fallen apart and social anthropology had emerged as the basic discipline, with ethnology as a bridge to physical anthropology.[55]

The advent of the war brought a halt to normal anthropological activities, but the worldwide scope of the war made heavy demands on anthropological knowledge and anthropologists emerged with a new position in social science, as well as with new ideas and sometimes new careers.

The influx of graduate students with government support burst the seams of American universities. For their field research they deserted the American Indians in favor of Africa, India, Oceania, or Southeast Asia. Great Britain established research centers in colonial regions as a preliminary to independence, with some American staff members. In addition, exchange of professors and of graduate students began to give anthropology a more international character.

In the postwar decades field studies more and more followed the model developed by Malinowski, but utilized, also, the structural framework developed by Radcliffe-Brown, as well as new ideas concerning the organization of culture. The colonial research centers in Africa were particularly concerned with the problems faced by emerging nations and concentrated much of their attention on political development and modernization; and the new roles of African chiefs and the problems of conflict in relation to social order had a prominent place in the research designs.[56]

The senior social anthropologists in Great Britain have produced an excellent series of monographs on African and other tribes, and considerable progress has been made in understanding lineage systems and other structural features. But the depth of detail has inhibited the correlative needs for comparison, and Radcliffe-Brown's hoped-for generalizations have not been forthcoming. Younger anthropologists are beginning to take a broader view of their discipline and to develop new methods for its study, including the use of historical documentation and the observation of change over time.

In this country the great expansion of anthropology in all its branches makes any brief characterization difficult. But by the time of the Wenner-Gren symposium "Anthropology Today" in 1952,[57] it was apparent that ethnology in its traditional sense was rapidly losing ground. The historical approach still loomed large, but it was clear that archaeology was taking over the historical interests and was utilizing ethnographical data to interpret its findings. On the other hand, documentary data were being increasingly utilized and ethnologists and some historians were joining forces in the new discipline of ethnohistory. The term "cultural anthropology" has gradually replaced ethnology as the general term for both historical and processual interests with respect to culture, but social anthropology has come to have almost equal weighting. The term "socio-cultural" anthropology is often used to refer to both interests—with the emphasis on the social system being balanced against culture as a patterned organization or symbol system, and their interrelationships deemed more important than their separation.

Another development came about through the establishment of closer working relations with other social scientists. The Institute of Human Relations at Yale had earlier brought together anthropologists, sociologists, psychologists, and psychiatrists for the study of behavioral problems; and, at the end of the war, Harvard established a Department of Social Relations which included social anthropology, sociology, and social psychology, the disciplines soon to be called the "behavioral sciences." Here Kluckhohn and his associates had greater scope, and Kluckhohn expanded his Navaho studies and began the Values Project, which was to compare and contrast the value systems of five southwestern groups.[58] Kluckhohn's primary

interest remained in culture, and particularly in its organization and relationships with personality. He had little interest
in social structure, but his associate, Talcott Parsons, has developed structural-functional theory in a sophisticated manner.
Kluckhohn's extended service as Director of the Russian Research Center and his premature death prevented him from
completing most of his projects, but his Navaho studies and his
essays testify to his outstanding abilities as a theorist and field
worker.

At Chicago there were no administrative innovations, but
close relations were maintained with sociology through Redfield and Warner, and the Committee on Human Development
included some anthropologists. Redfield continued his research on the folk-urban continuum and peasant cultures, but
soon shifted to the comparative study of civilizations. My own
researches have tended to follow the model of Radcliffe-Brown,
but with a greater utilization of historical data and within
smaller regions where it is possible to achieve greater control
over the frame of comparison.

A number of other developments during these thirty years
have attracted attention and some adherents. Leslie A. White's
revival of evolutionary theory has not only restored Morgan in
his rightful place as a major figure, but has led to a re-examina-
tion of both cultural and social evolution, and to an important
distinction between macro-evolution and micro-evolution.[59] Evolution as an adaptive process also plays an important role in
Julian Steward's conception of cultural ecology, which has
given us a new vantage point from which to view the interrelations of technology, social organization, and the environment.
Some of Steward's views of cultural causality have recently
been confirmed by Robert McC. Adams' recent comparison of
the development of early Mesopotamia with that of prehispanic
Mexico.[60]

The postwar period has also seen a considerable development of quantitative methods in cultural anthropology. These had their origins in Tylor's pioneer investigation of the relations between residence rules and kinship avoidances; and Driver and Kroeber had applied quantitative methods to interpret the results of the California culture element survey in the 1930's. But Murdock's *Social Structure* (1949), which used statistical methods to test functional hypotheses and to establish correlations between social traits, has stimulated a great amount of research on social systems. Cross-cultural research utilizing quantitative methods has also been facilitated by such organizations as the Human Relations Area Files, a consortium of some twenty universities, and by the development of computer technology, but such research is complicated by the lack of clear-cut units, difficulties of coding, and problems of sampling.[61]

The integration of social and cultural anthropology has been developed in new directions by Claude Lévi-Strauss under the rubric of "structural anthropology." A philosopher by training, but a disciple of Mauss, Lévi-Strauss went to Brazil in the 1930's on a cultural mission; there, field research among the Brazilian Indians led him to become a social anthropologist. His structural analysis derives in part from linguistic research and is concerned with the development of models abstracted from empirical reality and compared on a number of levels and transformations. He is concerned with basic mental processes, of which social and cultural institutions are empirical manifestations, and he is searching for general principles which should be applicable to all societies. Elaborating on Mauss's principle of reciprocity, Lévi-Strauss has examined social structures, primitive systems of classification, and mythology in a highly productive way.

Lévi-Strauss's first important work was *Les Structures élé-*

mentaires de la parenté (1949), a massive study of cross-cousin marriage in terms of exchange theory, which has revolutionized kinship studies and led to much productive controversy, from which Dumont and Leach have developed alliance theory as an alternative to descent. His more recent renovation of totemic theory and his clarification of *The Savage Mind* (1966), along with his current studies of mythological systems and their interpretations, have opened up exciting vistas for anthropologists, and are certain to arouse new controversy. Whatever the ultimate outcome, it is clear that Lévi-Strauss has added a new dimension to social anthropology.[62]

THE PRESENT AND THE FUTURE

The 1960's show a number of new developments which, in retrospect, may be as important as those of the 1860's for the future of anthropology. Today there is enough personnel to engage in long-term projects which will consolidate and develop the pioneer insights which anthropology has so far achieved. The gradual merging of social and cultural anthropology involves a basic acceptance of structural-functional theory, but without the extremes of Radcliffe-Brown, Malinowski, or Leslie White. A number of contributions have become landmarks since the early observations of Tylor and Morgan: van Gennep's conceptualization of the rites of passage; Malinowski's and Mauss's formulation of reciprocity as a basic pattern for interaction; the concept of social integration and the lineage principle, as formulated by Radcliffe-Brown and developed by Fortes and others; and more recently the development of alliance theory by Lévi-Strauss, Dumont, and Leach. In the last few years, the principle of binary opposition, borrowed from the linguists, has been utilized by Lévi-Strauss and others to give further understanding of social and cultural institutions, and of the mind, as well.[63]

Looking back on a century of anthropology, we can see that there have been major changes in the relations between data and theory. The evolutionary theories were initially developed in the relative absence of anthropological facts, and new data led to the abandonment of the classical stages. At the beginning of this century the collection of data became a primary preoccupation and the anthropological disciplines were differentiated in part because of the different techniques utilized for gathering the facts. With the growing realization that theory did not automatically develop from the data, new methods for ordering and interpreting the data were consciously sought, utilizing the models of history or science, and a new realignment of disciplines came about in terms of ultimate objectives—generalizations or "descriptive integration." Data and theory were more closely interrelated, and social anthropology became differentiated from cultural anthropology in both objectives and methodology. Today there are greater tendencies for fusion and for the development of a more comprehensive point of view and a single set of assumptions.[64]

Social and cultural anthropology continues to be both a generalizing discipline and a historical one—the tensions between history and science have not been resolved, but the differences have become less important. While, in the German-speaking world, cultural anthropology continues as the handmaiden of history, of American ethnologists only Paul Radin has favored Maitland's view that "by and by anthropology will have the choice between being history and being nothing." Evans-Pritchard, while arguing that social anthropology is closer to some kinds of history than to natural science, accepts Maitland's dictum only if it is also reversed. Benedict, Kluckhohn, and Redfield have all considered themselves to be humanists in varying degrees, and Kroeber envisages cultural anthropology as taking over the data of the humanities and generalizing them. In England, Fortes has criticized Evans-Pritchard's views, holding that "there are regularities independent of period and place in social organization and culture" and that "the main aim of social anthropology is to investigate the general tendencies, or laws, manifested in them."[65]

Radcliffe-Brown, who originally had taken a rather intransigent view of "conjectural" history and had emphasized the search for synchronic laws, modified his position in his later writings: "It is only by the use of the comparative method that we can arrive at general explanations. The alternative is to confine ourselves to particularistic explanations similar to those of the historians. The two kinds of explanation are both legitimate and do not conflict; but both are needed for the understanding of societies and their institutions."[66]

And Evans-Pritchard believes that diachronic laws must be established before we can validate synchronic laws. My own contribution has been to look at social structures as they change over time, in order to evaluate more clearly the factors operating in a given situation and to describe the processes involved in general terms. As Spoehr has put it: "The very meaning of functional dependence is that change in one variable results in change in a dependent variable."[67]

The fear expressed in some quarters that anthropology might disintegrate has not been realized, though there is increasing difficulty in maintaining close relations between cultural anthropology and physical anthropology, which are largely separate on the continent and in England. On the other hand, within social and cultural anthropology, there is an increasing development of specialties which will influence their future organization and affect their relations with the social and behavioral sciences.

We have already noted the growing communication between ethnology and archaeology, and their joint interest in ethno-history; in the field of culture history the historians are beginning to meet the cultural anthropologists halfway. There is also a new relationship developing between museums and the universities in terms of cooperative training and research. The interest in culture and personality studies has been carried forward by Hallowell and others through the incorporation of new findings in psychology and psychiatry, and the utilization of psychological tests.[68] The resulting psychological anthropology is currently using life-history studies, projective tests, dream analysis, and cross-cultural surveys to develop a central body of theory with regard to personality which will intermesh with that of the psychiatrists and social psychologists. Political anthropology has developed as social anthropologists have become concerned with the problems of power and social control in emerging nations and large-scale tribes. Here they have had to become acquainted with political theory and join forces with the students of political behavior and comparative politics, who have emerged since the war. Economic anthropology, pioneered by Herskovits and recently elaborated by Karl Polyani and his associates, has begun to attract the attention of professional economists and to result in more sophisticated studies of primitive economics.[69]

We can begin to see a new organization for anthropology emerging, centering on man and his works and providing a spectrum of specialized fields which interlock with those of the social and behavioral sciences. Ultimately, there will be no sharp boundaries—as there are none in the biological and physical sciences today—but culture, society, and personality will be

major foci of attention, both individually and in their interrelationships. What the role of anthropology will be in this larger
field is not yet clear, but its broad comparative treatment of
social and cultural phenomena should assure it a central position.

The directions of anthropological research in the next few
decades are to be found in the work currently under way. I have
not attempted an analysis of the journals and doctoral theses,
but I had the good fortune to attend a meeting of the British
Association of Social Anthropologists in 1963 at Cambridge,
England, to which a group of younger American anthropologists
had been invited. The sessions were organized in terms of four
major topics: (1) the relevance of models for social anthropology;
(2) political systems and the distribution of power; (3) anthropological approaches to the study of religion; and (4) the social
anthropology of complex societies. The papers and the discussion confirmed our conclusions with regard to the growing unity
of social and cultural anthropology on both sides of the Atlantic;
they also indicate some of the trends and developments in
anthropological research.[70]

The history of anthropology has been one of gradually
increasing complexity as race, language, and culture were first
differentiated, and, later, culture, society, and personality were
conceptualized. The central problems of anthropology remain,
and we keep returning to them periodically with new methods
and new data. The interrelations of biological, psychological,
social, and cultural factors and the problems of adapting to
varied geographical and social environments make anthropology
a complicated science indeed. But the simpler formulations of
the past have not sufficed, and we will make progress only as
we develop new ideas and new ways to cooperate with other
disciplines. Radcliffe-Brown has said: "It will be only in an
integrated and organized study in which historical studies and

sociological studies are combined that we shall be able to reach a real understanding of the development of human society."[71] And Eric Wolf, asserting his belief that it is the task of anthropology to create a true science of man, notes that "in the process of creating that science of man that will underwrite the new world culture and its new possibilities, anthropology will also change itself, and change itself beyond recognition. Some of these changes are already under way. To make them possible, in a world of necessity, is our obligation."[72]

Floyd G. Lounsbury / One Hundred

Years of Anthropological Linguistics

1866 and 1966

IT MAY BE OF INTEREST, and appropriate to this occasion, to scan the scene in the field of anthropological linguistics as it was a hundred years ago, in the mid-1860's, and for a decade or two immediately thereafter. This can provide a background against which to view more recent developments.

Among the linguistic topics that commanded attention during that period, from the 1860's on into the 1880's, and that are (or were) of anthropological interest, the following deserve to be accorded special mention.

1. *Questions about the origin of language.* This was an old theme for speculative linguistics, centuries old; but it was again, or still, in the forefront of thought and was heavily published on in the two decades at the beginning of the period we are marking. Although this was a topic of debate whose primary relevance was for philosophical and theological inquiries into the nature of language, it was of anthropological interest also; and there is, as will be seen, a special reason for its inclusion in this list.

2. *Problems of Indo-European historical and comparative linguistics.* This domain of investigation had a history of just eighty years, as of 1866. By that time it embraced a number of special but related inquiries, among which, of particular relevance to this survey, were the attempts to uncover the prehistory of the Indo-European peoples—their phylogeny, and traits of their common ancestral culture—through detailed study and comparison of their languages; and, also, as one of the results of this effort, the development of a general theory of the processes of change in language. And, in connection with the latter, one must mention especially the formulation of the

NOTE: Floyd G. Lounsbury is Professor of Anthropology at Yale University.

153

"neogrammarian" hypothesis and the method of linguistic comparison and reconstruction that is based on it. All of these led to culminations in the two decades under consideration. Moreover, they furnished a model and established a goal for later work in other families of languages that were to become more intimately a part of the anthropological concern.

3. _Questions concerning the significance of language differences._ During the initial decades of the period of our review the primary concern in regard to language differences was with morphological typology, and with interpreting the evolutionary significance of typological differences. This theme had been current for over half a century; but at this particular time a new view of the evolution of language was gaining credence—one that was soon to turn the older one upside down. A still newer view of the significance of language differences, which has been dominant in anthropology in recent history, had not yet appeared on the scene.

4. _The development of the science of phonetics._ This was as yet a relatively minor theme in linguistics. The 1860's and 1870's, however, saw the appearance of some of the works that laid a foundation for the new science. This was also a period in which the need for phonetic knowledge and theory was being very keenly felt in connection with a number of other linguistic pursuits: especially in historical and comparative linguistics (in order to understand the nature of phonetic changes), in anthropological and missionary enterprises involving hitherto unwritten languages, and in the practice of foreign-language teaching.

5. _Studies of the languages of primitive peoples._ At a time when the principal task of anthropology was taken to be the reconstruction of the unrecorded past, "linguistic anthropology" (reconstruction of the past from linguistic evidence) was

viewed by some as one of its most promising branches. To this end, significant starts had been made toward the description and classification of native languages in each of the major ethnographic areas of the world: North and South America, Oceania, Africa, and the various non-Indo-European regions of Asia and Europe.

Starting from these five problem areas of anthropological linguistics, as subdivided for the period of a century ago, it is possible to trace certain continuities and developments of ideas up to the present, as well as to see certain dead ends, shelving of old problems and discovery of new ones, and a realignment of interests and redefinition of goals.

The accounting for the origin of language—that once irresistible subject—lost its attraction for scholars, and the whole matter was quite generally shelved by the early decades of the twentieth century. Thereafter, it was only occasionally to be taken up in an attempt to make a relevant point. The linguistic and philosophical contributions to the problem had seemingly been exhausted, and to little avail. But, interestingly, the two principal issues that had motivated much of the old debate on this subject, and in terms of which the question was generally argued, have continued to reappear as fundamental issues for linguistic theory. These were the question of priority as between *thought* and *language,* and the question of *innate* versus *experiential* determination of the structure of language. They are with us again at the time of this writing, having survived their former theological-philosophical context and reappearing now in contexts of grammatical theory and the psychology of language. Meanwhile, the problem of the origin of language has been redefined as the problem of the attainment of *the capacity* for language by *Homo sapiens,* a problem to be taken up by a number of more relevant disciplines: comparative neural anatomy and neurophysiology, primate ethology, and physical anthropology. The older theories of the origin of language, after all, never did have as their goal to account for the origin of the *linguistic faculty*—the uniquely human condition—but only for an initial appearance of language in the behavior of an organism in which the necessary faculty was assumed already to be present. Whether linguistic science may yet contribute to the problem as newly defined is a question for the future. Some see the potential contribution of linguistics as being that of specifying precisely what the behavioral capacities are that have to be accounted for.

Indo-European historical and comparative linguistics has flourished for another century since 1866. It is a vigorous and exacting discipline, with remarkable achievements to its credit. Being a specialty in its own right, it is not usually reckoned as "anthropological linguistics" (though by any reasonable definition of the latter, it certainly must be included). But the problems encountered by researchers in the domains of other language families, in which anthropology has by tradition and preference a more intimate concern, reproduce the most crucial ones that had been faced by the Indo-European comparativists. The experience gained in the earlier field could be transferred to the newer ones.

The concern with language differences took on a new and different aspect in the twentieth century as morphological typology, having undergone great refinement on the one hand, but apparent loss of significance on the other, dropped to a lower place and gave way to new interests in a different aspect of language variability: the differences in the categorizations of meaning that are presented by different languages, and the psychological significance of these. Out of the investigations of this phenomenon there has grown a theory of "linguistic relativity" and a view of the relationships between culture and language, and between language and thought, rather different from that envisioned by the typologists.

Researches into phonetics produced results of immediate utility to ethnographers, linguists, and others who had need to record hitherto unwritten languages. Systems of phonetic transcription of great flexibility and adaptability were devised, which could encompass the diversity of possible speech sounds, and could allow for discriminations as fine as might be necessary in accommodating the (to the European) unexpectedly strange or subtle bases for contrast in previously unknown languages. With this equipment, and training in the use of it, new generations of field linguists and ethnographers made immense improvements over their predecessors in the quality and adequacy of their recordings of linguistic data and of native-language ethnographic texts. But, in the process of refinement of phonetic discriminations, it very soon came to be appreciated that some of these, which it is crucial to recognize in one language because they differentiate linguistic signs, may in another language be quite superfluous to recognize because, even though present, they lack the word-differentiating function, and are determined instead by other phonetic variables in their immediate contexts (being dependent, rather than independent, variables). Thus in the phonetic organization of languages there was found another domain of "linguistic relativity": a variability from language to language in the assignment of "distinctiveness" (cue value, semantic discriminatory function) to features of phonetic difference. Out of this recognition came the "phonemic principle" and the theories and methods of phonology ("functional phonetics," "phonemics"). Phonology has proved to be a fertile ground for the growth of linguistic theories and for the development of analytic methods. Some of the latter have proved their utility in transfer to other domains—most notably in recent times to semantic analysis, in describing the phenomena of distinctiveness and the oppositional structures built out of them in this other domain of language structure where a "relativity" has been found.

The study of the languages of primitive peoples has continued, more or less steadily, but yet at a rate wholly incapable of matching the rate of extinction of these languages in certain areas of the world, especially in the Americas. The motivations for study of these languages have been varied. They have derived, of course, from the major aims of anthropology and of linguistics. But these aims also have diversified and undergone change during the hundred-year period we are considering. As noted above, in the early years of this period the historical goals predominated. This was as true in the discipline of linguistics as it was in that of anthropology. The most immediate of the historical goals in the study of aboriginal languages was the classificatory one: ordering the languages into families and subfamilies to reveal an outline of their prehistoric phylogenies. Other orderings, such as areal ones that cross-cut the family-tree classifications (possibly reflecting the geography of diffusion and long-term mutual influences), or typological ones (open to several historical interpretations), also enter into the historical problem. Beyond the immediate classificatory goals, a second and more distant possibility has motivated much comparative work: the reconstruction of lexical forms and of grammar, as well as phonological patterns, of ancient ancestral languages (proto-Algonquian, proto-Muskogean, and so forth), employing the methods developed and tested in the Indo-European field. Evidence from such reconstructions can—in principle—then be used to push the classificatory program much deeper into prehistory, performing on millennia-old protolanguages the kind of comparison and grouping first performed on present-day contemporary languages. But goals other than the historical ones have also given motivation to intensive work with aboriginal languages. Ethnographic pursuits have furnished many of these: recording and describing key concepts in the various aspects of culture; the need to understand the thoughts of one's subjects; and the documentation of a legacy of mythological explanation, oral folk-literature, verbal ritual in religion and medicine, oratory, and other ceremonial aspects of social and political forms—all of these require and contribute to the documentation of a native language. In more recent years, as ethnography has taken on functional and psychological orientations, and as linguistics has become "descriptive," "structural," and "generative," the study of aboriginal languages has reflected these movements. Particularly important have been the several goals of structural description: description for its own sake; for psychologically oriented "ethnolinguistics"; for the novelty and inherent interest of the particular specimen at hand; for the excitement and satisfaction derived from solving structural problems, that is, from finding principles that reveal internal order and explain an otherwise seemingly chaotic set of data; for developing descriptive methodology; or for providing a context for validating one's theory of language. Most recently the goal of discovering and defining the universal properties of all languages—or of writing "general grammar"—has gained ascendancy in linguistics and has motivated many of the students of aboriginal languages, as well as other linguists, whose object of study is English or some other modern literary or national language.

This brief overview of the main components in the anthropological linguistics of a century ago, and of the bridges to the present, may serve as an index to the sections which follow in this review. Not all of these topics can be treated equally here, however. Nor is it possible to present here a history of the substantive results from a hundred-year accumulation of anthropologically relevant linguistic studies. Even if I were qualified for such a task, the limitations of time and space would prohibit the attempt. Rather, the aim in what follows is to present something—however sketchily—from the history of ideas about language that have developed during the course of these pursuits. While some of these may have less permanent value than the substantive labors that provided contexts for their development, they represent nonetheless something of the spirit that has animated this new science during its growth out of an infancy that is still not very far in the past.

THE "ORIGIN" OF LANGUAGE

A history of the inquiry into the origin of human language might take as its starting point almost any period, as many centuries back as one might wish to carry it. For the present occasion it is not only appropriate, but also convenient, to pick up the subject at a point just a century ago.

In 1865 Edward B. Tylor, one of the founders of the science of cultural anthropology, published his first major work, defining the content and discussing some of the principal topics in this new science. It was his book *Researches into the Early History of Mankind*.[1] Significantly, a good half of this book was concerned with language and its manifestations. It is worth noting some of the linguistic topics that appear in it. The range is wide, but well focused, with topics including the relation of language to thought, the nature of the capacity for language, the manifestations of this capacity in the spontaneous "gesture language" of deaf-mutes, the relevance of this gesture language for the question of the origin of spoken language, the processes that may be assumed to have been involved in that origin, certain apparently analogous processes in the invention and development of writing, the relation between symbols and their objects, language as a vehicle of culture and as an instrument of its development, and the subject of myth. Parts of this book are striking, even today; and some parts of it represent a contribution of lasting value. In the year following the appearance of the book, in 1866, Tylor published a further article, "On the Origin of Language," in which he developed still other lines of thought on this subject that were of interest in the middle of the nineteenth century.

It was no doubt inevitable that a work such as Tylor's, dealing with the roots and the growth of civilization, should have focused to a considerable extent upon language, and that he should have given attention to the question of origin. Few questions about language had been debated more zealously than this, and the debate was especially lively in Tylor's time. It was one of those perennial questions, that had long been regarded as fundamental, and as basic to many other questions in humanistic inquiry. And it was one that had engaged the minds of philosophers, almost continuously, during the century and a half before Tylor wrote. It was still a vital issue, prompting numerous publications by authors of diverse views and several professional backgrounds.

Before drawing together what we may take to be Tylor's conclusions on this subject, some attention should be given to their historical context. The middle and the third quarter of the eighteenth century—a hundred years before Tylor's writing, and a time of great speculation on the origin of language—had provided a legacy of philosophical issues that were involved over and over again in the debates on this subject. The contributors included several of the notable thinkers of that age, for example, Condillac (1746), Rousseau (1750), Maupertuis (1752), Adam Smith (1761), Leibnitz (1765), Süssmilch (1766), Herder (1772), Lord Monboddo (1773).[2] Again, a century later—in the middle and third quarter of the nineteenth century, both preceding and following Tylor—there was another intensification of debate and publication on this sub-ject, the participants this time including several noted scholars from the newly-founded science of linguistics, as well as repre-sentatives of the older philosophical and theological disciplines. Just preceding Tylor's publication, one might note Grimm (1851), Steinthal (1851), Renan (1858), Farrar (1860), Max Mueller (1861), and Schleicher (1863, 1865);[3] and following immediately or shortly thereafter, Wedgwood (1866), Bleek (1869), Geiger (1869), Whitney (1873, 1875), Noiré (1874), Marty (1875), Hale (1886).[4] In the midst of all this appeared Darwin's publications: *Origin of Species* in 1859, *The Descent of Man* in 1871, and *The Expression of the Emotions in Man and Animals* in 1872. Although Darwin's theories were opposed by some (for example, Max Mueller) and accepted and elabo-rated by others (for example, Wilhelm Bleek), it is of interest to note that on the whole they affected the character of the speculations, or of the debate, relatively little. Whatever issues were raised by Darwin's theory for the origin of language had in fact been anticipated and posed as problems long before, even though in a different general framework. Darwin, in fact, drew his suggestions about the origin of language largely from the linguists and philosophers who were his contemporaries (he mentions Wedgwood, Farrar, Schleicher, Whitney, and, on the contrary side, Mueller); and since he saw no sharp dis-continuity in kind between the vocal expressions of other animals and those of man, and was only able to give a La-marckian-type explanation for the development of the language capacity, he was not able to frame some of the essential aspects of the problem. His principal contribution was to put the question in an entirely naturalistic context and to allow for an immensely expanded time scale. After 1887 this subject appears no longer to have held the attention either of linguists or of philosophers and theologians as it had in the past. The rate of publication on it dropped off rather sharply, and the debate, if it can still be called that, lost its former acrimony. It was no longer a vital issue. Nonetheless it has come up for treatments of one sort or another in occasional works since then, right up to recent times; for example Jespersen (1894), Sapir (1907, only indirectly), Wundt (1911), DeLaguna (1927), G. H. Mead (1934), Wilson (1937), Révész (1946), Rosenkranz (1961).[5]

One might wonder how in pre-Darwinian days there could have been any debate on the question of the origin of language, that is, what conceivable alternative there might have been to the belief in divine endowment. Actually there were several alternatives within the general frame of orthodoxy. One was that man was endowed at creation with his essential nature, but that thus endowed he had to discover that nature and its capacities, including the capacity he employed in inventing and developing a language—placing this interpretation on the symbolic account or "parable" in *Genesis*, picturing the Creator as if standing by to see what Adam would name the animals: "And whatsoever he named every living creature, that was the name thereof." According to another alternative, more or less within the frame of orthodoxy, man before the fall was endowed with language, as with all other necessities, but (as for example Lord Monboddo would have it), after his fall he was in a very low state, not much better off than the apes (to which he might be seen to have some affinity), and so he had to create his life anew by the sweat of his brow, inventing and developing by slow degrees the means of satisfying his needs—physical, mental, and social—and therewith also inventing anew and slowly evolving a language to serve his social communication needs. Still another alternative was provided by the account of the tower of Babel, where the confusion of tongues was taken to mean not a sudden differentiation of one language into many, but rather a degeneration or total dis-integration of language—a true "babel," or "babble"—making human communication and social cooperation no longer pos-sible, resulting in a disintegration of society and a scattering of the people, and leaving them in a state where societies and languages had to be re-formed from scratch.

But all of these alternative theories—which would have man inventing language rather than being divinely endowed with it—even though cast in one way or another in a framework of seeming orthodoxy, were nonetheless viewed askance by ad-herents of a more traditional orthodoxy and seen as bordering dangerously on heresy. The more orthodox contended either for direct endowment of man with language as a part of the act of creation, or else for a special gift of language to man by direct revelation consequent to creation.

These alternatives provided the cause for debate. But it is the nature of the arguments that concerns us more here. The espoused issue—natural versus supernatural origin of language —provided an arena for the clash between rationalist and sen-sationist theories of knowledge, and for the clash between the metaphysical-deductive and the empirical-inductive philosoph-ical biases. The arguments about the basis of knowledge have had a continuity of their own, surviving these as well as other particular contexts. Only recently they have again come to the fore in linguistic theory.

One of the issues that was involved in the earlier debate was whether the elementary ideas, necessary for language, under-standing, thought, and reason, are an innate endowment of the mind, or whether they are acquired through sense experience. Another was whether thought is, or is not, possible without language—whether language should be regarded as an instru-ment for the expression of thought, or whether thought is in essence a linguistic phenomenon, thinking being dependent on speaking (including of course internal speech). Still another was the nature of the circumstance that caused man to need and to develop language, whether primarily "psychological" (innate necessity of vocal as of other forms of self-expression) or "sociological" (requirements of social contact and coopera-tion). Other issues turned on whether the first root vocables may have been derived from natural cries of the organism, from the imitation of sounds correlated with things in nature, or from vocal accompaniments to pointing and other indexical gesture signs (the "expressive," "onomatopoeic," and "gesture" theories, respectively); and, further, on how a transition might be made from any of these natural, iconic, and indexical signs to a language whose root elements consist entirely of arbitrary signs.

If one considers the positions that may be taken on these various questions, and their possible combinations, one may have an idea of the varieties of views that were put forward in these speculations. In general, the naturalist philosophers were on the side of acquired ideas and the social matrix of the invention of language, while the strict rationalists were on the side of innate ideas. And if, along with the latter position, one held to the identity of thought and language, one was led to the position of divine imposition of language on man. If, on the other hand, one held to the priority of thought over lan-guage, then there was room within the rationalist position for a human rather than divine origin of the latter. The mold established for these arguments in the eighteenth century shaped also those of the nineteenth. Certain of the basic issues, however, have a still longer continuity. One may see them in the seventeenth century, in the opposed positions of Bacon and Descartes, of empiricists and rationalists; and one acquainted with the twentieth-century history of linguistic theory can only be reminded of the longevity and irreconcilability of the opposition.

We may return now to Tylor, after this digression into the historical context of his work. It appears that he was well acquainted with at least some of the voluminous literature on the origin of language that was current in his day, and he was out of sympathy with its tenor and appropriately skeptical of its value. He was moved to write: "We know very little about the origin of language, but the subject has so great a charm for the human mind that the want of evidence has not prevented the growth of theory after theory; and all sorts of men, with all sorts of qualifications, have solved the problem, each in his own fashion."[6]

And, of these speculative solutions, he said: "It may indeed be brought forward as evidence to prove something that matters far more to us than the early history of language, that it is of as little use to be a good reasoner when there are no *facts* to reason upon, as it is to be a good bricklayer when there are no bricks to build with."[7] Tylor was declaring his interest in a *data*-based science, not in further metaphysical speculation, whether about language or about human culture. Why then should he have taken up the question of the origin of language?

The answer is that he *had* some data, on a subject that was too interesting and too apparently relevant to pass over. He had made himself acquainted with the literature that had been accumulated over the course of the preceding three quarters of a century on the gesture communication of deaf-mutes, mostly in institutions in Germany and in France. And he had made further personal inquiries into the matter and had come to some conclusions of his own. The main points to be drawn from Tylor's discussion of this matter, relevant to the problem of the origin of language, may be summarized as follows.

With each, brief illustrative excerpts are quoted from his writing.

First: it was apparent from the data on deaf-mute "gesture language" that a working system of communication by signs, adequate for a very wide range of elementary social needs and functions—that is, *a language* (though a nonvocal one in this case)—can be made up entirely of *iconic* and *indexical* signs.

> Under the two classes "pictures in the air" and things brought before the mind by actual pointing out, the whole of the sign-language may be included.[8]

> In the gesture-language the relation between idea and sign not only always exists, but is scarcely lost sight of for a moment.[9]

Second: the arbitrary signs of spoken language cannot be assumed to have been primary, but may be assumed rather to have been derived in the first instance out of nonarbitrary ones.

> At the root of the problem of the origin of language lies the question, why certain words were originally used to represent certain ideas, or mental conditions, or whatever we may call them . . . That the selection of words to express ideas was ever purely arbitrary . . . is a supposition opposed to such knowledge as we have of the formation of language.[10]

> It is as bearing on the question of the relation between idea and word that the study of the gesture-language is of particular interest. We have in it a method of human utterance independent of speech, and carried on through a different medium, in which, as has been said, the connection between idea and sign has hardly ever been broken, or even lost sight of for a moment.[11]

Third: a working system of signs, adequate for human communication, can be made up of signs with concrete reference only, without "parts of speech," without any specifically grammatical signs, and with only the "natural syntax" of stimulus dominance.

> In these [deaf-and-dumb] institutions, however, there are grammatical signs used in the gesture-language which do not fairly belong to it. These are mostly signs adapted, or perhaps invented, by teachers who had the use of speech, to express ideas which do not come within the scope of the very limited natural grammar and dictionary of the deaf-and-dumb. But it is to be observed that though the deaf-and-dumb have been taught to understand these signs and use them in school, they ignore them in their ordinary talk, and will have nothing to do with them if they can help it.[12]

> So far as I can learn, few or none of the factitious grammatical signs will bear even the short journey from the schoolroom to the playground.[13]

> In the gesture-language there seems no distinction between the adjective, the adverb which belongs to it, the substantive, and the verb.[14]

> It has however a syntax, which is worthy of careful examination. The syntax of speaking man differs according to the language he may learn . . . But the deaf-mute strings together the signs of the various ideas he wishes to connect, in what appears to be the natural order in which they follow one another in his mind, for it is the same among the mutes of different countries, and is wholly independent of the syntax which may happen to belong to the language of their speaking friends.[15]

The fundamental principle which regulates the order of the deaf-mute's signs seems to be that enunciated by Schmalz, "that which seems to him the most important he always sets before the rest, and that which seems to him superfluous he leaves out."[16]

Fourth: thought, in the human being, is not necessarily or totally dependent on spoken language, but may have other forms or manifestations.

As Steinthal admits, the deaf-and-dumb man is the living refutation of the proposition, that man cannot think without speech, unless we allow the understood notion of speech as the utterance of thought by articulate sounds to be too narrow.[17]

Recognition of this, however, does not necessarily lead to acceptance of a nonphysical or nonmotor theory of thought.

Though, however, the deaf-and-dumb prove clearly to us that a man may have human thought without being able to speak, they by no means prove that he can think without any means of physical expression. Their evidence tends the other way.[18]

Fifth and finally: given the nature of the human mind, language is inevitable. If the individual inherits this mind, but is deprived of the means of acquiring (socially inheriting) the linguistic legacy of the community, he can and does invent a new language to express and communicate his thought. Thought will "out."

The evidence of the best observers tends to prove that they (the deaf-and-dumb) are capable of developing the gesture-language out of their own minds without the aid of speaking men.[19]

One may note that Tylor's observations bear on the principal issues that animated the earlier (and subsequent) debate on the origin of language, namely, the question of the relation between thought and language (in man with his present capacities), the question of innateness versus social acquisition of language capacity in the individual, the primary roles of deixis and imitation in founding a language, and the secondary development of arbitrary signs. There is one further issue that Tylor's data and discussion bear on. This is the question of the "grammarless language," without inflections, parts of speech, or pure-relational signs, that was the hypothetic starting point for the evolutionary interpretation of the well-known, or once well-known, linguistic typology (see section below, "The Significance of Language Differences").

That Tylor's observations and the conclusions that he drew from them may not have been totally in error, and that these may still have relevance to the inquiry concerning the bases for language, is suggested by a recent publication, almost a century later, by Eric Lenneberg. He writes:

> Just as we can say with assurance that no man inherits a propensity for French, we can also say with equal confidence that all men are endowed with an innate propensity for a type of behavior that develops automatically into language, and that this propensity is so deeply ingrained that language-like behavior develops even under the most unfavorable conditions of peripheral and even central nervous system impairment.[20]

It is of interest to quote one further paragraph from Lenneberg, because of the similarity of his observations to those of Tylor and his predecessors:

> Recently I had occasion to visit for half a year a public school for the congenitally deaf. At this school the children

were not taught sign language on the theory that they must learn to make an adjustment to a speaking world, and that the absence of sign language would encourage the practice of lip-reading and attempts at vocalization. It was interesting to see that all children, without exception, communicated behind the teacher's back by means of "self-made" signs. I had the privilege of witnessing the admission of a new student, eight years old, who had recently been *discovered* by a social worker who was doing relief work in a slum area. This boy had never had any training, and had, so far as I know, never met with other deaf children. This newcomer began to "talk" sign language with his contemporaries almost immediately upon arrival. The existence of an innate impulse for symbolic communication can hardly be questioned.[21]

The important lack in all of the efforts to solve the "origin of language"—a gap that could no more be filled with Tylor's evidence than with that from which other writers had proceeded—was the implicit assumption that it was *Homo sapiens,* biologically endowed as he is today, that developed language in the first instance. But although missing the central problem, these efforts had a relevance for certain peripheral problems. And perhaps one may now suppose that if the impermissible experiment of King Psammetichos were to be repeated, a new language would be created, in accord with principles fairly well understood, and would undergo development and be passed on to succeeding generations.

For present-day anthropology the relevant problem is not that of the origin of language, but rather that of the origin of the capacity for language. This is a problem that belongs to a number of biological sciences, though linguistics may be expected to contribute to the specification of the capacity. It is perhaps a century too early to be reviewing this subject; and in any case it would require another writer. Attention may be directed, however, to a few items of recent literature that bear in one way or another on the problem. Lenneberg (in 1960, 1964, 1966, and 1967)[22] has assembled evidence from his studies of speech development and speech disorders that leads him to posit a *specific* language capacity in man—rather than simply a greater *general* capacity of (nonspecific) intelligence —and that leads him thus to attribute the acquisition of language by the individual more to biologically determined maturational processes than to the learning processes as such. Geschwind (1964, 1965)[23] has proposed a theory of a neural basis for the object-naming capacity, ascribing this to a human capacity for forming associations between non-limbic stimuli (in addition to those between nonlimbic and limbic stimuli). Penfield and Rasmussen (1950),[24] Penfield and Roberts (1959)[25] and Roberts (1966)[26] present essential data on cortical function relevant to speech that derive from studies of cortical lesions and experiments in cortical stimulation. Chauchard (1963)[27] gives comparative neurological data and interpretations relating to neural processes in vocal-auditory behavior. Marler (1963, 1965)[28] gives important comparative behavioral data on vocalization and communicative behavior in primate species. Hockett (1960)[29] has specified design features that are crucially characteristic of human language and that must be taken account of in theories of the biological basis and origin of language. Reynolds (1967)[30] relates evidence from neurological and behavioral studies to the explication of three of the most crucial design features indicated by Hockett —namely, phonematization, semantic openness, and displacement—in an attempt to avoid positing a specific language capacity in man, as Lenneberg does, and to resolve this into components relating to several more general capacities. These are but a few of the items that might be cited here, but they may suffice for the present as evidence of renewed interest in the old question, of new definition of the problem, and of new possibilities for evidence and interpretation.

COMPARATIVE AND HISTORICAL LINGUISTICS

In the early decades of the nineteenth century a new kind of linguistics was being developed. By the end of the 1860's it was well under way and had already achieved some notable results. This was *historical* or *comparative* linguistics. The terms have special meanings here. The "linguistics" was Indo-European; the "comparison" was between languages of that family, already determined to be related to each other (not a general comparison of any and all languages); and the "history" was that which could be reconstructed by inference from the relations of forms in the languages compared, as well, of course, as that directly attested in source materials of mediaeval and ancient languages. It generally went under the name of "comparative grammar" (*vergleichende Grammatik*), but it involved the comparative study of lexicon as well—and as much —as of grammar. In marked contrast to the traditions of deductive philosophical grammar and speculative solutions to the problem of the origin of language which had dominated linguistic thought in the seventeenth and eighteenth centuries, the new comparative linguistics was conceived of as being *empirically* based. Linguists, by the end of the 1860's, had already espoused the "inductive method of science," which was now being regarded as superior to that of reasoning from first principles. "First principles" were suspect, being felt now—at least by some—to be far from self-evident. Instead of providing the starting points for scientific inquiry into language, their discovery was to be held off as a possible *ultimate* goal, to be attained, inductively, only after the solution of many more *particular* linguistic problems of a historical sort. Through its empirical approach and inductive method, linguistics was expected to be first a branch of natural history, and then ultimately—as "laws" were discerned in history—a branch of natural science.

The event that is generally regarded as the starting point for historically oriented comparative linguistics is one whose date is 1786. It was in that year that Sir William Jones, in a paper delivered before the Bengal Asiatic Society, announced his conviction that Sanskrit, the ancient and the religious language of India, bears to Greek and to Latin "a stronger affinity, both in the roots of verbs and in the forms of grammar, than could have been produced by accident; so strong that no philologer could examine all the three without believing them to have sprung from *some common source* which, perhaps, *no longer exists*. There is a similar reason, though not quite so forcible, for supposing that both the Gothic and the Celtic . . . had the same origin with the Sanskrit."[31]

To appreciate the full impact of Jones's declaration (which saw publication in 1788), one should recall what conceptions of linguistic history were current before that time. In the first place, all of linguistic history had been conceived of as taking place within the supposedly fewer than six thousand years since the creation. Further, it was generally assumed that Hebrew, or some immediate congener of Hebrew, was *the original language*; and that the Oriental languages (meaning usually those of the Near East, but sometimes including those of more distant lands as well) were *closer* to the "original language" than were those of Europe. Ancient Greek was also imagined to be closer to the original language than were the vernaculars of Western Europe. The diversity of the world's languages was accounted for by assuming varying degrees and manners of *degeneration* from the original language, or—for those who believed in the

human invention of the original language—by assuming varying degrees and manners of *progressive advancement* over that
original.

The effect of Jones's discovery (of a relationship that was indeed, for one who would examine into the matter, as apparent
as he said it should be) was to usher in a whole new conception of linguistic history and of language phylogeny, as well
as an understanding of the processes of linguistic change.

In the period spanning the years from 1814 to 1868, the
works of Rask, Grimm, Bopp, Pott, Schleicher, and Fick (and
yet others) had established the new science and prepared the
way for what is commonly regarded as "the most significant
decade in the history of modern linguistics, the 1870's."[32] The
1870's were the decade of epoch-making publications by
Verner, Leskien, Brugmann, Schmidt, Saussure, and Paul. The
history of the individual contributions of these scholars has
been told many times[33] and it need not be recounted in any
detail here. It will suffice to give only brief mention to some
of the ideas about language, and about linguistics, that developed during these years.

One of these was the notion of *regularity in language change*—
as if changes occurred in obedience to some general principles,
or "natural laws," operating independently of human volition.
Such regularities—for example, those of the common-Germanic
and the High-German consonant shifts, noted by Rasmus Rask
(1814) and Jakob Grimm (1819, 1822)[34] and now generally
known as "Grimm's law"—came to be one of the principal
objects of study and furnished the foundation facts for the
"neogrammarian" movement of the 1870's and following (see
below).

Of interest in this connection also is the *organismic view of
language* that was congenial to many of this period and that
seemed appropriate to express a growing appreciation of the

systematic and supraindividual aspects of language and its changes. An early expression of this was Franz Bopp's (1827): "Languages must be regarded as natural organisms which arise according to definite laws, carry within them the principle of their life according to which they unfold themselves, and gradually die."[35]

A close paraphrase of Bopp's expression of this idea was stated by August Schleicher in his famous tract, *Die Darwinsche Theorie und die Sprachwissenschaft* (1863, 1869)[36], in which he stressed also the independence of the course of language from the human will, and its possession of "that succession of phenomena to which one ordinarily applies the term 'life' "; and from which he concluded that "linguistic science is therefore a 'natural science'; its method is, on the whole and in general, the same as that of the other natural sciences."

From this, it followed of course that languages could be treated as species; and Schleicher, and others after him, proceeded to express the (inferred) prehistoric phylogeny of the Indo-European languages and their putative ancestors in the form of a *family tree (Stammbaum)*. The original idea and the first attempt to carry it out were Schleicher's. August Fick followed, employing lexical data for this purpose—in contrast to Schleicher's primary morphological basis.[37] As might be imagined, however, not all scholars were willing to accept the organic analogy. There were those who regarded it as an overstatement of the facts, who held metaphor to be inherently dangerous to clear thinking, who were unwilling to see human volition ruled out of the development of speech behavior, or who were interested in characterizing language rather as a phenomenon of folk-psychology. Still other grounds for objection became clear later (see below, in reference to J. Schmidt).

Another product of this period was the conception of the possibility, and of a method, not only for reconstructing the phylogeny of languages (and so, inferentially, of ethnic groups), but also for reconstructing the *forms of words* of extinct, prehistoric, ancestral languages. The "neogrammarians" a decade later provided the fundamental assumptions, and methods based on these, that gave precision to this enterprise. The reconstruction of prehistoric ancestral forms, such as must be assumed to underlie the separate major branches—and even the whole—of the Indo-European family, became and has remained one of the several major goals of comparative linguistics.

The "neogrammarian" hypothesis is that *the laws of phonetic change admit of no exceptions*. It was stated by August Leskien in 1876 and proclaimed with fanfare (and some lack of tact) by Karl Brugmann in 1878.[38] It was a product of the thinking of a group of students at Leipzig, and soon took on the character of a movement in linguistics, both attracting followers and alienating others. Even today, although it has largely won the field, it still has detractors as well as defenders. The movement took on the nickname of the Leipzig group, "*die Junggrammatiker*," a term whose use and special sense might be best given in American idiom as "the Young Turks of comparative grammar." But a translation as "neogrammarian" has become standard as the English term. A statement of the hypothesis by Hermann Paul in 1879 exemplifies the spirit of this movement and its approach to the history of language: "*Every phonetic law operates with absolute necessity; it as little admits of an exception as a chemical or physical law.*" On the face of it the neogrammarian hypothesis appeared to ignore, and to be flatly contradicted by, the known exceptions to every one of the major regularities of phonetic correspondence between related languages (so that these correspondences had been judged by some, seemingly more prudently, as *tendencies* rather than absolute rules). The point of the neogrammarian approach, however, was that the "exceptions" were only *appar-*

ently such, and were rather the result of insufficiently accurate understanding and statement of the rules of correspondence, or else were due to insufficient control of other historical facts in the case. In modern phraseology the matter might be put in the following way. (1) Rules of phonetic development are rarely, if ever, context-free rules; rather, they are context-sensitive rules. (2) If such a rule is too crudely stated, that is, without sufficiently accurate delimitation of the contexts in which it is operative, then spurious "apparent exceptions" are bound to appear. (3) A methodological corollary follows from this: if apparent exceptions to a rule are at hand, then look to the statement of the rule; assume that its context restrictions have been improperly determined, rather than assuming that the nature of such rules—and the nature of language—in principle allow of sporadic and random exceptions; assume that there is an order also in the exceptions. A procedure for dealing with exceptions—often known as the "method of diminishing residues"—was recognized, based on this last assumption. But this is only a part of the neogrammarian procedure. Explanation of correspondences by means of postulated historical phonological developments ("phonetic laws," *Lautgesetze*) can be valid only if the correspondences at hand actually are the result of such developments, which is not necessarily the case, and is something that cannot always be ascertained in advance. There are other possibilities: words giving evidence of deviant correspondences may have been borrowed from another language (a matter usually not too difficult to detect) or from another adjacent and closely related dialect (sometimes more difficult to be sure of); or they may go back to competing alternative forms in a nonhomogeneous original speech community (a still more difficult matter); or their shapes may have been altered by analogical leveling and re-formation. According to the neogrammarian method, all of these possibilities have to be entertained and tested in the treatment of residues of exceptions, of exceptions to exceptions, and so forth. One may or may not succeed in reducing the residue to zero, but one does not surrender the basic hypothesis of the regularity of phonetic changes. One waits for further evidence.

The kinds of historical changes in word forms that the neogrammarians recognized, then, were the phonetic changes and the analogical changes. The former were regarded as "physiological" in origin and the latter as "psychological." The former were expressable as "laws." These were special, not general, phonetic laws—inasmuch as they applied to a particular language at a particular period of its history, and affected particular sounds in particular contexts. Besides these two historical processes, there was also need to recognize a third—namely, borrowing.

The neogrammarian development tends to overshadow others of the same period. Two of these—the two which are perhaps of the most general anthropological interest—remain to be mentioned. These are the beginning of areal linguistics, and the reconstruction of prehistoric culture content.

The first of these arose in recognition of an inherent difficulty in determining the proper sequence of branchings when attempting to set up a family tree of the Indo-European languages. Schleicher had proposed two quite different arrangements on different occasions, and other scholars, in succeeding years, proposed still different arrangements. They were encountering the difficult problem of the *subclassification* of languages within a family. Different diagnostics lead to different results. The nature of the family-tree diagram, and the concept of history that is implied by it, required a hierarchy of branchings ordered along a dimension of relative time. This poses quite a different problem from that involved in a simple classification of languages into families, where relative distances of relation-

ship and inferences about prehistoric movements of peoples
are not at issue. The fact is that the products of historical
changes in languages are rarely found distributed as they would
be if they had resulted from clean and decisive splits in speech
communities. Thus the family-tree scheme is not an entirely
appropriate model for the portrayal of linguistic relationships.
Within a speech community, different linguistic innovations
often have separate points of origin and attain different—and
overlapping—spheres of geographic diffusion, resulting in
incipient dialect differentiations along many and cross-cutting
lines. The cumulative result of such processes over a period of
time within a language area is a gradual transition through
local dialects, each of which resembles most closely those geographically closest to it or most accessible to it, with those
that are geographically distant becoming more and more unlike
and reaching the point of mutual unintelligibility—a situation
such as is found, for example, among the numerous local dialects of the area of High German, Low German, and Dutch still
today. Johannes Schmidt, in an influential work in 1872,
posited a somewhat similar state of affairs as having existed
also in the proto-Indo-European speech area, thus conceiving of
it as a dialectically nonhomogeneous community with gradual
transitions between adjacent incipient dialects. Yet, as is obvious, major branchings did take place (Germanic, Italic, Celtic,
Balto-Slavic, Greek, Albanian, Armenian, Indo-Iranian), and
within most of these still further significant branchings developed. And there remains the temptation to order these by
relative chronology. But given an initial nonhomogeneous base
with incipient dialect differences, any fission that develops
within it must surely cut across other lines of incipient fission;
and so, different and disagreeing hypothetic trees of relationships must result from different selections of diagnostics.
Schmidt turned his attention to the question of how the Indo-

European speech area might have been changed from one of continuous dialect variation to one of discrete language isolates. There are of course various circumstances under which permanent and ultimately deep fissures may be introduced into a speech community. An obvious one is separation by distant migration of a part of the community, cutting itself off from the remaining part. Another is splitting of an original community by intrusion of an alien people into its area. Events of these sorts have of course happened in the histories of various societies. But there is a third process which Schmidt recognized— one that may yield a comparable final result. It is, moreover, one of historical importance, inasmuch as it must relate to factors of social development. It is the ascendance to dominance (political, commercial, and cultural) of a few growing centers of influence within an area, with consequent social ascendance of the particular dialects of these centers. These become the dialects of social prestige, and are gradually adopted in adjacent parts within their respective spheres of influence, and *the intermediate local dialects die out.* The gradual transition between dialects thus disappears, and what are left are discrete and more distantly separated political languages. (This is what has been taking place in modern history in the German-Dutch area, for example, and at an accelerating rate in recent years.) Schmidt posited such a process to account for the linguistic discontinuities that must be recognized among the major branches of the Indo-European family, and to account for the irreconcilability of different proposed family trees based on different linguistic diagnostics. He proposed that the tree diagram be abandoned. But not all of his contemporaries agreed, even though many of them granted the validity of the kind of initial situation and the process that he posited. The disconcerting criteria were after all few in comparison with the numbers of criteria that might be adduced, and the changes that they represented presumably antedated the major pre-historic branchings. One could thus attribute them to the ancestral base, as dialect differences within it, without totally abandoning the concept of tree-like branching thereafter. And the tree concept could be modified so as to attribute a special significance to the spatial arrangement of the branches.

The remaining development of nineteenth-century historical and comparative linguistics that must be mentioned here is the one that pertains most directly to the ethnographic part of culture-history. It is the attempt to reconstruct, from linguistic evidence, the elements that can be ascribed to the culture of the ancestral Indo-European speech community. This developed as a by-product of the philological and comparative-linguistic studies and was drawn together, and reached an early culmina-tion, in the work of Otto Schrader. His *Sprachvergleichung und Urgeschichte* appeared first in 1883, and in revised editions in 1889 and 1907. An English translation from the second edition was published in 1890 under the title *Antiquities of the Aryan Peoples.* Schrader's hope was that, with "the aid of the same Comparative Philology, to which such startling results were due in the domain of words and their forms, it might also be possible to penetrate somewhat more deeply into the history of *the things denoted by those words*."[39] To this effort he gave the name "linguistic palaeology" (or "palaeontology"). It was to provide the basic tool for "a third science . . . that of Com-parative Antiquities," which was to join with archaeology and etymology in order to "pass beyond the bounds of history" and "to distinguish between what, on the one hand, [the individual Indo-European peoples] have jointly inherited in the way of manners and customs, of private, public, and religious institu-tions, and what, on the other hand, in this connection may be termed their recent acquisitions, whether loans from abroad or the results of their own independent evolution."[40] Aspects of culture dealt with in Schrader's work cover a wide range: metals, metallurgy, and weapons; wild and domestic animals; forest trees and cultivated plants; animal breeding and agriculture; time reckoning; food and drink, clothing, and dwellings; commerce and travel; the family; kindred and tribe; law; religion; and evidences for place of origin. He also founded a journal, *Wörter und Sachen,* devoted to Indo-European linguistic ethnography and culture-history.

Close to a century has passed since the developments that have been briefly described here. The foundations of historically oriented comparative linguistics were well laid in this initial period, so that the record from then to the present is one largely of continuity of effort and accumulation of results. The neogrammarian hypothesis is still the working assumption of most comparative linguists, but they use it in full awareness of the possible special conditions under which it can fail to produce a correct historical solution. The record of verification of its results is so impressive, however, that it is regarded as poor strategy (to say the least) to begin with a contrary initial assumption. Not only have results accumulated in the Indo-European field, but the method has been adopted in other linguistic fields as well—in Semitic, Malayo-Polynesian, several American Indian language families, Bantu, and, in more recent times, still others. It is the method that offers the possibility of obtaining reliable historical depth in these areas. One of its successes that has become known as a classic case is a prediction made by Bloomfield for Proto-Algonquian on the basis of a single deviant correspondence. Instead of admitting of possible irregularity in a sound law, and seeing no basis for an assumption either of analogical change or of dialect mixture, he ventured to set up a feature of the Proto-Algonquian phonological system on the basis of this single instance of a "deviant" phonetic correspondence in a form from one of the Algonquian languages. Confirmation came later, on more than one occasion, when additional comparative materials from other languages were made available. The case was so striking that Sapir made it the basis for an article on linguistic methodology.[41]

The problem of "subclassification" of languages remains an important one, both for historical linguistics and for culture-historical anthropology. It is a matter of concern not only for Indo-European, but for any language family in which one may have interest. It has not been necessary to abandon the family-tree view of language phylogeny in its entirety, for there are situations in which it can be granted a certain degree of validity, even though it is never adequate to represent all of the pertinent historical facts. But this model of relationships is supplemented by other types drawn from dialect geography: "chains," "nets," and so forth. The problem of subclassification is now generally conceded to be one for quantitative evaluation, requiring a large amount of data rather than just a few handy diagnostics. As a result there has been in recent years an increasingly heavy reliance on counts of cognate lexical items in the more "basic" areas of vocabulary, that is, of lexical items referring to the most basic and universal objects of experience. Not all are agreed, however, about the proper criteria for subclassification. Some historical linguists would give more weight to the isoglosses of shared phonetic change.

Out of the experimentation with lexical counts, there was developed by Morris Swadesh (1950, 1951)[42] a method for estimating approximate time depths for the branchings within a family. This rested on an observation that the apparent rate of loss (and replacement) of items from a basic-vocabulary list tended to vary within a much smaller range than one would have supposed. And it was both a smaller range and a much slower rate than the averages for vocabulary in general (covering the many areas of cultural objects and culturally developed concepts). Lees (1953)[43] calculated the average rate for the list that Swadesh had used, deriving the figure from comparisons of recent with earlier stages of a number of historically documented languages. The early results of this work were of immediate interest to historically oriented anthropologists, and the method seemed to open up possibilities for approximate dating of the prehistoric separations of ethnic groups. The limits of the reliability of the work have been, and still are, in dispute; but it is clear that the reliability is greater within the range from 500 to 5000 years than it is at either shallower or deeper time-depths, where the number of losses (in the one case) or the number of retentions (in the other) is too small to provide an adequate sample for statistical purposes. An excellent review of the first ten years of work on this subject was given by Hymes in the first number of *Current Anthropology*.[44] Bergsland and Vogt (1962)[45] submitted a rejoinder. It remains a subject of disagreement and controversy. Objections have been raised by opponents on several grounds.[46] Defenders of the method, however, feel that virtually all of these can be answered satisfactorily. One of the most serious defects in the early formulation was the implicit or working assumption of equal average viability for all items of the list, which gave appreciably foreshortened estimates for time-depths greater than those that went into the first calculation of the rate. This problem was early recognized by Swadesh and measures to compensate for it, or to correct it, have been proposed by him (1955), Joos (1964), and Van der Merwe (1966).[47] Dyen's work on testing the cross-linguistic comparability of rate-based subdivisions of the list also contributes to the solution of this problem, as well as to determining the degree of confidence that can then be placed in the assumption of a "constant" rate. But quite aside from the question of the validity of the method of approximate dating by glottochronology, lexicostatistic computations employing a "basic-vocabulary" list are a major and effective tool for establishing the subclassification of related languages within a family and for revealing the kinds of special connections that are not readily accommodated in a simple family-tree model. The concept of "basic vocabulary" has been—in spite of recent objections to the idea—accepted and used in comparative linguistics ever since Rask (1814) first enunciated the principles for judging relationship. It was the first of his three criteria: "A language, however mixed it may be, belongs to the same branch of languages as another when it has the most essential, concrete, indispensable words, the foundation of the language, in common with it."[48]

His other two criteria had to do with consistency of phonetic correspondences and with morphological similarities. These three criteria have been in use for more than a century and a half. The first is the one that has lent itself most readily to quantitative and statistical treatment. The most ambitious lexicostatistical project undertaken so far, for purposes of subclassification in an area where the prehistoric relations were unclear, has been Dyen's computer-assisted treatment of some five hundred Malayo-Polynesian languages.[49]

THE SIGNIFICANCE OF LANGUAGE DIFFERENCES:
MORPHOLOGICAL TYPOLOGY

We turn here to another topic: a third focus of attention, of anthropological interest, in the linguistics of the nineteenth and early twentieth centuries. This is a concern with differences among languages (in this case, with the more striking typological differences), and an attempt to discern the mental and cultural significance of these.

The growth of ideas surrounding this topic was roughly synchronous with the development of historical and comparative Indo-European linguistics, and it was an important side interest and furnished a general overview of language for many of those whose primary effort was directed toward the strictly historical enterprise. It was, in fact, initiated and developed by some of the same scholars. Yet its leading ideas, and especially its methods, were in some ways a diametric opposite of those of the historically oriented science. It was "comparative," but in a *synchronic* and *nonhistorical* sense. Still, its interpretation was not without a time dimension—at least an imagined one— for the interpretation was *evolutionary*: "evolutionary" in the same sense as that in which anthropologists have spoken of "cultural evolution" with "stages of development" (as opposed to "culture history" in the particularistic sense). The matter to which I am referring is what has so often been referred to (nowadays frequently with scorn or amusement) as "the nineteenth-century typology."

As we shall see, interest in this topic has persisted right up to the present—among at least some anthropologists and linguists—in spite of a general loss of popularity and an increase in skepticism concerning its possible significance. Early in this century, however, many linguists (though not all) and most anthropologists began to drop the evolutionary interpretation that had been placed on the matter. The importance of this break cannot be overestimated, so far as the history of anthropological linguistics is concerned. For American anthropology, we can place the cleavage quite appropriately between Franz Boas and his chief predecessor in matters of linguistic and anthropological philosophy, John Wesley Powell of the Bureau of American Ethnology. At least the contrast between Boas's view and Powell's is most striking; and it is Boas's that has survived. But Powell's position also was revolutionary in its way, and for its day (it was presented in 1880). It reflects an earlier break, and an advance, in the interpretation of the typology. We shall come to this shortly, after a review of the earlier thinking that led up to it.

As already indicated, and as will be seen further, the concern with language differences—and with the typology and evolutionary interpretations to which this gave rise—was a component in the thinking of the historically oriented scholars of the nineteenth century. But it received a strong impetus from one whose main linguistic work was descriptive and philosophical. This was Wilhelm von Humboldt (elder brother of the naturalist and explorer, Alexander von Humboldt). It is Humboldt who is often credited (or blamed) for the "nineteenth-century typology." Yet it was not he who originated it. Its origins are earlier.

The story starts with Friedrich Schlegel, a literary figure and one of the influential leaders of the romantic movement in both Germany and France. In 1803 he had gone to Paris to study; and there he began the study of Sanskrit, making use of source materials in the Paris library, and studying under the tutelage of an English orientalist whose name was Alexander Hamilton. In 1808 Schlegel published his first work based on this study, "On the Language and Ancient Philosophy of the Indians" (Über die Sprache und Weisheit der Indier). This work is best known for establishing the concept, as well as the term, "comparative grammar." Here he laid the groundwork for the comparison of cognate roots between Sanskrit and the classical European languages and for the use of this as an indication of their original ethnic unity. But the method of proof for such relationships (the "neogrammarian" method), by exploiting the phenomenon of regularity of phonetic correspondences, had not yet taken shape; and the phylogenetic interpretation placed on these cognate roots might thus be open to doubt by some, and challenged with the alternative hypothesis of borrowing and language mixture. To anticipate and forestall this possible objection, Schlegel appealed to another line of evidence which, he felt, "completely decides this matter and puts it beyond doubt . . . This decisive point, which will clear up everything, is the *structural plan* of the languages, or their *comparative grammar*, by which we obtain an entirely new insight into the genealogy of languages, much in the same way in which *comparative anatomy* has cast light on more advanced branches of the natural sciences."[50]

And so he called attention to the grammatical similarity—the similarity of "structural plan"—between Sanskrit and the classical languages of Europe. Now, there was already current at this time enough information (and of course misinformation also) about a surprising number of *non-Indo-European* languages (Hebrew, Turkish, Hungarian, Finnish, Malay, Chinese, Manchu, Quechua, Tupi, Nahuatl, and yet others) so that the typological comparison which he was about to draw had force. The Indo-European languages appeared to be unique among the known languages because of their patterns of "flexion"— with their high degree of union of root and grammatical determination into "formed" words that did not offer themselves to easy segmentation—and with their morphologically marked differentiation into form-classes. It was the Indo-European *ablaut* alternations and the fusion of radical and grammatical elements into wholes not easily dismembered that were seen as the hallmark of these languages. The differentiation of word-forms Schlegel saw as working from inside to out. "Roots" were what the name might imply if the metaphor were taken almost literally: elements endowed with the power of growth and differentiation; and their flexion he likened to "organic growth." This kind of structure seemed to him to stand in marked contrast to those of all other languages on which he had information, where grammatical determination appeared to be *added from the outside,* by means of the loose and "mechanical" accretion of words, particles, or affixes, to inert and unbending roots, rather than being developed from the inside as he felt the Indo-European to be. And so there arose a dichotomy between languages with an "organic" structure and those with a merely "mechanical" one. Hierarchic implications and evaluative judgments were not difficult to draw from the metaphors of this typological opposition. Schlegel noted that it could not be denied that the American native languages, for example, belonged to a lower level,[51] and that Chinese belonged to the lowest of all.[52]

This dichotomy of "organic" and "mechanical" was soon to yield to a trichotomy; one introduced by Friedrich's elder brother, August Wilhelm von Schlegel, in his "Observations on the Provençale Language and Literature" (*Observations sur la langue et la littérature provençales*), published in 1818.[53] The Chinese language, which had occupied the lowest position among the so-called "mechanical" languages, was here singled out as a separate type; for it did not possess even the fastened-on grammatical affixes for the expression of case, or of person, number, tense, mode, and so forth, with which the other languages of the mechanical type were generally equipped. And so there came into being the trichotomy. In August Schlegel's terms the types were: (1) "languages without grammar," (2) the "affixing languages," and (3) the "inflectional languages." These are of course the "isolating," the "agglutinating," and the "inflecting" of the classic trilogy. Chinese, with its monosyllables, was the example of the lowest and supposedly "grammarless" order; the Indo-European languages, together with the somewhat problematic Semitic languages (which Friedrich had not admitted into this category), became the representatives of the highest order; and the rest of the languages of the Old World and the New World, so far as they were known, were taken to be representatives of the middle category. But there was a problem with some of the modern European vernaculars, and a work on a Romance language and folk literature could hardly avoid facing it. These modern languages seemed to have lost some of the abundant inflectional growth of their ancestors, developing certain other resources instead: auxiliary verbs in place of the corresponding categories of verb inflection; more use of prepositions, in compensation for the loss of case inflections of nouns; adverbs for forming the comparative and superlative degrees of adjectives, instead of inflected forms; the use of articles with nouns; and so forth. And so the "inflectional" category of the trilogy was bifurcated into two subtypes: the "synthetic" and the "analytic," the former being the Indo-European prototype, and the latter being a modern development in some of its branches.

This typology has had a long life, in spite of the various attempts to modify or refine it. Franz Bopp, for example, had rather different ideas. He saw less of a gulf between the "mechanical" and the "organic," and suspected even Sanskrit of being at least partially "mechanical" or "affixing" in origin. So he minimized this distinction; and instead (in 1820, and again in 1857) set Semitic apart because of its disyllabic, triliteral root structure. His trichotomy was essentially Chinese versus Semitic versus all else. But Bopp's version proved to be less attractive to followers.

It was Wilhelm von Humboldt who introduced an explicit theory of linguistic development to go along with the concepts on which Schlegel typology was based. In 1822, in an essay "On the Origin of Grammatical Forms and Their Influence on the Development of Ideas" (*Über das Entstehen der grammatischen Formen und ihren Einfluss auf die Ideenentwicklung*)[54] he distinguished four principles of linguistic structure which might be seen as a developmental sequence. In the first, language expresses objects only, leaving it to the understanding to supply (or to infer from the situation) the unexpressed relations between the "object-words." There was supposed to be in this stage, however, experimentation with the use of object-words as an expedient toward the expressing of relations. In the second stage these expedients are regularized and the object-words that doubled as relation indicators become half-material and half-formal (or alternately material and formal). In the third stage they begin to lose their independence and become loose affixes, but the whole—that is, they and a word to which they may be appended—is not yet a unity, but only an aggregate. In the fourth and highest stage, the evolution of grammatically formed words is complete; the word is a unit and each word is grammatically individuated. Humboldt's first stage was quite hypothetic. No known language could be said to exemplify it. Yet it was the logical starting point necessary to provide the resources for the second stage. For an example we would have to appeal to our imagination. But, interestingly, although it would be a vocal language, it would otherwise have precisely the character that Tylor and others, both before and after him, have ascribed to the so-called "spontaneous gesture-language" of deaf-mutes, with its "natural syntax" of situational dominance, and in which purely grammatical signs are reportedly nonexistent. One is drawn inevitably back to the earlier speculations on the origin of language. Beyond Humboldt's hypothetic first stage, the remaining ones are simply the classic three—isolating, agglutinating, and inflecting—but with what appears to be the implication of a developmental sequence from each to the next. The illustrative examples are as before, except that Humboldt, being more aware and appreciative of the great variety of differences among languages, was apparently less willing to think in terms of *pure types*. His was more a typology of principles and of processes than of static structures. He admitted that languages might not be assignable unequivocally to one or another of the types, and that more than one type of structure might be found in a single language. In fact he concluded that a precise typological classification of all languages was hardly to be attained. Nonetheless, Humboldt did add one new "type" to the previous three, and the trilogy became henceforth, for many writers, a foursome. Humboldt had acquainted himself with data on a number of American Indian languages, especially the Nahuatl of Mexico, and he felt it necessary to take account of the curious pattern of noun incorporation, or object incorporation, that so many of these exhibited; and so the fourth type was established, the so-called incorporating languages.

"Incorporation" is indeed quite a striking phenomenon; and I can remember my own astonishment on encountering it, when as a student I first began work on Iroquoian. Rather than defining the phenomenon, let me illustrate it with an example or two from Oneida. The word for "I eat" (or "I am eating") is *i·kéks*; the word for "fish" is *kéⁿtsyuⁿ*; but the word for "I eat fish" (or "I am eating fish") is *kítsyaks*; and for "I ate fish" is *waʔkítsyakeʔ*. Similarly, *i:laks* "he eats"; *kéⁿtsyuⁿ* "fish"; *léⁿtsyaks* "he eats fish"; *wahéⁿtsyakeʔ* "he ate fish"; etc. Or, with personal-object incorporations: *wahi·kéⁿ*: "I saw him"; *wahákkeⁿʔ* "he saw me"; *waʔkhe·kéⁿ*: "I saw her (or them)"; *waʔúⁿkkeⁿʔ* "she (or they) saw me"; *wáskeⁿʔ* "you (singular) saw it (thing or animal) or her (woman in child-bearing years)"; *wesa·kéⁿ*: "it (animal) or she (woman in childbearing years) saw you (singular)"; etc. These are all single words. No part of any one of them can be uttered alone or would mean anything by itself. The Iroquoian languages can be taken as prime examples of Humboldt's "incorporating" type.

Other typologists generally took their departure from Humboldt's formulation, while reading new significances into it, or modifying it in one way or another. August Friedrich Pott

(1848)[55] recognized the four types of Humboldt, but concluded that the flexional one was the normal one for a human language, and that the isolating and agglutinating types were infranormal while the incorporating languages were transnormal, the latter having exceeded the proper goal in the growth of form. August Schleicher (1848)[56] elaborated a deductive rationale for the three major classes in the typology, all of this being built on a Hegelian mode of reasoning. He was also most explicit in stressing the idea of a developmental sequence from one state to another, from the lowest to the highest. And, following Schleicher, the sequence came to take on more and more connotations of societal as well as mental evolution. In 1854 Max Mueller (of Oxford), in a lengthy essay incorporated into Christian Charles Bunsen's *Outlines of the Philosophy of Universal History*,[57] proceeded from Humboldt's principles and erected a theory of the relation of the language types to stages in societal evolution. The isolating languages (the Chinese type) were seen as a product of the "family stage" of social development; the agglutinating languages (the Turanian type) were the product of the "nomad stage"; and the flexional languages (the Aryan type) were the product of "political" or "state" society. And, after quoting Pott's opinion that even the Sanskrit might have been preceded by simpler stages in its history, Mueller remarks: "I should say that, in the same manner as in every body-politic, traces of a former nomadic or even family life can be discovered, we may really discover in all Arian languages traces of a Turanian and Chinese formation through which they had passed. Nay, during periods of anarchy, conquest, and migration, political languages seem to relapse into nomadic unsettledness, and during periods of apathy and stagnation nomadic languages may fall back into a state of Chinese helplessness. But what interests us here is the ascending scale, the primary growth of languages, not their secondary formations and reformations."[58] In his famous _Lectures on the Science of Language_ (1862),[59] Mueller popularized still further this scheme of correlating the typology with stages of social development, and he expounded again his theory of the necessary character of "nomadic" languages.

William Dwight Whitney (of Yale), although a long-time antagonist of Max Mueller's, accepted the typology and some of its evolutionary connotations, while rejecting, however, the explicit correlation with societal stages.[60]

Another term, and type, which sometimes appeared in the typologies around this time was "polysynthetic." This is of course still a widely used term. It was coined by the French-American scholar of American aboriginal languages, Peter Stephen (or Pierre Étienne) DuPonceau, and was used by him in various works (for example, 1819 in a report to the American Philosophical Society, and 1838 in an essay published in France)[61] to apply to those American native languages in whose words a great many morphological elements are joined, and many features of meaning are specified, so that it requires a lengthy phrase or a sentence to translate one of them into an ordinary European language. These are the so-called "sentence words" of certain American languages. Almost from the beginning it came to be regarded that all of the American languages were of this polysynthetic type, and, on this basis, there was constructed an argument for their historical unity.[62] Many of the Americanists of the mid-nineteenth century accepted this view (besides DuPonceau, there were, for example, Albert Gallatin, John Pickering, and Robert G. Latham). And the term, together with the view of the unity of the American languages, was widely current in European circles as well. Some writers used Powell's term "holophrastic" for this type. It may be noted that in accepting the term and the type "polysynthetic," the agglutinating-versus-fusional distinction was being quietly ignored; for polysynthesis might be found (and of course actually is found) in languages of both of these types. For example, Quechua or Eskimo must surely be judged to go with the "agglutinative" type, but Iroquoian just as surely would have to go with the "inflectional."

Just as the polysynthetic American languages amazed the nineteenth-century scholars for their high degree of elaboration of word morphology, the Chinese pattern remained incomprehensible to them for an opposite reason. They were all struck by its oddity, and could see in it only the manifestation of a primitive degree of linguistic development. It was not only the lack of paradigms of inflected forms that stigmatized Chinese for them; but, even more, the fact that grammatical relations were indicated by words whose basic meanings were thought to be referential and "material": that verbs meaning "give," "use," "go," and so forth should double as prepositions meaning "for," "with," "to," and so forth; or that nouns should double as adverbs or locative postpositions. In all of these cases, it seemed to them, abstract relational concepts were being expressed only by means of concrete metaphors, or being suggested by material concepts. As William Dwight Whitney put it: "The Chinese word admits of employment indifferently as one and another part of speech, and plainly by an inherent non-distinction of their various offices."[63]

There were embarrassing implications in all this. How could the American aborigines have developed languages that exceeded even the Greek and the Sanskrit in their delicate differentiations of morphological form? And how was it that the Chinese, for all of their linguistic "poverty" and "primitivity," should yet have been the developers and possessors of a great civilization? As for the latter question, various ingenious explanations were offered. For William Dwight Whitney it could be explained by two general phenomena: the independence of thought from language (which was a bone of contention between him and Max Mueller), and the remarkable power of conservatism. Regarding the former, Whitney says: "The Chinese language is therefore, in one most important and fundamental respect, of the very lowest grade of structure and poverty of resource. But it is also the most remarkable example in the world of a weak instrumentality which is made the means of accomplishing great things."[64]

As for the relation between resources and creativity, Whitney notes by way of an appropriate simile: "A few scratches on a board with a bit of charcoal by a skilled artist may be more full of meaning, may speak more strongly to the imagination and feeling, than a picture elaborated by an inferior hand with all the resources of a modern art-school."[65] The preservation of their primitive linguistic instrument by the Chinese, then, was laid to the genius with which they used it, and to a remarkable conservatism and persistency which Whitney regarded as a national trait of the Chinese—enabling them to preserve their language "substantially unchanged from the very dawn of history."

Friedrich Schlegel had another, though not unrelated, idea: "The language of this otherwise so refined nation stands therefore at the very lowest level; perhaps because their so extremely artful system of writing had caused it to become fixed too early in its infancy."[66]

The matter about the languages of the American Indians was eventually handled in another way. It was out of this, and out of the problem of the so-called "analytic" languages like English and French, that a new note came to be injected into the interpretation of typology. This was the notion of "efficiency," and of its opposed trait, "cumbersomeness." One of the first works to make this concept explicit, and to provide a new rationale for the ranking of languages, was the *Introduction to the Study of Indian Languages*, by John Wesley Powell of the Bureau of American Ethnology, published in 1880. Powell introduces the subject in this way: "The assumed superiority of the Greek and Latin languages to the English and other Modern civilized tongues, has in part been the cause of many erroneous conceptions of the rank of Indian tongues. When the student discovers that many of the characteristics of the classic languages appear in the Indian, which are to a greater or less extent lost in the modern civilized languages, he has at once assumed the superiority of the Indian tongue; and when he has further discovered that some of these characteristics are even more highly developed than in the classic ones, he has been led to still further exalt them. . . . The many curious linguistic devices by which great specification of expression is attained has led some scholars into undue admiration, *as they have failed to appreciate the loss in the economy and power which these peculiar methods entail.*"[67]

Powell set forth a typology of grammatical processes and their functions, and a view of the organization of language and the historical processes in its development. The principles of the old typology were incorporated into this, under one subcategory of the types of processes. But Powell took these as representing a continuous scale on which no well-defined "planes of demarcation" could be drawn. And his was a typology of on-going processes, all of which might be found at work simultaneously in any one language at any period of its development. It might thus seem to be less susceptible to a general evolutionary interpretation. But not so. It still recognized differences in the predominating character of different languages, and Powell—strongly influenced by Lewis Henry Morgan—was an avowed cultural evolutionist. His criterion of "efficiency" in language enabled him, he believed, to rank languages. And on this basis he could also turn the old order of ranking upside down. After describing the elaboration of inflectional paradigms in certain American languages, he comments: "A Ponca Indian, in saying that a man killed a rabbit, would have to say the man, he, one, animate, standing, in the nominative case, purposely killed, by shooting an arrow, the rabbit, he, the one, animate, sitting, in the objective case; for the form of a verb to kill would have to be selected, and the verb changes its form by inflection and incorporated particles to denote person, number, and gender as animate or inanimate, and gender as standing, sitting, or lying, and case; and the form of the verb would also express whether the killing was done accidentally or purposely, and whether it was by shooting or by some other process, and, if by shooting, whether by bow and arrow, or with a gun; and the form of the verb would in like manner have to express all of these things relating to the object; that is, the person, number, gender, and case of the object; and from the multiplicity of paradigmatic forms of the verb to kill, this particular one would have to be selected. Perhaps one time in a million it would be the purpose to express all of these particulars, and in that case the Indian would have the whole expression in one compact word; but in the nine hundred and ninety-nine thousand nine hundred and ninety-nine cases, all of these particulars would have to be thought of in the selection of the form of the verb, when no valuable purpose would be accomplished thereby."

He concluded: "In the development of the English, as well as the French and German, linguistic evolution has not been in vain. Judged by these criteria, the English stands alone in the highest rank."[68]

This reversal of the arrow of "progress" in language became generally accepted toward the end of the nineteenth century and well into the twentieth. William Dwight Whitney (1875, 1889) expressed a similar opinion about the form of American

Indian languages: "As it is, it makes upon us the impression of as much exceeding the due medium of formal expressiveness as the Chinese comes short of it; it is cumbrous and time-wasting in its immense polysyllabism."[69] (This, of course, sounds like an echo of Pott's "infranormal," "normal," "transnormal" classification of languages.) André Lefèvre, a professor in the Anthropological School in Paris, also took up this point of view. In a book about the typology and evolution of language (*Race and Language*, 1894),[70] he devoted two chapters to describing the development and the virtues of French and English, in which "simplified languages . . . the word is even more the willing servant of the thought." And, in this connection, we can hardly neglect to mention the great Danish scholar of the English language, Otto Jespersen, who in several writings (from 1894 to 1949),[71] defined progress as the stripping down of the old elaborate morphology that he regarded as the true relic of primitive times. Progress was now seen as morphological simplification.

This takes us through what might be called the second chapter in the history of language typology. But there is a third. It begins with Franz Boas, and then Edward Sapir, with a continuation more recently by Joseph Greenberg and Charles Hockett, which brings us up to the present. We can be brief on this, since the recent history is well known to all. The present state of the problem merits some comment, however.

It was mentioned earlier in this section that a break in the interpretations of typological differences in language came with Franz Boas. Boas himself did not minimize the typological differences. In fact he stressed the variability and illustrated it in some of his writings. He also granted a certain validity to the varieties distinguished in the traditional typology. And on one occasion[72] he gave a Kwakiutl example that might almost rival Powell's Ponca illustration. There is even a slight trace of

Powell's evolutionary interpretation in one of his statements, where, in speaking of the classifications given by obligatory categories, which, as he says, "set off languages sharply from one another," he notes that "Such ancient classifications continue to exist in modern languages and we have to think in their forms." But Boas, after asking the question whether the form of a language (whatever its morphological impedimenta) might in any way hinder clear thought or the formulation of generalized ideas, concluded that this could not be the case. Rather, a language might be regarded as adapted to the culture and needs and circumstances of life of the society speaking it. But it could not be regarded as limiting the forms of thought.

It might be felt that this was not so much of a break after all, for the conditioning implied by some of the earlier typologists was from culture to language also; and at least Whitney allowed that thought was independent of the form of a language and not necessarily impeded by its (supposed) deficiencies. But if one reads through this literature, one can only conclude that there is indeed a new element in Boas's position. He was formulating, on what he felt to be good evidence, a view that anticipated those later to be known as cultural and linguistic relativism. But Boas's linguistic relativism rested on a doctrine of universals in language, and on a belief in the essential equality amongst languages so far as their fundamental and psychologically relevant aspects are concerned. This is contrary, in spirit at least, to the evolutionary interpretation of Powell.

Recent generations of students of language have been trained in an intellectual atmosphere in which the old problem of the typology has dropped out of sight, and they have grown up more or less ignorant of its past. This was not yet so in Edward Sapir's day, and the typological problem forms the main theme of his book Language (1921).[73] When he wrote, he could doubtless assume knowledge of the nincteenth-century back-ground of this problem, and so he could devote his attention to a new attempt to unravel its tangled threads, without ever mentioning the names of the nineteenth century typologists whose formulations he was trying to improve on. All of this apparently was part of the public domain at that time. Chapter IV of his *Language,* on "Grammatical Processes," actually fol-lows the outline of Powell's treatment of the same subject, though Sapir elaborated and illustrated certain aspects of the subject more fully. Chapter V, "Grammatical Concepts," is an attempt to deal with the fundamental dichotomy that was at the root of nineteenth-century typology, the expression of material and relational meanings. Sapir's treatment made a brilliant contribution to the understanding of this topic; and it was based on a far more intimate knowledge of languages, and more penetrating insight into their working, than were the earlier treatments. And, in Chapter VI, "Types of Linguistic Structure," Sapir attempted to formulate a better basis for a typology of language structures, separating out as independent variables a number of factors that had not been clearly dis-tinguished from one another in the earlier attempts. For ex-ample, the scale of synthetic types (analytic, synthetic, poly-synthetic) and that of kinds or degrees of fusion (isolating, ag-glutinative, fusional, and internal-flexional—the last of which he called "symbolic") were for the first time separated out clearly as separate dimensions of variation. Neither of these, or even both taken together, did he regard as adequate for a typology, no matter how strikingly languages might differ from one another in these respects; for the first of these scales was, as he put it, "merely quantitative," and the second was concerned with "technical externals." The most important in-gredient in Sapir's typology, as he envisioned it, was the way in which a language handled the expression of the various essential kinds of concepts: radical, pure-relational, concrete-and mixed-relational, and derivational.

Sapir's typological endeavor has been a source of enlightenment to some, but of confusion to others. Those who have worked with languages of types very different from our own have especially appreciated Sapir's discussion of typology. But those who have come to these chapters unprepared, without knowledge of the nineteenth-century history that lay behind them, or without the field-work experience of trying to find one's own way into a new and strange language, have often been left in bewilderment.

Sapir perceived with greater clarity than any of his predecessors the separate ways in which languages could be morphologically different; and he appreciated the extent of the differences. It should be interesting, then, to note what significance he attached to these differences. In this, in the interpretation of his typology, he was even less of an evolutionist and more of a relativist than Boas: "Nor can I believe that culture and language are in any true sense causally related. Culture may be defined as what a society does and thinks. Language is a particular how of thought. It is difficult to see what particular causal relations may be expected to subsist between a selected inventory of experience . . . and the particular manner in which the society expresses all experience."[74]

And just prior to this was his statement: "The latent content of all languages is the same—the intuitive *science* of experience. It is the manifest form that is never twice the same, for this form, which we call linguistic morphology, is nothing more nor less than a collective *art* of thought." This "morphology" of languages he saw as subject to long-term self-perpetuating tendencies of change, which he called "drift." But the directions of drift might be different in different languages. Since morphology was not to be related to cultural level, the direction of drift could hardly be either.

After Sapir's *Language*, I know of no further significant contribution to the matter of linguistic typology until the early 1950's, when Joseph Greenberg and Charles Hockett (independently) devised a series of indices which could be used to quantify the variables in Sapir's typology. Such quantification could be used not only to compare the degrees of synthesis, of fusion, of recourse to derivational devices, and so forth, in different languages, but also to compare different periods in the histories of single languages for which there are literary documents extending over sufficiently long periods of time. In this way there could also be obtained a quantification of the "drift" tendencies that Sapir spoke of.

As matters stand now, we have Sapir's and Greenberg's and Hockett's refinements of the typology of languages, but, ironically, the typology has been shorn of any significance. The evolutionary interpretations, whether in the direction indicated by the Schlegels, Pott, Humboldt, Schleicher, Mueller, Whitney, and so many others, or whether in the reverse direction indicated by Powell, Lefèvre, and Jespersen, have been disavowed. And neither Boas nor Sapir was willing to attribute any deep psychological significance to the thought-ways given by different language structures. To be sure, Whorf, and quite possibly Sapir in his later years, and quite a number of linguists and anthropologists of more recent decades, have taken a different view of the matter, seeing the structure of a language as implying a metaphysics or world-view; and some have sought an understanding of the underlying postulates of a culture by this means. But this has always been a matter of controversy. As of right now, with the current ascendance of new theories of grammar that sharply distinguish between "deep structure" and "surface structure" in language, I think there would be a general reluctance to ascribe much in the way of psychological significance to typological differences among languages; for the typologies have to do with "surface grammar," not with "deep grammar." Can it be then that the typology—with all its recent refinements—ends up by being a typology with no known significance?

Perhaps we can recognize at least this much significance: that it shows and measures the *latitude* of the human capacity for speech: the immense leeway that the anatomy and neural organization of man allow for the organization of language. This may well be a measure of the difference between the biological endowment of *Homo sapiens* and that of all other species, in which latter the range of possibilities is next to zero.

Perhaps there may be found yet another significance. Not every linguist is willing to discard as irrelevant the types of developmental processes sketched by Humboldt and his successors, and by Powell. There is a possibility that gross typological differences reflect, if not thought or culture, then something of the accidents of the social histories of speech communities, as these have created periods and circumstances in which traditional linguistic structures were, one might say, destroyed, and languages rebuilt, putting (as Powell and so many others had expressed it) "old materials to new uses." It may be of interest in this connection that the purest "analytic" and "isolating" languages known are the Pidgins and Creolized languages. These have long been the unwanted step-children of linguistic science. But it is in these that one can see most clearly something like the first principle in the building of grammar that was posited by the evolutionary typologists. One may note that the historical circumstances that gave birth to the Pidgins and Creolized languages were far more drastic and destructive of continuity of tradition in language than were those that gave impetus to change in the modern "an-alytic" Romance vernaculars, or in early modern English.

THE SIGNIFICANCE OF LANGUAGE DIFFERENCES:
CATEGORIES OF MEANING

Our survey of the history of the typology has brought us to the point of apparent denial of any significant mental or cultural differences being correlated with structural differences in languages, even though these differences are impressive in number, variety, and magnitude, and remain fascinating in their own right to students of language. Thus Boas could conclude: "It does not seem likely, therefore, that there is any direct relation between the culture of a tribe and the language they speak";[75] and Sapir could express a similar opinion: "Nor can I believe that culture and language are in any true sense causally related."[76] Yet, as we know, these same writers also expressed views seemingly to the contrary, to the effect that different languages embody—in their individual peculiarities and differences—the special cultural background and habits of thought of the peoples who use them; and that a language may be seen as presenting a key to the most unconscious aspects of a culture, and providing a guide to what is taken for granted in a particular world view. Moreover, anthropological linguists who have followed Boas and Sapir, from Whorf on down to the "cognitive-theorists," "ethnoscientists," and "structural-semanticists" of the present, have a continuing tradition of language-and-culture studies, both theoretical and applied, in which one looks to language as an aid in penetrating the conceptual world of a society. These have followed in the direction indicated by Boas when he wrote, concerning the "theoretical importance of linguistic studies," that "the purely linguistic inquiry is part and parcel of a thorough investigation of the psychology of the peoples of the world. If ethnology is understood as the science dealing with the mental phenomena of the life of the peoples of the world, human language, one of the most important manifestations of mental life, would seem to belong naturally to the field of work of ethnology."[77] And by Sapir when he stated that: "We may think of language as the symbolic guide to culture."[78]

One may gain an impression of inconsistency in reading Boas and Sapir—as if they were at one moment taking the position of linguistic universalists, and, at another, the position of relativists. There is no real inconsistency in this, however. It is necessary to see their various statements in proper context, and to remember always the importance in the anthropology of Boas, and his students, of the distinction between *nature* and *nurture*. The essential nature of language—what it is, or the properties that it has (that all languages have), by virtue of the common nature of the human species—is one thing; how languages differ from one another, because of their separate histories of cultural development, is another. Boas and Sapir were, without contradiction, both universalists and relativists. If there is apparent confusion, it is only that when they spoke of thought patterns, or psychology, or mental processes in language, they might in one context be referring to those that correspond to the *essential* character of language, as given by the nature of all humanity, and in another context referring to the particular intellectual content and the special conventions and habits of reference that are unique to the use of each individual language. They recognized both human universals and cultural variables in the structure of language. Both were seen as having relevance for the psychology of language. Thus, from Boas, concerning certain psychological universals in language: "The occurrence of the most fundamental grammatical concepts *in all languages* must be considered as proof of the unity of fundamental psychological processes."[79]

And just preceding this, his view on the psychological relevance of the differences among languages: "It seems well worth while to subject the whole range of linguistic concepts to a searching analysis, and to seek in the peculiarities of the grouping of ideas in different languages an important characteristic in the history of the mental development of the various branches of mankind."[80]

From Sapir on the universal capacity of all languages: "We may say that a language is so constructed that no matter what any speaker of it may desire to communicate, no matter how original or bizarre his idea or his fancy, the language is prepared to do his work. . . . The world of linguistic forms, held within the framework of a given language, is a complete system of reference."[81]

And on the different predispositions imposed by particular languages: "No two languages are ever sufficiently similar to be considered as representing the same social reality . . . We see and hear and otherwise experience very largely as we do because the language habits of our community predispose certain choices of interpretation."[82]

It is worth recalling something of the background against which Boas wrote. Behind him were an anthropology which was *"Rassenkunde"* (in an early sense of this term) and another which was "cultural evolution" (in the manner of the stage-sequence theorists), as well as a third tradition of environmental determinism. These points of view, in varying proportions, affected the thinking of a very large part of the professional and amateur anthropologists, as well as lay opinion, in the several decades preceding Boas's influence. It was habitual to ascribe different "temperaments" or "psychic traits" to the various ethnic groups—primitive or civilized—and to see such traits, as well as their supposed manifestations in the organization and character of particular languages, as being somehow determined by biological race, or stage of cultural evolution, or physical environment, or some causal concatenation of these. These assumptions colored the broader generalizations of even those scholars who were most meticulous in their attention to the more minute details and small-scale problems in their own special subjects of investigation and who were otherwise cautious in their descriptive and historical treatments of these. To Boas the evidence against the racial, cultural-evolutionary, and environmental explanations of language differences was clear. But since this was not yet in the domain of general knowledge or accepted opinion, it was necessary for him to devote many pages to disabusing his readers of these notions and to demonstrating the lack of necessary dependence among the racial, cultural, environmental, and linguistic variables. These pages[83] now seem rather tedious reading, since the points made and illustrated there seem so obvious and self-evident. (Yet we receive frequent reminders—even today—that there are still those who have not learned this first lesson of anthropology.) Against this background it was necessary for Boas to present the findings of those who had worked intimately with the languages of primitive peoples, to the effect that all of these languages show the same capacity as instruments of thought and the same potential for the development of more advanced cultural content. From this derives the "universalist" component in Boas's thinking and teaching about language. At the same time it was also necessary to provide some account or theory of how languages could be so unlike one another and so varied and uneven in their existing cultural content. In giving the answer to this question, Boas developed his theory of classification in language, and his explanation of classifications in terms of needs and utility, which together are the essence of his theory of linguistic variability. A few fragmentary quotations must suffice here to illustrate these ideas. First, on the phenomenon of classification:

The total number of possible combinations of phonetic elements is . . . unlimited; but only a limited number are used to express ideas. This implies that *the total number of ideas that are expressed by distinct phonetic groups is limited in number.* (We will call these phonetic groups "word stems.")

Since the total range of personal experience which language serves to express is infinitely varied, and its whole scope must be expressed by a limited number of phonetic groups, it is obvious that *an extended classification of experiences must underlie all articulate speech.*

This coincides with a fundamental trait of human thought. In our actual experience no two sense-impressions or emotional states are identical. Nevertheless we classify them, according to their similarities, in wider or narrower groups the limits of which may be determined from a variety of points of view . . . Thus the limitation of the number of phonetic groups expressing distinct ideas is an expression of the psychological fact that *many different individual experiences appear to us as representatives of the same category of thought.*[84]

And now on the variability, or relativity, of classifications: "It seems important at this point of our considerations to emphasize the fact that the groups of ideas expressed by specific phonetic groups show very material differences in different languages, and *do not conform by any means to the same principles of classification.*"[85] Finally, the variability of linguistic classifications as given by the lexicons of different languages, and as imposed through obligatory grammatical categories, might be viewed in terms of considerations of the relevance of these, given the conditions of life of a people. Proliferation of distinctions in certain semantic areas might represent a response to practical interests (or the legacy of a history of such responses), while apparent deficiencies in other areas, whether of differentiating specific terms or of generalizing cover terms (class abstractions), probably indicate nothing more than their irrelevance to the given conditions of life. In Boas's words, the lack of generalizing terms "does not prove inability to form them, but it merely proves that the mode of life of the people is such that they are not required; that they would, however, develop just as soon as needed."[86]

Boas went on to demonstrate that the three alleged deficiencies of "primitive" languages—supposed indeterminacy of sounds, lack of generalizing capacity, and holophrasis—were a mirage. The "indeterminacy of sounds" he had shown more than two decades earlier (1889)[87] to be an artifact of the outside observer's habits of perception of speech sounds and not a deficiency of language of the primitive. It merely demonstrated the relativity principle in yet another domain of language, namely, in phonology. The absence of terms for certain "general" concepts was now also shown to be due to no incapacity of the primitive mind or inherent deficiency of language, but merely a matter of adaptation that hinged on questions of relevance. And even holophrasis was a relative matter. If one attended to defining categories, it was possible to show that many expressions in any language could be shown to be "holophrastic" in comparison with corresponding ones of some other language. "Thus," Boas says, "we have found that language does not furnish the much-looked-for means of discovering differences in the mental status of different races."[88]

Sapir followed the lead of Boas, and restated, or developed further, many of the ideas of his teacher. For example, Chapter X of Sapir's book *Language* (1921), which is entitled "Language, Race and Culture," is largely a reiteration of the content and arguments of Chapter V, "Race and Language," of Boas's *The Mind of Primitive Man* (1911) and of the section bearing the same title in Boas's "Introduction" to the *Handbook of*

American Indian Languages (1911), showing once more how a language type is not determined by the racial heredity of a people, or by the stage of development or the content of their culture. And Sapir's article on "Language and Environment" (1912) is directed against environmentalist explanation of language structures (both grammatical and phonetic), as was Boas's section entitled "Influence of Environment on Language" in the Introduction to the *Handbook*. Sapir's article, however, explored this subject more fully and developed lines of thought barely touched on by Boas. Environmental influences on language, according to Sapir, are to be seen only in the content of vocabulary, and not in phonetics or in the morphological patterns of language (he followed Boas on both of these points), or even in the classificatory categories of particular grammatical systems. As for the latter, he argued that, even if these had arisen in response to environmental pressures of some sort, it was in the nature of such systems that they should long outlive whatever factors may have contributed to their shaping. Linguistic structures, in his view, were by nature conservative and changed much more slowly than cultural elements. This he attributed "to the subconscious character of grammatical classification." "One necessary consequence of this," he continued, "is that the forms of language will in time cease to symbolize those of culture, and *this is our main thesis.*"[89] He was agreeing, essentially, with Boas's belief that "historical influences are much stronger than geographical influences."[90]

Sapir's Chapter IX of *Language*, "How Languages Influence Each Other," develops further the theme of Boas's section on "Mutual Influences of Languages" in the Introduction to the *Handbook*. This chapter is often seen as containing the germ of an idea that was eventually to run counter to Boas's when applied to the problems of the classification of languages, since Boas tended to be somewhat more partial to diffusionist explanations of linguistic (as well as cultural) similarities than was Sapir.[91] Yet Sapir elaborated the argument and adduced evidence for mutual influences between adjacent languages in their phonology, lexicon, and derivational affixes even more fully than did Boas; and Boas was almost as cautious (in the Introduction to the *Handbook* at least) about attributing such influences in "the most fundamental morphological traits of language" as was Sapir. The final impact of Sapir's chapter, however, is to show that languages influence each other much less than a diffusionist might think, and that the influences that do occur are only those that can be accommodated without essential changes in the structural pattern of a language and that do not run counter to the direction of its already established drift.

Sapir repeatedly stressed the unconscious (or subconscious) nature of language patterns. In this also he followed Boas. In fact, for Boas it was precisely this aspect of language that distinguished it from all other subjects of ethnological investigation: "If the phenomena of human speech seem to form in a way a subject by itself, this is perhaps largely due to the fact that the laws of language remain entirely unknown to the speakers, that linguistic phenomena never rise into the consciousness of primitive man, while all other ethnological phenomena are more or less clearly subjects of conscious thought."[92]

Sapir followed Boas also in his concept of linguistic relativity. His development of this, and of the language-thought relationship, was especially important in the history of anthropological linguistics in America. His view of the matter is best presented in his own words. One of Sapir's most succinct statements of this was in a brief note in *Science* (1931): "The relation between language and experience is often misunderstood. Language is not merely a more or less systematic inventory of the various items of experience which seem relevant to the individual, as is so often naively assumed, but is also a self-contained, creative symbolic organization, which not only refers to experience largely acquired without its help but actually defines experience for us by reason of its formal completeness and because of our unconscious projection of its implicit expectations into the field of experience . . . Such categories as number, gender, case, tense, mode, voice, aspect and a host of others, many of which are not recognized systematically in our Indo-European languages, are, of course, derivative of experience at last analysis, but, once abstracted from experience, they are systematically elaborated in language and are not so much discovered in experience as imposed upon it because of the tyrannical hold that linguistic form has upon our orientation in the world. Inasmuch as languages differ very widely in their systematization of fundamental concepts, they tend to be only loosely equivalent to each other as symbolic devices and are, as a matter of fact, incommensurable in the sense in which two systems of points in a plane are, on the whole, incommensurable to each other if they are plotted out with reference to differing systems of coordinates. The point of view urged in this paper becomes entirely clear only when one compares languages of extremely different structures, as in the case of our Indo-European languages, native American Indian languages, and native languages of Africa."[93]

In all of these matters—the universalist and the relativist components in a view of language (that recognizes the universal and apparently equal capacity of all languages for the intellective processes, but also the unique mold of each individual language into which these are cast), the recognition of the unconscious character and the conservatism of grammatical systems, and the assertion of the freedom of these and of language type from racial, cultural, or environmental determination, as well as (within the stated limits) from the influences of diffusion—in all of these, there is a strong bond of continuity between the views of Boas and those of Sapir. One can measure here the impress of the anthropologist field worker and teacher upon the Germanist student who, changing his field, came to study under him. The recognition of this continuity, however, must not be allowed to diminish our appreciation of the importance or the novelty of Sapir's own contributions, either to the understanding of linguistic relativity and the psychology of grammar, or to the wider content of anthropological linguistics. Especially important were his contributions to the theory of the phoneme[94] and the immense quantity of his documentation, analysis, and comparative-historical study of American Indian languages. And his influence on his students was every bit as profound as was Boas's on his. One of his students was Benjamin Lee Whorf.

Whorf came under Sapir's direct influence in 1931 when Sapir moved from Chicago to New Haven. Although Whorf's professional employment was in another field, outside the academic circle, he was already possessed of a wide variety of interests in language and of skills in linguistics developed largely on his own; and he had also undertaken field work on Nahuatl (on the advice of Alfred M. Tozzer) in Mexico in 1930. When Sapir offered his first course on American Indian linguistics at Yale, Whorf made arrangements to be enrolled and commuted to New Haven to attend. Under Sapir's influence and in the circle of graduate students then receiving professional training in linguistics and anthropology, Whorf was brought into the mainstream of these disciplines. In 1932 he began his studies of the Hopi language, working at first with a Hopi Indian informant who was then residing in New York City, and then later, in 1938, on a trip to the Hopi reservation in Arizona.

Whorf is perhaps best known for his efforts to express, in readable form and for a wide audience, the principle of linguistic relativity; and these writings of his, or excerpts from them, are much quoted. For example: "When linguists became able to examine critically and scientifically a large number of languages of widely different patterns, their base of reference was expanded; they experienced an interruption of phenomena hitherto held universal, and a whole new order of significances came into their ken. It was found that the background linguistic system (in other words, the grammar) of each language is not merely a reproducing instrument for voicing ideas but rather it is itself the shaper of ideas, the program and guide for the individual's mental activity, for his analysis of impressions, for his synthesis of his mental stock in trade. Formulation of ideas is not an independent process, strictly rational in the old sense, but is part of a particular grammar, and differs, from slightly to greatly, between different grammars. We dissect nature along lines laid down by our native languages. The categories and types that we isolate from the world of phenomena we do not find there because they stare every observer in the face; on the contrary, the world is presented in a kaleidoscopic flux of impressions which has to be organized by our minds—and this means largely by the linguistic systems in our minds. We cut nature up, organize it into concepts, and ascribe significances as we do, largely because we are parties to an agreement to organize it in this way—an agreement that holds throughout our speech community and is codified in the patterns of our language. The agreement is, of course, an implicit and unstated one, *but its terms are absolutely obligatory;* we cannot talk at all except by subscribing to the organization and classification of data which the agreement decrees."[95]

Whorf was convinced of a close relation of language to thought, of a dependence of thought on language patterns; but yet he was wary of a motor theory of thought. A motor theory— at least according to his understanding of that notion as then

current in Watsonian psychology and among some linguists—
seemed to leave out of consideration the vast and intricate
network of *unuttered relations* between linguistic elements:
relations that he attempted to describe under such terms as
"rapport," "linkage," and "reactance." To him the motor theory
of thought seemed to be deficient in a way that would not (or
should not) even be acceptable in a grammar: "an analysis of
silent thinking into motor quiverings corresponding to sup-
pressed words and morphemes would no more be a real analysis
of thinking than the analysis of a language into actual words
and morphemes would be a real analysis of the language. The
crudest and most amateurish grammar analyzes more effectively
than that, and any scientific grammar is necessarily a deep
analysis into relations."[96]

It may of course be questioned whether he had a correct understanding of the motor theories of thought. But this question
need not detain us here. We will concern ourselves rather with
his contribution to the semantic correlates (and "psychology")
of grammar.

Whorf's penetrating insights into the most subtle aspects of
semantic structure in language are probably his most valuable
contribution. The articles and sketches in which he developed
these were not published during his lifetime, although they
were written even before those in which he popularized the
relativity principle and before his grammatical sketches of Hopi
and Aztec—in none of which these ideas received any exposition. They are developed in two articles ("A Linguistic
Consideration of Thinking in Primitive Communities," and
"Grammatical Categories") and in a personal letter (now published under the title "Discussion of Hopi Linguistics"), all
written around 1936–1937, but published only posthumously—
"Grammatical Categories" in 1945 and the others in 1956, fifteen
years after his death. In these he takes the reader beyond the

more obvious overtly marked and "phenotypic" categories of a language to show him how much semantic structure there is, and how many semantic classes and categories there are which may be isolated on the basis of linguistic evidence, but which are not represented by any words or morphemes in the language, being given instead by various kinds of *relations* between morphemes. He described and illustrated several of these kinds of relations, and drew from them aspects of the structure of meaning that are of great subtlety and that do not readily meet the eye (or ear, or conscious awareness) of even the native speaker. It was in these exploratory pieces that Whorf was making his most original contribution to both the theory of semantic structure and the techniques of linguistic analysis. The relations that he appealed to were of two major sorts: what we should now call those of commutability and contrast between morphemes, and those of co-occurrability or potential compatibility of morphemes in construction. Among the former, moreover, that is, among the relations of contrast, his examples illustrated both those of semantic exclusion (the opposition of different items on the same hierarchic level in a taxonomy), and those of semantic inclusion (contrasts between items belonging to different hierarchic levels, where the lower is subsumed under the higher). These are not the terms used by Whorf to describe such relations: he was struggling to find an appropriate terminology. But he saw quite clearly the kinds of relations that were involved. The co-occurrability criterion came to be quite widely used in linguistic analysis beginning a decade or so after Whorf wrote these articles (though the articles were still unpublished). It fitted in well with the distributionally-oriented linguistics being developed at that time. But there was an important difference between this use and Whorf's. The linguistics of this period was in the middle of a phase in which it tried at all costs to avoid coming to grips with problems of meaning directly, and co-occurrence (or privilege of occurrence) could be used as a dodge, as an "objective" criterion, to escape having to define linguistic classes in terms of meaning or meaning-correlates. Whorf, on the other hand, was using it as an aid to discover the organization of meaning (the hidden as well as the obvious) that is given in a language. This was his avowed goal; meaning was to be sought, not avoided: *"The very essence of linguistics is the quest for meaning*, and, as the science refines its procedure, it inevitably becomes, as a matter of this quest, more psychological and cultural, while retaining that almost mathematical precision of statement which it gets from the highly systemic nature of the linguistic realm of fact."[97]

Whorf spoke of "covert categories" and "cryptotypes" when referring to the classes and categories that could be defined by various kinds of relations between morphemes, opposing these to "overt categories" and "phenotypes"—these latter being "the 'classical' morphological category." He observed, correctly, that: "Grammatical research up to the present time has been concerned chiefly with the study of phenotypes. A certain type of grammar proceeds as if linguistic meaning dwelt wholly in them. The anthropologist should not be satisfied with such a grammar . . . It can be shown that, in some languages at least, linguistic meaning results from the interplay of phenotypes and cryptotypes, not from phenotypes alone."[98]

Whorf's writings had a powerful influence, not only on anthropological linguists (who by and large may have been among the least receptive of the anthropologists at that time), but also on the profession of cultural anthropology, which was becoming, at that time and in the years following, more and more oriented toward psychology (partly through Sapir's influence) and increasingly hopeful of the contribution that the psychological disciplines—and a psychologically oriented linguistics—might make to it. Whorf's writings nourished that hope.

Professional linguistics in America at that time and in the immediately following decade or more had embarked, however, on a different course, oriented away from psychology (though like the contemporary psychology it was "behaviorist" in method and outlook), and disavowing meaning as its object of study. The prevailing view was that "meaning" was something too vague and imprecise, too complex a phenomenon, and too inaccessible to observation, to be susceptible to scientific treatment. Whether a linguist was working on an exotic language or on his own language, he was considered to be in much the same position. Either he had to rely on his informant's intuition about meanings, or on his own. And intuition—or rather, the retrieval and verbalization of intuitive knowledge on demand—was not trusted as a reliable guide. The emphasis therefore was on the analysis of the uttered form of speech. Methods were being devised for isolating its units at its major levels of organization, and for describing the combinatorial properties of such units. The starting point was phonology. Given these assumptions, it was natural that a great deal of interest and effort should be devoted to the formulation of *phonological* theory and method, and that the theory and method for the higher levels was patterned to a considerable extent by analogy with those of phonology. Anthropological linguists were among the major contributors to this development. Bloomfield, whose views and influential work were in large part responsible for setting this course, was himself a devoted researcher in both Philippine and Algonquian languages. And those who shaped the further development of linguistics along these lines were for the most part students of Sapir or of Bloomfield, and also were heavily committed to original researches in American Indian languages and were concerned with related anthropological problems.

While this development seems to have been quite contrary to the direction indicated by Whorf, it is probably fair to say that linguists—at least the majority, and the anthropologists

among them—retained in their view a large part of the aims
and assumptions expressed by Whorf. There remained the view
that an adequate description of a language *in its own terms*
would ultimately approximate the unconscious thought patterns
of its speakers, and that it might also furnish a guide (perhaps
the only guide) to the organization of meaning.

What was distinctive of linguistics in America during this
period (that is, of its dominant trend) was the acceptance of
Bloomfield's view of meaning. This rested on a behaviorist
definition: "We have defined the meaning of a linguistic form
as the situation in which the speaker utters it and the response
which it calls forth in the hearer."[99] These variables of stimulus
and response, in the human situation, are of course beyond the
investigator's control and are in large part unknowable. Even
Bloomfield's more restricted concept of "distinctive" or "linguistic" meaning ("the semantic features which are common to
all the situations that call forth the utterance of a linguistic
form")[100] could not escape this difficulty; and he did not anticipate that it should. Rather, he concluded: "The signals can be
analyzed, but not the things signalled about. This re-enforces
the principle that linguistic study must always start from the
phonetic form and not from the meaning. Phonetic forms . . .
can be described in terms of phonemes and their succession . . . ; the meanings . . . could be analyzed or systematically listed only by a well-nigh omniscient observer."[101]

But the turning away from the study of meaning by Bloomfield and by those who followed—the so-called post-Bloom-
fieldians—cannot be laid wholly to the accident of a particular
choice for a definition of "meaning." It was in larger part a re-
action against a long tradition of philosophical and semantic-
ally based grammar which, at least in its application if not also
in conception, was inept. It was the same tradition that Boas
earlier had reacted against when he insisted that a language
should be described in terms of its own explicit categories (his

"analytical treatment" of languages) instead of in terms of those of classical or philosophical grammar. Although the philosophical approach is undergoing rehabilitation today,[102] it was quite out of consonance with the behaviorism and operationalism of the period in which Bloomfield's ideas developed and took hold. However, had a suitable theory of meaning been drawn upon (instead of the stimulus-response theory), and had Bloomfield's concept of "differential meaning" been proposed within such a frame, the outcome could well have been different. It would not then have been supposed to require "omniscience" to study meaning; and distinctive semantic features might have been isolated with little more difficulty than distinctive phonetic features were, and by principles and methods quite analogous. As it was, the concept of reference was undeveloped in the Bloomfieldian approach. "Structural semantics" was to come later, with contributions from two different sources: first from ethnographers and ethnologists concerned to understand conceptual categories in primitive cultures,[103] and then further from new approaches in linguistic theory. In each case, attention was turning to lexicography—the presentation of meaning in vocabulary. Especially in the anthropological work, interest has returned to the "classifications" that Boas spoke of as being made by the lexical items of a language.

It is of interest to note in this connection that Sapir had never expressed (at least not in writing) very much interest in vocabulary as such. When he did have occasion to mention the subject, it was often in terms of "only in vocabulary," or "merely in vocabulary," as if this were not really a very interesting matter for a linguist. For example: "It goes without saying that *the mere content* of language is intimately related to culture. A society that has no knowledge of theosophy need have no name for it . . . The linguistic student should never make the mistake of identifying a language with its dictionary."[104]

It was grammar that interested Sapir. So it was also with

Whorf. Yet Whorf was moving toward the isolation of semantic components in vocabulary items when, as in the posthumously published articles referred to earlier in this section, he defined selection classes and other covert form-classes and drew out components of class meaning.

Recent anthropological work has been devoted to the study of meaning in culturally sensitive areas of lexicon. The aim has been to do for the study of meaning what "structural phonetics" (that is, phonemics) was intended to do for the structure of sounds in language, namely, to isolate its distinctive features and build descriptions on these. There has always been an assumption that the distinctive features of meaning have a special cultural relevance and psychological significance, even though the features themselves may not be in the domain of conscious awareness for speakers of the language. The model for the first experiments in the structural analysis of meaning was consciously an analogical adaptation of that which had been developed for phonemic analysis. More than one of those who were involved in the early phases of this experiment have acknowledged that the stimulus to it, as well as the eye-opener as to how it might be done, came from a combination of their training in phonemics and their reading of Charles W. Morris's *Foundations of the Theory of Signs*. The latter provided concepts that were needed for a structural treatment of meaning, while the former provided a view of the strategy for discovering distinctive features, a model for their formulation, and a standard of rigor to be adhered to. Among the culturally sensitive areas of vocabulary that are especially germane to ethnography and ethnology are vocabularies of kinship, and it was with these that the work was begun. The first concrete demonstration of the method and its possibilities (as well as its limits) was in Goodenough's *Property, Kin, and Community on Truk*. A number of other attempts were in progress about this time and in the years that immediately followed Goodenough's publication. The method came to be known as "componential analysis of meaning," on the analogy with the method of componential analysis of phonological and paradigmatic grammatical systems where it had been previously employed. After these applications to kinship terminologies, the method was extended to other lexical subsystems. Reviews of some of this work, by Sturtevant (1964), Colby (1966), and Hymes (1964), as well as collections of papers edited by Romney and D'Andrade, and by Hammel,[105] may be consulted as a guide to some of the history and the varieties of this work. The new attention to semantic theory within linguistics, notably in works by Weinreich, Katz and Fodor, Lamb, Lyons and Katz,[106] has given additional stimulus to these attempts to discover the organization of meaning in language. The possibility that the whole of the lexicon of a language may be susceptible to structural analysis is beginning to appear a reality—something that was hardly imaginable two decades ago. Componential analysis is only one of several methods available now for different tasks in semantic analysis, which include the analysis of metaphor, semantic extension, and polysemy. One no longer supposes that the "classifications" given by lexical items represent the only conceptual realities. These are but the "phenotypes" described by Whorf—the gross historical product of the generalization of names on the basis of perceived similarities among objects. The conceptual grid given by the cryptotypes and covert categories in language turns out to be considerably finer in structure.

It is important to note that a number of European linguists during the past four decades were attempting somewhat similar approaches toward structural analyses of meaning. There it developed in the field of historical philology, rather than in anthropology; and it can be traced in part to the influence of Wilhelm von Humboldt's ideas about the "inner form" of language. A concept of "semantic fields," covered by sets of lexical items, was suggested by Ipsen and was developed into a method and was applied by others—notably Trier, Jolles, and Porzig. Trier's "field" was essentially that of a contrast set, somewhat as in the approach of American anthropologists; Jolles's was more limited, based rather on reciprocal oppositions; Porzig's was based on syntagmatic and conceptual associations. Pervading much of this European work is a view of the nature and role of language that is very similar to that of the Boas-Sapir-Whorf linguistic-relativity hypothesis, with all of its cultural and psychological implications. Language is seen as providing a world of concepts mediating between man and the objective world about him, and affecting his experiencing of this world. Different languages mediate in different ways, reflecting different cultures. Ullman (1963), Spence (1961), Basilius (1952), Öhman (1953), and Waterman (1957) have reviewed this European work.[107]

The differences among languages in respect to their lexical classifications are as profound as any that can be found in grammars, and often far more overwhelming. There are not many who doubt that these classifications bear upon the conceptual ordering of experience. Unlike the differences in grammatical structure, which in the view of Sapir (as quoted earlier) cannot easily be held to reflect differences in culture, the differences in the semantic structure of vocabulary—including of course its cryptotypes—can often be convincingly demonstrated to do so. And unlike the categorizations of grammar, those in vocabulary seem to be quickly sensitive to cultural changes and to adapt accordingly. They are of especial significance for cultural anthropology. But, among the variables of semantic categorization in languages, there now appear also to be a few constant or repeatedly recurring bases for major categorical distinctions in lexicon. If there are universal properties here, as there are also in grammar, this too is of interest—to *general* anthropology.

Notes

1. For this, I have drawn upon lecture notes from a course given by the late W. D. Strong (1939–1940 at Columbia University); a syllabus, *The Foundations of American Archaeology* (1965), prepared by J. S. Belmont and Stephen Williams (Peabody Museum, Harvard University); and, most especially, a paper, by D. W. Schwartz, "North American Archaeology in Historical Perspective," in *Proceedings of the Eleventh International Conference for the History of Science* (Warsaw, in press). See also J. B. Griffin, "The Pursuit of Archaeology in the United States," *American Anthropologist*, Vol. 61, no. 3 (1959), pp. 379–389, for another historical summary of United States archaeology.

2. I follow D. W. Schwartz ("North American Archaeology") in terminology, at least in part; however, he lumps what I have called "descriptive" and "descriptive-historic" into a single "descriptive-historic" orientation. Schwartz emphasizes that he is recognizing trends or "orientations," not periods, and that these orientations overlap, substantially, through time. I recognize this, also; but, for my presentation, which is essentially historical, the concept of period is more convenient.

3. D. W. Schwartz (*ibid.*) refers to this "orientation"—which he dates as beginning a little earlier than I do—as the "scientific." I understand his meaning, but, since I consider all of American archaeology from the beginning of the Descriptive Period forward as "scientific," I prefer the term "comparative-historic." History is still an objective, but it is now history-become-process.

4. See S. F. Haven, *Archaeology of the United States* (Washington, 1856). For another review of "speculative" archaeology, see Justin Winsor, ed., *Narrative and Critical History of North America*, Vol. I: *Aboriginal America* (Boston, 1889).

5. S. F. Haven, *Archaeology of the United States*, pp. 27–28.

6. Edward Kingsborough, *Antiquities of Mexico* (London, 1831). See also Robert Wauchope, *Lost Tribes and Sunken Continents* (Chicago, 1962), for a thorough discussion of the fantastic theories of the times.

7. Charles Stephen Brasseur de Bourbourg, *Quatre Lettres sur Le Mexique* (Paris, 1868).

8. Caleb Atwater, "Description of the Antiquities Discovered in

227

the State of Ohio and Other Western States," *Transactions and Collections of the American Antiquarian Society* (Worcester, Mass., 1820).

9. Bernal Diaz del Castillo, *The True History of the Conquest of New Spain*, 5 vols. (London, 1908–1916), trans. A. P. Maudslay; Pedro de Cieza de Leon, *Parte Primera de la Cronica del Peru* (Madrid, 1932). These accounts were both written in the sixteenth century.

10. Diego Garcia de Palacio, "Description de la province de Guatemala," *Recueil de documents et mémoires originaux sur l'histoire des possessions Espagnoles dans l'Amerique* (Paris, 1840), written in 1576, pp. 5–45; Antonio Del Rio, *Description of the Ruins of an Ancient City, Discovered near Palenque in the Kingdom of Guatemala, in Spanish America*, with a *Teatro Critico Americano* by P. F. Cabrera (London, 1822).

11. J. L. Stephens, *Incidents of Travel in Central America: Chiapas and Yucatan*, 2 vols. (New York, 1841); *Incidents of Travel in Yucatan*, 2 vols. (New York, 1843).

12. William Bartram, *Travels in Georgia and Florida: 1773–74, A Report to Dr. John Fothergill* (Philadelphia, 1943).

13. Thomas Jefferson, *Notes on the State of Virginia* (Philadelphia, 1801).

14. E. G. Squier and E. H. Davis, *Ancient Monuments of the Mississippi Valley* (Washington, 1848).

15. I am indebted to the late W. D. Strong for calling my attention to this interesting and important, but little known, work.

16. C. J. Thomsen, "The Various Periods to Which Heathen Relics Can Be Assigned," *Man's Discovery of His Past: Literary Landmarks in Archaeology*, ed. R. F. Heizer (Englewood Cliffs, N.J., 1962), originally published in 1837, pp. 21–26.

17. Charles Lyell, *Principles of Geology* (New York, 1889), originally published in 1830–1833; Jacques Boucher de Perthes, *Antiquités celtiques et antediluviennes* (Paris, 1857–1864).

18. Specifically, an article by A. Morlot, "General Views on Archaeology," *Annual Report*, Smithsonian Institution (Washington, 1861), pp. 284–288, 291–293, 321–323, described excavations in Danish shell middens and in Swiss lake dwellings. Later, an article by J. J. Jones described excavations in shell mounds in Nova Scotia,

and refers to the influence of the Morlot article. See *Annual Report, Smithsonian Institution* (Washington, 1864).

19. See *Guide to the Peabody Museum of Harvard University* (Cambridge, Mass., 1898); Jeffries Wyman, "An account of the Fresh-Water Shell-Heaps of the St. Johns River, Florida," *American Naturalist*, 2 (1868), 393–403, 449–463.

20. C. C. Abbott, "On the Discovery of Supposed Paleolithic Implements from the Glacial Drift in the Valley of the Delaware River, near Trenton, New Jersey," *Tenth Annual Report, Trustees of the Peabody Museum of American Archaeology and Ethnology* (Cambridge, Mass., 1876), vol. II; Florentino Ameghino, "Une Nouvelle Industrie lithique," *Anales, Museo Nacional*, 20 (1911), 189–204, would be representative of early man claims that did not withstand close scrutiny. Representative critiques are A. Hrdlicka, *Skeletal Remains Suggesting or Attributed to Early Man in America* (Washington, 1907); A. Hrdlicka *et al.*, *Early Man in South America* (Washington, 1912). See also E. N. Wilmsen, "An Outline of Early Man Studies in the United States," *American Antiquity*, vol. 31, no. 2 (1965), pp. 172–192, for a review of this period.

21. Cyrus Thomas, "Who Were the Mound Builders?" *The American Antiquarian and Oriental Journal*, ed. S. D. Peet, vol. 6, no. 2 (1884), pp. 96–97; "Report on the Mound Explorations of the Bureau of American Ethnology," *Annual Report*, Bureau of American Ethnology, 12 (Washington, 1894), 3–370.

22. F. H. Cushing, "Preliminary Notes on the Origin, Working Hypothesis and Primary Researches of the Hemenway Southwestern Archaeological Expedition," *Seventh International Congress of Americanists* (Berlin, 1890), pp. 151–152, 163, 167, 170–172. See also Cushing, *A Study of Pueblo Pottery as Illustrative of Zuni Culture Growth*, *Annual Report*, Smithsonian Institution (Washington, 1886), pp. 467–521.

23. F. W. Putnam, "The Ancient Cemetery at Madisonville and Its Peculiar Ash Pits," report of lecture, *Kansas City Review*, vol. 6, nos. 9–10 (1883), pp. 529–531; "On Methods of Archaeological Research in America," *Johns Hopkins University Circular*, vol. 5, no. 49 (1886); "Prehistoric Remains in the Ohio Valley," *Century*, vol. 39, no. 5 (1890), pp. 698–703. This is a sampling of Putnam's numerous articles on American archaeology. His contributions to field

techniques, and so forth, were largely through instruction of students.

24. Charles Stephen Brasseur de Bourbourg, *Popol Vuh, le livre sacré et les mythes de l'Antiquité Americaine avec les livres heroiques et historiques des Quichés* (Paris, 1861); Ernst Förstemann, *Commentary on the Maya Manuscript in the Royal Public Library of Dresden* (Cambridge, Mass., 1906); Eduard Seler, *Gesammelte Abhandlungen zur Amerikanischen Sprach und Alterthumskunde* (Berlin, 1902–1923), vols. 1–5.

25. C. P. Bowditch, *The Numeration, Calendar Systems and Astronomical Knowledge of the Mayas* (Cambridge, Mass., 1910). See, for example, E. H. Thompson, *The Chultunes of Labna* (Cambridge, Mass., 1897); Teobert Maler, *Researches in the Central Portion of the Usumatsintla Valley* (Cambridge, Mass., 1903); or G. B. Gordon, *Prehistoric Ruins of Copan, Honduras* (Cambridge, Mass., 1896).

26. A. M. Tozzer, *A Comparative Study of the Mayas and the Lacandones* (New York, 1907); *A Preliminary Study of the Ruins of Nakum, Guatemala* (Cambridge, Mass., 1913); and see also the volume, *The Maya and their Neighbors,* ed. C. L. Hay *et al.* (New York, 1940), dedicated in Tozzer's honor.

27. Max Uhle, "La Antigua Civilización peruana," *La Industria* (Trujillo, Peru, 1900). J. H. Rowe in *Max Uhle, 1856–1944: A Memoir of the Father of Peruvian Archaeology,* University of California Publications in American Archaeology and Ethnology, vol. 46, no. 1 (Berkeley, 1954), cites this title as an important statement of Uhle's chronological scheme. See Rowe's memoir for other Uhle references, especially 1903b, 1910f, 1913c, and 1913e.

28. J. H. Rowe, "Problems in the History of Archaeology," read at annual meeting of the American Anthropological Association, Santa Monica, California, 1956.

29. Heinrich Schliemann, *Ilios, The City and Country of the Trojans: The Results of Researches and Discoveries on the Site of Troy from 1871–1879* (New York, 1881); W. H. Dall, "On Succession in the Shell-Heaps of the Aleutian Islands," *U. S. Geological and Geographical Survey, Contributions to North American Ethnology: I* (Washington, 1877), pp. 41–91.

30. A. L. Kroeber, *Anthropology* (New York, 1923), chap. 13.

31. *Ibid.,* fig. 36.

32. A. V. Kidder, *An Introduction to the Study of Southwestern*

Archaeology, with a Preliminary Account of the Excavations at Pecos (New Haven, 1924).

33. T. A. Joyce, *Mexican Archaeology* (London, 1914); *Central American and West Indian Archaeology* (London, 1916).

34. Manuel Gamio, "Arqueologia de Atzcapotzalco, D.F., Mexico," *Proceedings, Eighteenth International Congress of Americanists* (London, 1913), pp. 180–187; F. Boas, "Archaeological Investigations in the Valley of Mexico by the International School, 1911–12," pp. 176–179. See also R. E. W. Adams, "Manuel Gamio and Stratigraphic Excavation," *American Antiquity*, vol. 26, no. 1 (1960), p. 99.

35. N. C. Nelson, *Pueblo Ruins of the Galisteo Basin, New Mexico* (New York, 1914). See also R. B. Woodbury, "N. C. Nelson and Chronological Archaeology," *American Antiquity*, vol. 25, no. 3 (1960), pp. 400–401.

36. J. D. Figgins, "The Antiquity of Man in America," *Natural History*, vol. 27, no. 3 (1927), pp. 229–239.

37. E. B. Howard, "Evidence of Early Man in America," *The Museum Journal*, vol. 24, nos. 2 and 3 (1935); F. H. H. Roberts, Jr., *A Folsom Complex: Preliminary Report on Investigations at the Lindenmeier Site in Northern Colorado* (Washington, 1935); see also E. H. Sellards, *Early Man in America* (Austin, Texas, 1952); and H. M. Wormington, *Ancient Man in North America*, 4th ed. (Denver, 1957).

38. J. B. Bird, "Antiquity and Migrations of the Early Inhabitants of Patagonia," *Geographical Review*, 28 (1938), 250–275.

39. E. N. Wilmsen, "An Outline of Early Man Studies in the United States."

40. A. L. Kroeber, *Anthropology*, rev. ed. (New York, 1948), pp. 676–686.

41. *Ibid.*, chap. 18.

42. J. H. Steward, *Ancient Caves of the Great Salt Lake Region* (Washington, 1937); W. G. Haag, "Early Horizons in the Southeast," *American Antiquity*, 7 (1942), 209–222.

43. For examples, see F. H. H. Roberts, Jr., "A Survey of Southwestern Archaeology," *American Anthropologist*, 37 (1935), 1–33; H. S. Gladwin *et al.*, "Excavations at Snaketown," *Material Culture* (Globe, Arizona, 1937); E. W. Haury, *The Mogollon Culture of Southwestern New Mexico* (Globe, Arizona, 1936); J. O. Brew, "The First Two Seasons at Awatovi," *American Antiquity*, 3 (1937), 127–

137; H. S. Colton, "The Patayan Problem in the Colorado River Valley," *Southwestern Journal of Anthropology*, vol. 1, no. 1 (1945), pp. 114–121.

44. J. A. Ford and G. R. Willey, "An Interpretation of the Prehistory of the Eastern United States," *American Anthropologist*, vol. 43, no. 3 (1941), pp. 325–363; J. B. Griffin, "Culture Change and Continuity in Eastern United States," *Man in Northeastern North America*, ed. F. Johnson (Andover, Mass., 1946), pp. 37–95.

45. W. D. Strong, *An Introduction to Nebraska Archaeology* (Washington, 1935); W. R. Wedel, *An Introduction to Pawnee Archaeology* (Washington, 1936).

46. H. B. Collins, *Archaeology of St. Lawrence Island, Alaska* (Washington, 1937); Helge Larsen and F. G. Rainey, *Ipiutak and the Arctic Whale Hunting Culture* (New York, 1948).

47. The summary reference is G. C. Vaillant, *Aztecs of Mexico* (New York, 1941); however, his technical monographs begin as early as 1930.

48. For example, O. G. Ricketson, Jr., and Edith B. Ricketson, *Uaxactun, Guatemala, Group E: 1926–1931* (Washington, 1937); or J. E. S. Thompson, *Excavations at San Jose, British Honduras* (Washington, 1939).

49. M. W. Stirling, *An Initial Series from Tres Zapotes, Veracruz, Mexico* (Washington, 1940); Philip Drucker, *Ceramic Sequences at Tres Zapotes, Veracruz, Mexico* (Washington, 1943); Philip Drucker, *La Venta, Tabasco, A Study of Olmec Ceramics and Art* (Washington, 1952).

50. A. V. Kidder, J. D. Jennings, and E. M. Shook, *Excavations at Kaminaljuyu, Guatemala* (Washington, 1946).

51. W. C. Bennett, "The Position of Chavin in Andean Sequences," *Proceedings of the American Philosophical Society*, vol. 86, no. 2 (1943), pp. 323–327.

52. Irving Rouse, *Prehistory in Haiti: A Study in Method* (New Haven, 1939). See, also, *American Antiquity*, vol. 27, no. 1 (1961), for a series of articles by various authors reviewing the archaeology of the Americas for the years 1935–1960.

53. For examples, G. C. Vaillant, *Some Resemblances in the Ceramics of Central and North America* (Globe, Arizona, 1932); Philip Phillips, "Middle American Influence on the Archaeology of the Southeastern United States," *The Maya and Their Neighbors*, ed.

C. L. Hay and others (New York, 1940), pp. 349–367; E. W. Haury, "The Problem of Contacts Between the Southwestern United States and Mexico," *Southwestern Journal of Anthropology*, 1 (1945), 55–74; J. B. Griffin, "Meso-America and the Southeast: A Commentary," *The Florida Indian and His Neighbors*, J. W. Griffin, ed. (Winter Park, Florida, 1949), pp. 77–100.

54. H. J. Spinden, "The Origin and Distribution of Agriculture in America," *Proceedings, Nineteenth International Congress of Americanists* (Washington, 1917), pp. 269–276; *Ancient Civilizations of Mexico and Central America* (New York, 1928).

55. G. R. Willey and Philip Phillips, *Method and Theory in American Archaeology* (Chicago, 1958).

56. A. L. Kroeber, *Peruvian Archaeology in 1942* (New York, 1944); G. R. Willey, "Horizon Styles and Pottery Traditions in Peruvian Archaeology," *American Antiquity*, 11 (1945), 49–56.

57. Concern with this kind of archaeology is expressed in Robert Wauchope, ed., *Seminars in Archaeology: 1955* (Salt Lake City, 1956).

58. For examples, see V. G. Childe, *What Happened in History* (New York and Harmondsworth, 1942); J. G. D. Clark, *Archaeology and Society* (Cambridge, Mass., 1957), first published 1939.

59. See J. R. Caldwell, "The New American Archaeology," *New Roads to Yesterday*, ed. J. R. Caldwell (New York, 1966), first published 1959, pp. 333–347, for a summary of new attitudes.

60. Frederick Johnson, "Archaeology in an Emergency," *Science*, 152 (1966), 1592–1597.

61. For a summary of this, see G. R. Willey, *An Introduction to American Archaeology*, vol. 1: *North and Middle America* (Englewood Cliffs, N.J., 1966), chap. 2.

62. Stephen Williams and J. B. Stoltman, "An Outline of Southeastern United States Prehistory with Particular Emphasis on the Paleo-Indian Era," *The Quaternary of the United States, Seventh Congress of the International Association for Quaternary Research*, ed. H. E. Wright and D. G. Frey (Princeton, 1965), pp. 669–683.

63. B. R. Butler, "The Old Cordilleran Culture in the Pacific Northwest," *Occasional Papers of the Museum*, Idaho State College (Pocatello, 1961); "The Structure and Function of the Old Cordilleran Concept," *American Anthropologist*, vol. 67, no. 5 (1965), pp. 1120–1131.

64. G. H. S. Bushnell and Charles McBurney, "New World Origins Seen from the Old World," *Antiquity,* vol. 33, no. 130 (1959), pp. 93–101; H. M. Wormington, "A Survey of Early American Prehistory," *American Scientist,* vol. 50, no. 1 (1962), pp. 230–242; E. N. Wilmsen, "Flake Tools in the American Arctic: Some Speculations," *American Antiquity,* vol. 29, no. 3 (1964), pp. 338–344.

65. A. D. Krieger, "The Earliest Cultures in the Western United States," *American Antiquity,* vol. 28, no. 2 (1962), pp. 138–143; "Early Man in the New World," *Prehistoric Man in the New World,* ed. J. D. Jennings and E. Norbeck (Chicago, 1964), pp. 23–84.

66. For a summary of this, and references, see G. R. Willey, *An Introduction to American Archaeology,* chap. 2.

67. J. D. Jennings, *Danger Cave* (Salt Lake City, 1957).

68. R. S. MacNeish, *Second Annual Report of the Tehuacan Archaeological-Botanical Project* (Andover, Mass., 1962).

69. E. P. Lanning and E. A. Hammel, "Early Lithic Industries of Western South America," *American Antiquity,* vol. 27, no. 2 (1961), pp. 139–154; E. P. Lanning, "Early Man in Peru," *Scientific American,* vol. 213, no. 4 (1965), pp. 68–77; T. C. Patterson and E. P. Lanning, "Changing Settlement Patterns on the Central Peruvian Coast," *Ñawpa Pacha,* no. 2 (1964), pp. 113–123; A. R. Gonzalez, *La Estratigrafia de la Gruta Intihuasi Prov. de San Luis, R. A.* (Cordoba, Argentina, 1960).

70. J. L. Giddings, *The Archaeology of Cape Denbigh* (Providence, 1964).

71. Emilio Estrada and Clifford Evans, "Cultural Development in Ecuador," *Aboriginal Cultural Development in Latin America,* ed. B. J. Meggers and C. Evans (Washington, 1963), pp. 77–88; Carlos Angulo Valdes, "Cultural Development in Colombia," *ibid.,* pp. 55–66; C. F. Baudez, "Cultural Development in Lower Central America," *ibid.,* pp. 45–54; Gerardo Reichel-Dolmatoff, *Colombia,* ed. G. Daniel (New York, 1965); B. J. Meggers and Clifford Evans, *Archaeological Investigations at the Mouth of the Amazon* (Washington, 1957); D. W. Lathrap, "The Cultural Sequence at Yarinacocha, Eastern Peru," *American Antiquity,* vol. 28, no. 4 (1958), pp. 379–388.

72. B. J. Meggers, Clifford Evans, and Emilio Estrada, *Early*

Formative Period of Coastal Ecuador (Washington, 1965); Gerardo Reichel-Dolmatoff, *Excavaciones Arqueologicas en Puerto Hormiga* (*Depto. de Bolivar*) (Bogota, 1965).

73. Irving Rouse and J. M. Cruxent, *Venezuelan Archaeology* (New Haven, 1963); Gerardo Reichel-Dolmatoff, *Colombia*, ed. G. Daniel (New York, 1965); D. W. Lathrap, personal communication, 1965–1966.

74. See, for examples, C. C. DiPeso, "Cultural Development in Northern Mexico," *Aboriginal Cultural Development in Latin America*, eds. B. J. Meggers and C. Evans, pp. 1–16; J. C. Kelley and H. D. Winters, "A Revision of the Archaeological Sequence in Sinaloa, Mexico," *American Antiquity*, vol. 25, no. 4 (1960), pp. 547–561.

75. E. V. McMichael, "Veracruz, the Crystal River Complex, and the Hopewellian Climax," *Hopewellian Studies* (Springfield, 1964), pp. 123–132. R. P. Bullen has recently (1966 meeting of the Society for American Archaeology) reported the discovery of what appears to be a stela associated with one of the Crystal River mounds.

76. See D. S. Byers, "The Eastern Archaic: Some Problems and Hypotheses," *American Antiquity*, vol. 24, no. 3 (1959), pp. 233–256; Philip Drucker, *Indians of the Northwest Coast* (New York, 1955); C. E. Borden, "West Coast Crossties with Alaska," *Prehistoric Cultural Relations Between the Arctic and Temperate Zones of North America*, ed. J. M. Campbell (Montreal, 1962), pp. 9–19; Douglas Osborne, "Western American Prehistory: An Hypothesis," *American Antiquity*, vol. 24, no. 1 (1958), pp. 47–52.

77. M. D. Coe, "Archaeological Linkages with North and South America at La Victoria, Guatemala," *American Anthropologist*, vol. 62, no. 3 (1960), pp. 363–393.

78. G. R. Willey, "The Interrelated Rise of the Native Cultures of Middle and South America," *New Interpretations of Aboriginal American Culture History* (Washington, 1955), pp. 28–45; G. F. Ekholm and Clifford Evans, "The Interrelationships of New World Cultures: A Coordinated Research Program of the Institute of Andean Research," *Thirty-Fourth International Congress of Americanists* (Vienna, 1962), pp. 253–278.

79. B. J. Meggers, Clifford Evans, and Emilio Estrada, *Early Formative Period of Coastal Ecuador;* Emilio Estrada and B. J.

Meggers, "A Complex of Traits of Probable Transpacific Origin on the Coast of Ecuador," *American Anthropologist,* vol. 63, no. 5 (1961), pp. 913–939.

80. R. S. MacNeish, *Second Annual Report of the Tehuacan Archaeological-Botanical Project;* P. C. Mangelsdorf, R. S. MacNeish, and W. C. Galinat, "Domestication of Corn," *Science,* 143 (1964), 531–537; Alfred Kidder II, L. G. Lumbreras, and D. B. Smith, "Cultural Development in the Central Andes–Peru and Bolivia," *Aboriginal Cultural Development in Latin America,* ed. B. J. Meggers and Clifford Evans, pp. 89–102; G. R. Willey, "New World Archaeology in 1965," *Proceedings of the American Philosophical Society,* vol. 110, no. 2 (1966), pp. 140–145.

81. M. D. Coe and K. V. Flannery, "Microenvironments and Mesoamerican Prehistory," *New Roads to Yesterday: Essays in Archaeology,* ed. J. R. Caldwell (New York, 1966), pp. 348–360.

82. *Ibid.;* also, personal communication, R. S. MacNeish, 1965–1966.

83. K. V. Flannery's "The Ecology of Early Food Production in Mesopotamia," *Science,* 147 (1965), 1247–1256, has made a start in this direction.

84. R. M. Adams, *The Evolution of Urban Society, Early Mesopotamia and Prehispanic Mexico* (Chicago, 1966).

85. W. W. Taylor, *A Study of Archaeology* (Menasha, 1948).

86. G. R. Willey, *Prehistoric Settlement Patterns in the Viru Valley, Peru* (Washington, 1953). The Viru Valley field work was carried out in 1946, and, although Taylor's study was not published until 1948, I was familiar with parts of it, and with his ideas in general, before that date. See also the collection of essays, G. B. Willey, ed., *Prehistoric Settlement Patterns in the New World* (New York, 1956).

87. For examples, J. N. Hill, "A Prehistoric Community in Eastern Arizona," *Southwestern Journal of Anthropology,* vol. 22, no. 1 (1966), pp. 9–30; W. A. Longacre, "Changing Patterns of Social Integration: A Prehistoric Example from the American Southwest," *American Anthropologist,* vol. 68, no. 1 (1966), pp. 94–102.

88. James Deetz, *The Dynamics of Stylistic Change in Arikara Ceramics* (Urbana, 1965).

89. See especially, L. R. Binford, "Archaeology as Anthropology," *American Antiquity,* vol. 28, no. 2 (1962), pp. 217–225, and

"Archaeological Systematics and the Study of Cultural Process," *American Antiquity*, vol. 31, no. 2 (1962), pp. 203–210.

ONE HUNDRED YEARS OF OLD WORLD PREHISTORY

1. Gordon R. Willey, "One Hundred Years of American Archaeology," above.
2. T. D. Kendrick, *British Antiquity* (London, 1950).
3. Richard Colt Hoare, *The Ancient History of South Wiltshire* (London, 1812).
4. Rasmus Nyerup, *Oversyn over Foedrelandets Mindesmaerker fra Oltiden* (Copenhagen, 1806).
5. J. Frere, "Account of Flint Weapons Discovered at Hoxne in Suffolk," *Archaeologia*, 13 (1800), 204–205.
6. S. Toulmin and J. Goodfield, *The Discovery of Time* (London, 1965), pp. 60–110; G. E. Daniel, editorial in *Antiquity*, 1966, pp. 166–167.
7. Charles Lyell, *Principles of Geology* (London, 1830–1933), written in 1830.
8. G. E. Daniel, *The Three Ages* (Cambridge, England, 1943).
9. John Lubbock, *Prehistoric Times* (London, 1865).
10. Edward B. Tylor, *Primitive Culture* (London, 1871).
11. J. J. A. Worsaae, *The Primeval Antiquities of Denmark*, trans. W. J. Thoms (London, 1849), p. 10; Mortimer Wheeler, *Archaeology from the Earth* (Oxford, 1954).
12. G. E. Daniel, *A Hundred Years of Archaeology* (London, 1950).
13. *Materiaux pour l'histoire de l'homme*, 2 (1867), 469–528.
14. *Ibid.*
15. B. G. Trigger, "Sir Daniel Wilson: Canada's First Anthropologist," *Anthropologica*, n.s., 8 (1966), 1.
16. *Ibid.*
17. R. F. Heizer, *Man's Discovery of His Past: Literary Landmarks* (Englewood Cliffs, N.J., 1962), p. 72; B. G. Trigger, "Sir Daniel Wilson," p. 1.
18. G. de Mortillet, *Promenades préhistoriques à l'exposition universelle* (Paris, 1867).
19. *Ibid.*

20. E. B. Tylor, *Anahuac: or Mexico and the Mexicans.*
21. H. F. Seton-Lloyd, *Foundations in the Dust* (London, 1947).
22. W. M. Flinders Petrie, *Diospolis Parva* (London, 1901).
23. W. K. Loftus, *Travels and Researches in Chaldaca and Susiana* (London, 1857), p. 260.
24. Robert Wood, *The Ruins of Palmyra* (London, 1753).
25. *The Archaeological Journal*, 1 (1845), 289–291.
26. Joan Evans, *Time and Chance: The Story of Arthur Evans and His Forebears* (London, 1943).
27. A. Michaelis, *A Century of Archaeological Discovery* (London, 1908), p. 116; G. E. Daniel, *A Hundred Years of Archaeology*, p. 166.
28. A. Michaelis, *A Century of Archaeological Discovery*, p. 217.
29. S. Casson, *The Discovery of Man* (London, 1939), p. 221.
30. J. J. Myres, "The Cretan Labyrinth: A Retrospect of Aegean Research," *Journal of the Royal Anthropological Institute*, 1933.
31. J. J. Worsaae, *The Primeval Antiquities of Denmark*; A. Morlot, *General Views on Archaeology* (Washington, 1861).
32. J. L. Myres, "The Cretan Labyrinth."
33. H. St. George Gray, *Index to "Excavations in Cranborne Chase" and "King John's House, Tollard Royal"* (Somerset, 1905).
34. W. M. Flinders Petrie, *Methods and Aims in Archaeology* (London, 1904); *Seventy Years in Archaeology* (London, 1931); M. A. Murray, *My First Hundred Years* (London, 1964).
35. Mortimer Wheeler, *Archaeology from the Earth* (Oxford, 1954), p. 54; S. Piggott, *Approach to Archaeology* (London, 1959), p. 65.
36. Leonard Woolley, *Spadework: Adventures in Archaeology* (London, 1953), pp. 11–16.
37. *Ibid.*, p. 15.
38. Mortimer Wheeler, *Archaeology from the Earth; Still Digging* (London, 1955), p. 66; *Alms for Oblivion: An Antiquary's Scrapbook* (London, 1966), p. 105.
39. C. W. Phillips, *Antiquity*, March 1940; R. L. S. Bruce-Mitford, *The Sutton Hoo Ship Burial* (London, 1956); Charles Green, *Sutton Hoo: The Excavation of a Royal Ship Burial* (London, 1963).
40. M. E. Cunningham, *Woodhenge* (Devizes, 1929); R. J. C. Atkinson, C. M. Piggott, and N. Sandars, *Excavations at Dorchester, Oxon: Part I* (Oxford, 1951).

41. G. Bersu, "The Excavations of Woodbury, Wiltshire, During 1938," *Proceedings of the Prehistoric Society*, n.s., 4 (1938), 308.

42. B. Soudsky, *Bylany* (Praha, 1966).

43. Leonard Woolley, *Excavations at Ur: A Record of Twelve Years' Work* (London, 1954), p. 61.

44. P. V. Glob, *Les Hommes des Tourbieres* (Paris, 1966).

45. R. Martin, "Wooden Figures from the Source of the Seine," *Antiquity* (1965), p. 247.

46. G. F. Bass, *Archaeology Under Water* (London and New York, 1966).

47. O. G. S. Crawford and A. Keiller, *Wessex From the Air* (Oxford, 1928); G. E. Daniel, *A Hundred Years of Archaeology*, p. 294; J. P. S. Bradford, *Ancient Landscapes: Studies in Field Archaeology* (London, 1957); R. Chevallier, *L'avion à la découverte du passé* (Paris, 1965).

48. R. J. C. Atkinson, *Stonehenge* (London, 1956); J. F. S. Stone, *Wessex Before the Celts* (London, 1958), p. 82.

49. D. Brothwell and E. Higgs, eds., *Science in Archaeology* (London, 1963); E. Pyddoke, ed., *The Scientist and Archaeology* (London, 1965); M. J. Aitken, *Physics and Archaeology* (New York, 1961); F. Rainey, "New Techniques in Archaeology," *Proceedings of the American Philosophical Society*, 110 (1966), 146.

50. J. S. Weiner, K. P. Oakley, and W. E. Le Gros Clark, "The Solution of the Piltdown Problem," *Bulletin of the British Museum (Natural History), Geology*, 2 (1953), 141; J. S. Weiner, *The Piltdown Forgery* (London, 1955); K. P. Oakley, "Further Contributions to the Solution of the Piltdown Problem," *Bulletin of the British Museum (Natural History), Geology*, 2 (1955), 244–257.

51. G. E. Daniel, *A Hundred Years of Archaeology*, p. 176.

52. V. G. Childe, *The Dawn of European Civilization* (London, 1925).

53. W. M. Flinders Petrie, *Methods and Aims in Archaeology*.

54. W. M. Flinders Petrie, *Diospolis Parva*.

55. Bryant Bannister, "Dendrochronology," *Science in Archaeology*, ed. D. Brothwell and E. Higgs (London, 1963), p. 162.

56. G. De Geer, *Compte rendu Congrès géol. intern Stockholm 1910*, fasc. I (Stockholm, 1912), pp. 241–257; "Geochronology," *Antiquity* (1928), p. 308.

57. F. E. Zeuner, *Dating the Past*, 3rd ed. (London, 1953).

58. G. Libby, *The Testimony of the Spade* (New York, 1956).

59. W. Gentner and H. J. Lippolt, "The Potassium-Argon Dating of Upper Tertiary and Pleistocene Deposits," *Science in Archaeology*, ed. D. Brothwell and E. Higgs (London, 1963).

60. D. B. Ericson and G. Wollin, *The Deep and the Past* (London, 1966).

61. C. H. McBurney, a review of L. S. B. Leaky's *Olduvai*, *Antiquity* (1967), pp. 73–75.

62. E. Cartailhac, "Les Cavernes Ornées de Dessins: La Grotte d' Altamira. Mea Culpa d'un Sceptique," *L'Anthropologie*, 13 (1902), 348–352.

63. M. Breuil, *Four Hundred Years of Cave-Art* (Dordogne, 1952).

64. H. F. Seton-Lloyd, *Foundations in the Dust*.

65. H. Schliemann, *Ilios* (London, 1880); E. Ludwig, *Schliemann of Troy: The Story of a Goldseeker* (London, 1931); Carl W. Blegen, *Troy and the Trojans* (London and New York, 1963).

66. Joan Evans, *Time and Chance: The Story of Arthur Evans;* J. D. S. Pendlebury, *The Archaeology of Crete* (London, 1939); R. W. Hutchinson, *Prehistoric Crete* (Harmondsworth, 1962); R. J. Burrows, *The Discoveries in Crete and their Bearing on the History of Ancient Civilization* (London, 1907).

67. M. Ventris, "Deciphering Europe's Oldest Script," *The Listener*, July 10, 1952; J. Chadwick, *The Decipherment of Linear B* (Cambridge, England, 1958); L. Duel, *The Treasures of Time* (New York, 1961), p. 301.

68. A. M. Sayce, *The Hittites: The Story of a Forgotten Empire* (London, 1888); A. E. Cowley, *The Hittites* (London, 1912); J. Garstang, *The Hittites* (London, 1929); C. W. Ceram, *Narrow Pass: Black Mountain: The Discovery of the Hittite Empire* (London, 1956).

69. Mortimer Wheeler, "The Recording of Archaeological Strata," *Ancient India*, 3 (1947), 143.

70. Te-K'un Cheng, *Shang China* (Cambridge, England, 1960); Chi Li, *The Beginnings of Chinese Civilization* (Seattle, 1957); W. Watson, *China* (London, 1961).

71. R. J. Braidwood and B. Howe, *Prehistoric Investigations in Iraqi Kurdistan* (Chicago, 1960); R. J. Braidwood and G. R. Willey,

eds., *Courses towards Urban Life* (Edinburgh, 1962); J. Mellaart, *The Earliest Civilisations of the Near East* (London, 1965); K. M. Kenyon, *Digging up Jericho* (London, 1957); *Archaeology in the Holy Land* (London, 1960).

72. G. E. Daniel, *A Hundred Years of Archaeology*, p. 326.

73. J. Brøndsted, *Danmarks Oltid* (Copenhagen, 1938), p. 2.

74. R. Wauchope, *Lost Tribes and Sunken Continents: Myth and Method in the Study of American Indians* (Chicago, 1962); R. B. Dixon, *The Building of Cultures* (New York, 1928); Grafton Elliot-Smith, *Elephants and Ethnologists* (London, 1924); *Human History* (London, 1930); W. J. Perry, *The Growth of Civilisation* (London, 1924).

75. V. G. Childe, *What Happened in History* (Harmondsworth, 1942), p. 21.

76. Gordon R. Willey, "New World Archaeology in 1965," *Proceedings of the American Philosophical Society*, 110 (1966), 140; *Introduction to American Archaeology*, Vol. I: *North and Central America* (Englewood Cliffs, N. J., 1966); "One Hundred Years of American Archaeology," above; G. H. S. Bushnell, *Peru* (London and New York, 1958); B. Meggers, *Ecuador* (London and New York, 1965); M. Coe, *Mexico* (London and New York, 1964); *The Maya* (London and New York, 1966).

77. V. G. Childe, *Scotland before the Scots* (London, 1946).

78. V. G. Childe, *The Most Ancient East* (London, 1927); *What Happened in History; Social Evolution* (London, 1951).

79. C. F. C. Hawkes, *The Prehistoric Foundations of Europe to the Mycenean Age* (London, 1940).

80. V. G. Childe, *Man Makes Himself* (London, 1936).

81. Mortimer Wheeler, *Alms for Oblivion*, p. 47; G. E. Daniel, *Archaeology and the Origins of Civilisation* (London and New York, 1967); H. Frankfort, *The Birth of Civilisation in the Near East* (London, 1951).

82. C. O. Sauer, *Agricultural Origins and Dispersals* (New York, 1952); G. P. Murdock, *Africa, Its Peoples and Their Culture History* (New York, 1959).

83. W. W. Taylor, *The Study of Archaeology*, Memoir 69, American Anthropological Association (Menasha, 1948).

84. G. E. Daniel, *The Three Ages* (Cambridge, England, 1943); R. J. Braidwood, "Terminology in Prehistory," *Human Origins: An*

Introductory General Course in Anthropology: Selected Readings (Chicago, 1946), p. 32; F. Hole and R. F. Heizer, *An Introduction to Prehistoric Archaeology* (New York, 1965).

85. G. R. Willey and P. Phillips, *Method and Theory in American Archaeology* (Chicago, 1958).

86. S. Piggott, *Ancient Europe from the Beginnings of Agriculture to Classical Antiquity* (Edinburgh, 1965).

87. C. F. C. Hawkes, "British Prehistory: The Invasion Hypothesis," *Antiquity* (1966), p. 299.

88. T. G. E. Powell, *Prehistoric Art* (London, 1966).

ONE HUNDRED YEARS OF BIOLOGICAL ANTHROPOLOGY

1. Traditional physical anthropology might be defined by the content of Juan Comas, *Manual of Physical Anthropology* (Springfield, 1960) or Ashley Montagu, *An Introduction to Physical Anthropology*, 3rd ed. (Springfield, 1960). The content does not differ essentially from E. A. Hooton's *Up From the Ape* (New York, 1931 and 1946). The content of present-day anthropology is indicated by J. Buettner-Janusch, *Origins of Man* (New York, 1966) and by G. A. Harrison, J. S. Weiner, J. M. Tanner, and N. A. Barnicot, *Human Biology* (Oxford, 1964). It is clear from these and other books that the purposes of physical anthropology have always been much broader than the research techniques employed by those scientists labeled "physical anthropologists." In teaching about human evolution, no one would limit himself to anthropological information in the restricted sense, but would include information from many other sciences. I take "biological anthropology" to be even broader, to be the biological element in any anthropological problem.

In limiting this discussion primarily to the question of the origin of man, I do not want to suggest that physical anthropology has been limited to this question or that it should be so limited. Physical anthropological techniques are useful in studies of growth, variation, identification, and constitution. This might have considered race, rather than long-term evolution, as the major theme, and stressed regional variation and adaptation to climate and disease. Either technical advances or theoretical progress could easily fill an entire book, let alone a paper. Likewise, many important scientists are omitted (Coon, Hrdlicka, Krogman, Schultz, Vallois—to mention only a few). A more balanced account is given by J. S. Weiner, "Physical Anthropology: A Survey of Developments," A Hundred Years of Anthropology, ed. T. K. Penniman (London, 1965), pp. 285–320. My only essential point is that, with the synthetic theory of evolution, with fossils, and with the study of behavior, there has been major progress, and it is my belief that this progress will continue at a rapidly accelerating rate. The only important conclusion is that social science and biological science are inextricably interwoven in the study of human evolution.

The research for this paper is being carried out under a grant from the U. S. Public Health Service (No. MH 08623). I wish to thank Dr. Phyllis C. Jay for helpful criticism of the manuscript.

2. Charles Darwin. *The Descent of Man and Selection in Relation to Sex* (New York, 1871), p. 390.

3. B. Glass, O. Temkin, and W. L. Straus, Jr., eds., *Forerunners of Darwin, 1745–1859* (Baltimore, 1959).

4. J. Altman, *Organic Foundations of Animal Behavior* (New York, 1966); S. A. Altmann, ed., *Social Communication Among Primates* (Chicago and London, 1967); J. Buettner-Janusch, ed., *Evolutionary and Genetic Biology of Primates* (New York and London, 1963–1964); C. R. Carpenter, *Naturalistic Behavior of Nonhuman Primates* (University Park, 1964); I. DeVore, ed., *Primate Behavior: Field Studies of Monkeys and Apes* (New York, 1965); J. Goodall, "Chimpanzees of the Gombe Stream Reserve," *Primate Behavior: Field Studies of Monkeys and Apes,* ed. I. DeVore (New York, 1965), pp. 425–473; R. A. Hinde, *Animal Behavior* (New York, 1966); P. C. Jay, "Field Studies," *Behavior of Nonhuman Primates,* ed. A. M. Schrier, H. F. Harlow, and F. Stollnitz (New York and London, 1965), pp. 525–591; P. Marler and W. J. Hamilton III, *Mechanisms of Animal Behavior* (New York, 1966); T. E. McGill, *Readings in Animal Behavior* (New York, 1965); J. Napier and N. A. Barnicot, eds., *The Primates* (London, 1963); A. Roe and G. G. Simpson, eds., *Behavior and Evolution* (New Haven, 1958); G. Schaller, *The Mountain Gorilla: Ecology and Behavior* (Chicago, 1963).

5. G. P. Murdock, "The Common Denominator of Cultures," *The Science of Man in the World Crisis* (New York, 1945), pp. 123–142.

6. *Ibid.,* p. 125.

7. *Ibid.*

8. W. Goldschmidt, *Comparative Functionalism* (Berkeley and Los Angeles, 1966).

9. D. A. Hamburg, "Emotions in the Perspective of Human Evolution," *Expression of the Emotions in Man*, P. Knapp, ed. (New York, 1963), pp. 300–317.

10. Charles Darwin, *The Descent of Man and Selection in Relation to Sex* (New York, 1871).

11. E. Mayr, *Animal Species and Evolution* (Cambridge, Mass., 1963); T. H. Huxley, *Man's Place in Nature* (Ann Arbor, 1863). The revolution that the functional point of view of Malinowski and Radcliffe-Brown brought to social anthropology is very comparable to the change which came in biological anthropology with the advent of the synthetic theory of evolution. In both cases there was a repudiation of reconstructions which had minimum basis in recorded history. In both, interest changed from the description of unrelated items to actual behavior, pattern, and function.

12. G. L. Jepsen, E. Mayr, and G. G. Simpson, eds., *Genetics, Paleontology, and Evolution* (Princeton, 1949).

13. G. G. Simpson, *The Meaning of Evolution* (New Haven and London, 1949).

14. The Cold Spring Harbor Symposium, The Origin and Evolution of Man, organized by Dobzhansky, brought the new human revolutionary synthesis to the attention of all.

15. Darwin believed that the causes of evolution were selection, correlation of parts, sexual selection, and inheritance of acquired characteristics. In modifying his theory to meet criticisms, he reduced the emphasis on natural selection and actually weakened the theory from the modern point of view.

16. F. W. Jones, *Man's Place among the Mammals* (New York, 1929); W. K. Gregory in *Man's Place among the Anthropoids* (Oxford, 1934) criticized Wood Jones, but in retrospect it can be seen that the theoretical arguments could not be settled at that time.

17. This is the era in which physical anthropology took form as a distinct science, and in which degrees were given in physical anthropology. Hooton was trained in classics. Hrdlicka and Keith were medical doctors. The founders of the American Association of Physical Anthropologists were, for the most part, not anthropologists

in the restricted sense. The roots of the profession in anatomy and medicine tended to delay progress in both genetics and social science.

18. W. L. Straus, Jr., and A. J. E. Cave, "Pathology and the Posture of Neanderthal Man," *Quarterly Review of Biology*, vol. 32, pp. 348–363.

19. W. W. Howells, *Mankind in the Making* (New York, 1959); "Homo Erectus," *Scientific American*, 215 (1966), 46–53.

20. A. Keith, *A New Theory of Human Evolution* (New York, 1949).

21. T. Dobzhansky, "On Species and Races of Living and Fossil Man," *American Journal of Physical Anthropology*, 2 (1944), 251–265; E. Mayr, *Animal Species and Evolution*; G. G. Simpson, "The Meaning of Taxonomic Statements," *Classification and Human Evolution*, ed. S. L. Washburn (New York, 1963), pp. 1–31.

22. R. Dart, "*Australopithecus africanus*: The Man-Ape of South Africa," *Nature*, 115 (1925), 195–199.

23. Clearly anticipating this principle was E. A. Hooton's "The Asymmetrical Character of Human Evolution," *American Journal of Physical Anthropology*, 8 (1925), 125–141.

24. E. L. Simons, "New Fossil Apes from Egypt and the Initial Differentiation of Hominoidea," *Nature*, 205 (1965), 135–139.

25. W. E. L. Clark and D. P. Thomas, *Associated Jaws and Limb Bones of Limnopithecus Macinnesi* (London, 1951); J. Napier and P. R. Davis, "The Fore-Limb Skeleton and Associated Remains of *Proconsul africanus*," *Fossil Mammals*, 16 (1959), 1–78; Helmuth Zapfe, "The Skeleton of Pliopithecus (Epipliopithecus) vindobonensis" in *American Journal of Physical Anthropology*, 16 (1958), 441–455.

26. W. K. Gregory, "Were the Ancestors of Man Primitive Brachiators?" *Proceedings of the American Philosophical Society*, 67 (1929), 129–150.

27. Since all the recent evidence, reviewed by G. G. Simpson, "The Biological Nature of Man," *Science*, 52 (1966), 472–478, indicates that man's closest relatives are the African great apes, theories that our ancestors were other quadrupedal forms are not considered here, but see W. L. Straus, Jr., ed., "Riddle of Man's Ancestry," *Quarterly Review of Biology*, 24 (1949), 200–223, for an alternative point of view.

28. H. P. Klinger, J. L. Hamerton, D. Mutten, and E. M. Lang, "The Chromosomes of the Hominoidea" in *Classification and Human Evolution*, ed. S. L. Washburn.

29. M. Goodman, "Serological Analysis of the Phyletic Relationships of Recent Hominoids," *Human Biology*, vol. 35, pp. 377–436; A. S. Hafleigh and C. A. Williams, Jr., "Antigenic Correspondence of Serum Albumins among the Primates," *Science*, 151 (1966), 1530–1535.

30. V. Sarich and A. Wilson, "Immunological Time Scale for Hominid Evolution," *Science*, 158 (1967), 1200–1202.

31. E. L. Simons, "New Fossil Apes from Egypt and the Initial Differentiation of Hominoidea," *Nature*, pp. 135–138; L. S. B. Leakey, "An Early Miocene Member of Hominidae," *Nature*, 212 (1967), 155–163.

32. T. H. Huxley, *Man's Place in Nature*.

33. W. J. Sollas, *The Age of the Earth* (London, 1905).

34. A. Keith, *New Discoveries Relating to the Antiquity of Man* (London, 1931).

35. A. Knopf, "Time in Earth History," *Genetics, Paleontology, and Evolution*, ed. G. L. Jepsen, E. Mayr, and G. G. Simpson, pp. 1–9; "Measuring Geologic Time," *Study of the Earth*, ed. John F. White (Englewood Cliffs, N. J., 1962). The study of time shows the importance of techniques. In spite of great efforts by many competent scientists, it was not until the development of methods based on atomic disintegration that estimates of time became possible. Carbon 14 and potassium-argon have been particularly important in anthropology. Molecular biology gives great promise of the quantification of biological difference. Functional anatomy remains a primitive science, and, even after two hundred years, there is still no agreement as to how structures should be compared or differences evaluated (see Solly Zuckerman, "Myths and Methods in Anatomy," *Journal of the Royal College of Surgeons of Edinburgh*, vol. 11, pp. 87–114). Progress in statistical methods and computer analysis has not been matched by progress in the understanding of things measured.

36. G. E. Folk, Jr., *Introduction to Environmental Physiology* (Philadelphia, 1966).

37. Frederick Snyder, "Toward an Evolutionary Theory of Dreaming," *American Journal of Psychiatry*, 123 (1966), 121–142. It is

interesting to note that the biology of sleep suggests that the meaning of dreams and their frequency is independent of their content. Here is point of relation between biological and social anthropology. If the social scientist wants to collect dreams without the loss of detail and error that comes with remote recall, the dreamer should be awakened at the end of the Rapid Eye Movement state.

38. R. A. Hinde and N. Tinbergen, "The Comparative Study of Species-Specific Behavior," *Behavior and Evolution*, ed. A. Roe and G. G. Simpson, pp. 251–268.

39. D. A. Hamburg, "Emotions in the Perspective of Human Evolution," *Expression of the Emotions in Man*, ed. P. Knapp, pp. 300–317.

40. H. F. Harlow and M. K. Harlow, "Learning to Love," *American Scientist*, vol. 104, pp. 244–272.

41. C. R. Carpenter, "A Field Study in Siam of the Behavior and Social Relations of the Gibbon (*Hydlobates lar*)," *Comp. Psychol. Monogr.*, 16 (1940); J. O. Ellefson, *A Natural History of Gibbons in the Malay Peninsula* (Doctoral thesis, University of California, Berkeley, 1966).

42. S. L. Washburn and I. DeVore, "The Social Life of Baboons," *Scientific American*, 204 (1961), 62–71.

43. D. S. Sade, "Some Aspects of Parent-Offspring and Sibling Relations in a Group of Rhesus Monkeys, with a Discussion of Grooming," *American Journal of Physical Anthropology*, 23 (1965), 1–17; "Ontogeny of Social Relations in a Free-Ranging Group of Rhesus Monkeys" (Doctoral thesis, University of California, Berkeley, 1966).

44. S. M. Garn, ed., *Culture and the Direction of Human Evolution* (Detroit, 1964); J. N. Spuhler, ed., *The Evolution of Man's Capacity for Culture* (Detroit, 1959).

45. J. R. Napier, "The Locomotor Functions of Hominids," *Classification and Human Evolution* (New York, 1963), pp. 178–189.

46. G. Schaller, *The Mountain Gorilla: Ecology and Behavior* (Chicago, 1963).

47. J. Goodall, "Chimpanzees of the Gombe Stream Reserve," *Primate Behavior: Field Studies of Monkeys and Apes*, ed. I. DeVore, pp. 425–473; V. Reynolds and F. Reynolds, "Chimpanzees of the Budongo Forest," *Primate Behavior: Field Studies of Monkeys and Apes* (New York, 1965), pp. 368–424.

48. R. H. Tuttle, "Knuckle-Walking and the Evolution of Hominoid Hands," *American Journal of Physical Anthropology*, 26 (1967), 171–206.

49. J. van Lawick-Goodall, *My Friends the Wild Chimpanzees* (Washington, D.C., 1967).

50. P. R. Pilbeam, "Man's Earliest Ancestors," *Science Journal*, 3 (1967), 47–53.

51. J. B. Lancaster, "Primate Communication Systems and the Emergence of Human Language," *Patterns of Primate Behavior: Adaptation and Variability* (New York, 1967); E. H. Lenneberg, *Biological Foundations of Language* (New York, 1967).

52. J. Huxley in "The Future of Man—Evolutionary Aspects," *Man and His Future*, ed. G. Wolstenholme (Boston and Toronto, 1963), pp. 1–22, has stated that: "In place of separate subjects each with its own assumptions, methodology and technical jargon, we must envisage networks of co-operative investigation, with common methods and terminology, all eventually linked up in a comprehensive process of enquiry. This, of course, will mean a radical reorganization of scientific teaching and research."

ONE HUNDRED YEARS OF ETHNOLOGY AND SOCIAL ANTHROPOLOGY

1. I wish to record a special indebtedness to the participants in the conference on the History of Anthropology, held April 13–14, 1962, at the Social Science Research Council, New York, N. Y. I must thank the Harvard University Archives for permission to read Clyde Kluckhohn, "Some Aspects of Contemporary Theory in Cultural Anthropology" (Doctoral thesis, Harvard University, 1936). I have also read portions of Marvin Harris, "The Rise of Anthropological Theory, 1750–1965" (New York, in press). Of the papers in this centennial celebration, I have had the privilege of reading only Gordon Willey's on archaeology.

2. Sol Tax, "The Integration of Anthropology," *Yearbook of Anthropology* (New York, 1955), p. 315.

3. See, for example, T. K. Penniman, *A Hundred Years of Anthropology*, 2nd ed. (London, 1952); and A. C. Haddon, *History of Anthropology*, 2nd ed. (London, 1934).

4. A. L. Kroeber, *Configurations of Culture* (Berkeley and Los Angeles, 1944).

5. Thomas S. Kuhn, *The Structure of Scientific Revolutions* (Chicago, 1962).

6. M. J. Herskovits, "A Genealogy of Ethnological Theory," *Context and Meaning in Cultural Anthropology*, ed. M. E. Spiro (New York, 1965), pp. 403–415.

7. In addition to the accounts mentioned in note 3, reference should be made to R. H. Lowie, *History of Ethnological Theory* (New York, 1937), which has long been the standard account for ethnology.

8. See, especially, the publications of George W. Stocking, Jr., who is utilizing the Boas Collection in the Library of the American Philosophical Society to throw new light on the development of American anthropology.

The recent *Guide to Manuscripts Relating to the American Indian in the Library of the American Philosophical Society*, compiled by John F. Freeman (Philadelphia, 1966), indicates the riches available to the historian in these collections. The premature death of Freeman as he was about to embark on a career as a historian of anthropology is a severe loss.

9. J. S. Slotkin, *Readings in Early Anthropology* (New York, 1965), p. vii.

10. M. T. Hodgen, *Early Anthropology in the Sixteenth and Seventeenth Centuries* (Philadelphia, 1964); A. I. Hallowell, "The Beginnings of Anthropology in America," *Selected Papers from the American Anthropologists, 1888–1920*, ed. Frederica de Laguna (Evanston, 1960), pp. 1–90.

11. T. K. Penniman, *A Hundred Years of Anthropology*, pp. 20–21.

12. Summarized from F. Eggan, "Culture History Derived from the Study of Living Peoples," unpub. lecture, the University of Chicago, October 27, 1936.

13. L. H. Morgan, *League of the Iroquois* (New York, 1962). William Fenton, in his "Introduction" to this edition, quotes J. W. Powell to this effect.

14. F. Eggan, "Lewis H. Morgan in Kinship Perspective," *Essays in the Science of Culture in Honor of Leslie A. White*, ed. G. E. Dole and R. L. Carneiro (New York, 1960), pp. 179–201. See, also, F. Eggan, *The American Indian, Perspectives for the Study of Social Change* (Chicago, 1966).

15. Sol Tax, "From Lafitau to Radcliffe-Brown: A Short History

of the Study of Social Organization," *Social Anthropology of North American Tribes*, ed. F. Eggan, enlarged ed. (Chicago, 1955), pp. 443–481.

16. See Edward Lurie, *Louis Agassiz, A Life in Science* (Chicago, 1960), for an excellent account of these controversies, and for a view of the level of scientific development at Harvard and in the nation at mid-century.

17. K. E. Bock, "The Acceptance of Histories, toward a Perspective for Social Science," *University of California Publications in Sociology and Social Institutions*, vol. 3, no. 1 (Berkeley and Los Angeles, 1956), p. 10.

18. See the recently published account by Neil Judd, *The Bureau of American Ethnology, A Partial History* (Norman, Okla., 1967).

19. R. B. Dixon, "Anthropology 1866–1929," *The Development of Harvard University since the Inauguration of President Eliot 1869–1929*, ed. S. E. Morison (Cambridge, Mass., 1930), pp. 202–215.

20. F. H. Cushing's pioneer work is well known and does not need documentation. For Cushing's contribution to primitive classification, see E. Durkheim and M. Mauss, "De quelques formes primitives de classification: Contribution à l'étude des représentations collectives," *Année Sociologique*, 6 (Paris, 1903), trans. Rodney Needham as *Primitive Classification* (Chicago, 1963).

21. For the first adequate account of the career of Alice Fletcher, see Nancy O. Lurie, "Women in Early American Anthropology," *Pioneers of American Anthropology, The Uses of Biography*, ed. June Helm (Seattle, 1966), pp. 31–81.

22. T. K. Penniman, *A Hundred Years of Anthropology*, p. 206.

23. E. B. Tylor, *Primitive Culture* (London, 1871), p. 1. R. R. Marett, in *Tylor* (New York, 1936), has given us a preliminary estimate of his contributions. For a re-evaluation of Tylor's contributions to the concept of culture, see G. W. Stocking, Jr., "Matthew Arnold, E. B. Tylor, and the Uses of Invention," *American Anthropologist*, 65 (1963), 783–799.

24. E. Westermarck, *The History of Human Marriage*, 1st ed. (1891); 5th ed., 3 vols. (London, 1921).

25. F. Boas, "The Limitations of the Comparative Method of Anthropology," *Science*, n.s., 4 (1896), 901–908, reprinted in F. Boas, *Race, Language and Culture* (New York, 1940), pp. 270–280.

26. There is already a considerable literature on Franz Boas. Of particular relevance here are J. W. Gruber, "Horatio Hale and the Development of American Anthropology," *Proceedings of the American Philosophical Society*, vol. 3, no. 1 (Philadelphia, 1967), pp. 5–37; R. P. Rohner, "Franz Boas, Ethnographer on the Northwest Coast" in *Pioneers of American Anthropology*, ed. June Helm (Seattle, 1966), pp. 149–222.

27. See Boas's essays reprinted in *Race, Language and Culture* (New York, 1940).

28. For an account of the trials and tribulations of Putnam in connection with the World Columbian Exposition of 1893, see R. W. Dexter, "Putnam's Problems Popularizing Anthropology," *American Scientist*, 54 (1966), 315–332.

29. The letter, dated May 16, 1901, is given in full in Ross Parmenter, "Glimpses of a Friendship, Zelia Nuttall and Franz Boas," *Pioneers of American Anthropology*, ed. June Helm, pp. 98–101.

30. See, for example, C. Wissler, *The American Indian*, 2nd ed. (New York, 1922); *The Relation of Nature to Man in Aboriginal America* (New York, 1926).

31. See A. L. Kroeber, *Cultural and Natural Areas in Native North America* (Berkeley, 1939); L. Spier, "Problems Arising from the Cultural Position of the Havasupai," *American Anthropologist*, 31 (1929), 213–222.

32. W. H. R. Rivers has not been adequately assessed, so far as his contributions to anthropology are concerned, but the comments by R. Firth and D. M. Schneider in connection with a new edition of *Kinship and Social Organization* (London, 1914) promise to remedy the situation in part.

33. For a review of the theoretical position of the "Culture Circle" group, see Clyde Kluckhohn, "Some Reflections on the Method and Theory of the *Kulturkreislehre*," *American Anthropologist*, 38 (1936), 157–196. A drastic remodeling of its conclusions was foreshadowed in the discussions in Sol Tax *et al.*, eds., *An Appraisal of Anthropology Today* (Chicago, 1953); with the death of Peter Schmidt, the group has largely disbanded.

34. See the tribute to Roland B. Dixon in *Studies in the Anthropology of Oceania and Asia, Presented in Memory of Roland Burrage Dixon*, ed. C. S. Coon and J. M. Andrew IV (Cambridge, Mass., 1943).

35. R. B. Dixon, *Oceanic Mythology*, vol. IX, in *Mythology of All Races* (Boston, 1916); *The Building of Cultures* (New York, 1928).
36. Ralph Linton, *The Tree of Culture* (New York, 1955).
37. In M. Mead and R. Bunzel, eds., *The Golden Age of American Anthropology* (New York, 1960), p. 400.
38. E. Sapir, "Time Perspective in Aboriginal American Culture: A Study in Method," *Canada, Department of Mines, Geological Survey Memoir 90, Anthropological Series No. 13* (Ottawa, 1916).
39. C. Wissler, *The Relation of Nature to Man in Aboriginal America* (New York, 1923); A. L. Kroeber, *Anthropology* (New York, 1923); R. H. Lowie, "Plains Indian Age-Societies," American Museum of Natural History, *Anthropological Papers*, 11 (1916), 877–992; L. Spier, "The Sun Dance of the Plains Indians: Its Development and Diffusion," American Museum of Natural History, *Anthropological Papers*, 16 (1921), 451–529.
40. For this period, I am particularly indebted to E. E. Evans-Pritchard's excellent account in *Social Anthropology* (London, 1951); to M. Fortes, *Social Anthropology at Cambridge Since 1900: An Inaugural Lecture* (Cambridge, England, 1953). I have also made use of my earlier paper, "Social Anthropology and the Method of Controlled Comparison," *American Anthropologist*, 56 (1954), 743–763, which has a further bibliography.
41. His diary for the period 1914–1918, written originally in Polish, has just been published. B. Malinowski, *A Diary in the Strict Sense of the Term* (New York, 1967).
42. B. Malinowski, *Argonauts of the Western Pacific* (London, 1922); *The Sexual Life of Savages in Northwestern Melanesia* (New York, 1929); *Coral Gardens and Their Magic*, 2 vols. (London, 1935).
43. For a review and evaluation of Malinowski's contributions by his students and colleagues, see R. Firth, ed., *Man and Culture, An Evaluation of the Work of Bronislaw Malinowski* (London, 1957).
44. See A. R. Radcliffe-Brown, *The Andaman Islanders* (Cambridge, England, 1922).
45. For a compact view of Radcliffe-Brown's ideas, see his *Structure and Function in Primitive Society, Essays and Addresses* (London, 1952); *A Natural Science of Society* (Glencoe, Ill., 1957); and *Method in Social Anthropology: Selected Essays by A. R. Radcliffe-Brown*, ed. M. N. Srinivas (Chicago, 1958). For his influence see the

essays in F. Eggan, ed., *Social Anthropology of North American Tribes*, enlarged ed. (Chicago, 1955); and in M. Fortes, ed., *Social Structure: Essays Presented to A. R. Radcliffe-Brown* (Oxford, 1949).

46. Ruth Bunzel quotes Boas, who rarely made definite statements, as saying "diffusion is finished," *The Golden Age of American Anthropology*, ed. M. Mead and R. C. Bunzel, p. 574.

47. F. Boas, "Methods of Ethnology," *American Anthropologist*, 22 (1920), 311–322, reprinted in *Race, Language and Culture* (New York, 1940).

48. F. Boas, "Some Problems of Methodology in the Social Sciences," *The New Social Science*, ed. L. D. White (Chicago, 1930), p. 98.

49. Robert Redfield, "Introduction," *Social Anthropology of North American Tribes*, ed. F. Eggan, p. ix.

50. M. Mead, *An Anthropologist at Work: Writings of Ruth Benedict* (Boston, 1959), especially pp. 326 ff.

51. See W. Lloyd Warner, *Yankee City* (New Haven, 1963), for a summary of the "Yankee City" series; and A. Davis, B. Gardner, and M. Gardner, *Deep South* (Chicago, 1941).

52. See C. Kluckhohn, "Some Reflections on the Method and Theory of the *Kulturkreislehre*," pp. 157–196; "The Place of Theory in Anthropological Studies," *Philosophy of Science*, 6 (1939), 328–344; "The Conceptual Structure of Middle American Studies," *The Maya and Their Neighbors* (New York, 1940), pp. 41–51.

53. R. Redfield, M. J. Herskovits, and R. Linton, "A Memorandum for the Study of Acculturation," *American Anthropologist*, 38 (1936), 149–152.

54. See, for examples, C. Geertz, ed., *Old Societies and New States: The Quest for Modernity in Asia and Africa* (Glencoe, 1963); and E. H. Spicer, ed., *Perspectives in American Indian Culture Change* (Chicago, 1961).

55. M. Fortes, *Social Anthropology at Cambridge since 1900* (Cambridge, England, 1953), pp. 14–16.

56. See, for examples, the studies of Max Gluckman and his students, and particularly Gluckman, *Order and Rebellion in Tribal Africa* (London, 1963); L. A. Fallers, *Bantu Bureaucracy* (Cambridge, England, 1956); *The King's Men, Leadership and Status in Buganda on the Eve of Independence* (Oxford, 1964).

57. A. L. Kroeber, chairman, *Anthropology Today: An Encyclo-*

pedic Inventory (Chicago, 1953); and Sol Tax *et al.*, eds., *An Appraisal of Anthropology Today.* See also, *The Yearbook of Anthropology* (New York, 1955).

58. For two among many contributions from the Values Project, see F. R. Kluckhohn and F. L. Strodtbeck, *Variations in Value Orientations* (Evanston, 1961); and E. Z. Vogt and E. M. Albert, eds., *People of Rimrock, A Study of Values in Five Cultures* (Cambridge, Mass., 1966).

59. For an appreciation of Leslie A. White, see Gertrude Dole and R. L. Carneiro, eds., *Essays in the Science of Culture, in Honor of Leslie A. White* (New York, 1960). L. A. White, *The Evolution of Culture* (New York, 1959), presents his recent views; and M. D. Sahlins and E. R. Service, eds., *Evolution and Culture* (Ann Arbor, 1960), clarify and carry them further.

60. Julian Steward, *Theory of Cultural Change* (Urbana, 1955); Robert McC. Adams, *The Evolution of Urban Society* (Chicago, 1966). See also R. A. Manners, ed., *Process and Pattern in Culture, Essays in Honor of Julian Steward* (Chicago, 1964).

61. G. P. Murdock, *Social Structure* (New York, 1949). See, also, Frank W. Moore, ed., *Readings in Cross-Cultural Methodology* (New Haven, 1961).

62. See C. Lévi-Strauss, *Structural Anthropology* (New York, 1963), for a translation of his major essays and papers. *Les Structures élémentaires de la parente* (Paris, 1949) is in process of translation and *La Pensée sauvage* (Paris, 1962) has just been published as *The Savage Mind* (London, 1966).

63. See F. Eggan, "Social Anthropology: Methods and Concepts," in *Social Anthropology of North American Tribes;* A. van Gennep, *Rites de passage* (Paris, 1909), trans. as *The Rites of Passage* (London, 1960); M. Mauss, "Essai sur le don: forme et raison de l'échange dans les sociétés archaiques," *Année Sociologique,* n.s., 1 (1925), 30–186, trans. as *The Gift* (Glencoe, 1954).

64. See, for example, the now classic dispute between Boas and Kroeber with regard to the nature of "History and Science in Anthropology," *American Anthropologist,* 37 (1935), 539–569; and 38 (1936), 137–141. For modern developments, see S. F. Nadel, *The Foundations of Social Anthropology* (Glencoe, 1951).

65. See E. E. Evans-Pritchard, "Anthropology and History," *Essays in Social Anthropology* (Glencoe, 1963), pp. 64–65; and M.

Fortes, *Social Anthropology at Cambridge Since 1900* (Cambridge, England, 1953), p. 35. For the view that "anthropology is the most scientific of the humanities [and] the most humanist of the sciences," see Eric Wolf's *Anthropology* (Englewood Cliffs, N.J., 1964).

66. A. R. Radcliffe-Brown, *Structure and Function in Primitive Society* (London, 1952), pp. 113–114.

67. E. E. Evans-Pritchard, "Anthropology and History," *Essays in Social Anthropology*, p. 47; F. Eggan, *The American Indian, Perspective for the Study of Social Change* (Chicago, 1966); A. Spoehr, "Observations on the Study of Kinship," *American Anthropologist*, 52 (1950), 11.

68. For A. I. Hallowell's contribution, see M. E. Spiro, ed., *Context and Meaning in Cultural Anthropology* (New York, 1965).

69. For psychological anthropology, see Francis Hsu, ed., *Psychological Anthropology* (Homewood, Illinois, 1961); and Bert Kaplan, ed., *Studying Personality Cross-Culturally* (Evanston, 1961). On political anthropology, see M. J. Swartz, A. Tuden, and V. W. Turner, eds., *Political Anthropology: An Introduction* (Chicago, 1967). For economic anthropology, see M. J. Herskovits, *Economic Anthropology* (New York, 1952); K. Polyani, C. M. Arensberg, and H. W. Pearson, eds., *Trade and Market in the Early Empires* (Glencoe, 1957); June Helm, ed., *Essays in Economic Anthropology* (Seattle, 1965).

70. The results of the conference on new approaches in social anthropology has now been published as *Monographs 1–4, Association of Social Anthropologists*, under the general editorship of Michael Banton and with an "Introduction" by Max Gluckman and Fred Eggan: 1. "The Relevance of Models for Social Anthropology"; 2. "Political Systems and the Distribution of Power"; 3. "Anthropological Approaches to the Study of Religion"; 4. "The Social Anthropology of Complex Societies" (London and New York, 1965–1966).

71. A. R. Radcliffe-Brown, "The Comparative Method in Social Anthropology," *The Huxley Memorial Lecture for 1951*, Royal Anthropological Institute of Great Britain and Ireland (London, 1951), p. 22.

72. Eric Wolf, *Anthropology* (Englewood Cliffs, N.J., 1964), p. 97.

ONE HUNDRED YEARS OF ANTHROPOLOGICAL LINGUISTICS

1. E. B. Tyler, *Researches into the Early History of Mankind* (London, 1865, and Chicago, 1964). Following page references are to the 1964 edition.

2. E. G. Condillac, *Sur l'Origine des connaissances humaines* (Paris, 1946); J. J. Rousseau, *Essai sur l'origine des langues* (Paris, 1750); P. L. M. de Maupertuis, "Reflexions philosophiques sur l'origine des langues et la signification des mots," *Les oeuvres de M. de Maupertuis* (Dresden, 1752); Adam Smith, "Considerations concerning the First Formation of Languages, and the Different Genius of Original and Compounded Languages," *The Theory of Moral Sentiments*, 2nd ed. (London, 1761); G. W. v. Leibnitz, *Nouveaux essais sur l'entendement humain* (Paris, 1765); J. P. Süssmilch, *Versuch eines Beweises, dass die erste Sprache ihren Ursprung nicht von Menschen sondern allein vom Schöpfer erhalten habe* (Berlin, 1766); J. G. v. Herder, *Der Ursprung der Sprache* (Berlin, 1772); James Burnet, Lord Monboddo, *Of the Origin and Progress of Language* (Edinburgh, 1773).

3. Jakob Grimm, *Über den Ursprung der Sprache* (Berlin, 1851); Heymann Steinthal, *Der Ursprung der Sprache, im Zusammenhange mit den letzten Fragen alles Wissens: Eine Darstellung der Ansicht Wilhelm v. Humboldts, verglichen mit denen Herders und Hamanns* (Berlin, 1851); Ernest Renan, *De l'Origine du langage*, 2nd ed. (Paris, 1858); F. W. Farrar, *An Essay on the Origin of Language* (London, 1860); Max Mueller, *Lectures on the Science of Language* (Cambridge, England, 1861); August Schleicher, *Die Darwinsche Theorie und die Sprachwissenschaft* (Weimar, 1863) trans. A. V. W. Bickers as *Darwinism Tested by the Science of Language* (London, 1869); *Über die Bedeutung der Sprache für die Naturgeschichte des Menschen* (Weimar, 1865).

4. Hensleigh Wedgwood, *On the Origin of Language* (London, 1866); W. H. I. Bleek, *On the Origin of Language*, ed. E. Häckel, and trans. T. Davidson (New York, 1869); Lazarus Geiger, *Der Ursprung der Sprache* (Stuttgart, 1869); William D. Whitney, *Oriental and Linguistic Studies* (New York, 1873); *The Life and Growth of Language: An Outline of Linguistic Science* (New York, 1875); Ludwig Noiré, *The Origin and Philosophy of Language*, 2nd

ed., rev. and enlarged from earlier works of 1874 and 1879 (Chicago, 1917); Anton Marty, *Über den Ursprung der Sprache* (Würzburg, 1875); Horatio Hale, "The Origin of Languages and the Antiquity of Speaking Man," *Proceedings of the American Association for the Advancement of Science*, 35, (1886), 276–323.

5. Otto Jespersen, *Progress in Language, with Special Reference to English* (London and New York, 1894); Edward Sapir, "Herder's *Ursprung der Sprache*," *Modern Philology*, 5 (1907), 109–142; W. Wundt, *Völkerpsychologie, I: Die Sprache* (Leipzig, 1911); G. A. DeLaguna, *Speech: Its Function and Development* (New Haven, 1927); G. H. Mead, *Mind, Self, and Society* (Chicago, 1934); R. A. Wilson, *The Birth of Language: Its Place in World Evolution and Its Structure in Relation to Space and Time* (London, 1939); G. Révész, *Ursprung und Vorgeschichte der Sprache* (Bern, 1946), trans. J. Butler as *The Origins and Prehistory of Language* (New York, 1956); Bernhard Rosenkranz, *Der Ursprung der Sprache* (Heidelberg, 1961).

6. E. B. Tyler, *Researches into the Early History of Mankind*, p. 48.

7. *Ibid.*, p. 49.

8. *Ibid.*, p. 11.

9. *Ibid.*

10. *Ibid.*, p. 49.

11. *Ibid.*, p. 51.

12. *Ibid.*, p. 11.

13. *Ibid.*, p. 18.

14. *Ibid.*, p. 54.

15. *Ibid.*, p. 19.

16. *Ibid.*, p. 20.

17. *Ibid.*, p. 9.

18. *Ibid.*, p. 57.

19. *Ibid.*, p. 12.

20. E. H. Lenneberg, "The Capacity for Language Acquisition," in *The Structure of Language: Readings in the Philosophy of Language*, ed. J. A. Fodor and J. J. Katz (Englewood Cliffs, N. J., 1964), p. 589.

21. *Ibid.*

22. E. H. Lenneberg, "Language, Evolution, and Purposive Be-

havior," in *Culture and History: Essays in Honor of Paul Radin*, ed. S. Diamond (New York, 1960); "A Biological Perspective of Language," in *New Directions in the Study of Language*, ed. E. H. Lenneberg (Cambridge, Mass., 1964), pp. 65–88; "The Capacity for Language Acquisition," in *The Structure of Language*, pp. 579–603; "The Natural History of Language," in *The Genesis of Language: A Psycholinguistic Approach*, ed. Frank Smith and G. A. Miller (Cambridge, Mass., 1966); "Speech Development: Its Anatomical and Physiological Components," in *Brain Function, Vol. III: Speech, Language and Communication*, ed. E. C. Carterette (Berkeley and Los Angeles, 1966), pp. 37–58; *Biological Foundations of Language* (New York, 1967).

23. Norman Geschwind, "The Development of the Brain and the Evolution of Language," in *Monograph Series on Language and Linguistics*, 17 (Washington, 1964), pp. 155–169; "Disconnection Syndromes in Man and Animal" in *Brain*, 88 (1965), 237–294.

24. W. Penfield and T. Rasmussen, *The Cerebral Cortex of Man: A Clinical Study of Localization of Function* (New York, 1950).

25. W. Penfield and L. Roberts, *Speech and Brain Mechanisms* (Princeton, 1959).

26. L. Roberts, "Central Brain Mechanisms in Speech," in *Brain Function, Vol. III: Speech, Language and Communication*, ed. E. C. Carterette (Berkeley and Los Angeles, 1966), pp. 17–22.

27. F. Chauchard, "Emission and Reception of Sounds at the Level of the Central Nervous System in Vertebrates," in *The Acoustic Behavior of Animals*, ed. R. G. Busnel (Amsterdam, 1963).

28. Peter Marler, "Inheritance and Learning in the Development of Animal Vocalizations," *The Acoustic Behavior of Animals*, ed. R. G. Busnel; "Communication in Monkeys and Apes," in *Primate Behavior: Field Studies of Monkeys and Apes* (New York, 1965).

29. C. F. Hockett, "The Origin of Speech," *Scientific American*, September, 1960, pp. 88–111; "Logical Considerations in the Study of Animal Communication," *Animal Sounds and Communications*, ed. W. E. Lanyon and W. N. Tavolga (Washington, 1960).

30. P. C. Reynolds, "Evolution of Primate Vocal-Auditory Communication Systems," *American Anthropologist*, 70 (1968), in press.

31. William Jones, *Asiatic Researches*, vol. I (Calcutta, 1788).

32. John T. Waterman, *Perspectives in Linguistics* (Chicago, 1963), p. 40.

33. *Ibid.*; Holger Pedersen, *Linguistic Science in the Nineteenth Century,* trans. J. W. Spargo (Cambridge, Mass., 1931), reissued under title of *The Discovery of Language* (Bloomington, 1962); Hanns Oertel, *Lectures on the Study of Language* (New York and London, 1902).

34. Rasmus K. Rask, *Undersögelse om det Gamle Nordiske eller Islandske Sprogs Oprindelse* (Copenhagen, 1814); Jakob Grimm, *Deutsche Grammatik,* 2nd ed. (Göttingen, 1822).

35. Trans. quoted from Hanns Oertel, *Lectures on the Study of Language,* p. 57.

36. August Schleicher, *Die Darwinsche Theorie und die Sprachwissenschaft,* trans. A. V. W. Bikkers, *Darwinism Tested by the Science of Language* (London, 1869).

37. Otto Schrader, trans. F. B. Jevons, *Prehistoric Antiquities of the Aryan Peoples: A Manual of Comparative Philology and the Earliest Culture* (London, 1890), pp. 48–73.

38. Hanns Oertel, *Lectures on the Study of Language,* pp. 259–273; Holger Pedersen, *The Discovery of Language* (Bloomington, 1962), pp. 292 ff.; John T. Waterman, *Perspectives in Linguistics,* pp. 48–55.

39. Otto Schrader, *Prehistoric Antiquities of the Aryan Peoples,* p. iii.

40. *Ibid.,* p. iv.

41. Edward Sapir, "The Concept of Phonetic Law as Tested in Primitive Languages by Leonard Bloomfield," in *Methods in Social Science: A Case Book,* ed. Stuart Rice (Chicago, 1931), pp. 297–306; C. F. Hockett, "Implications of Bloomfield's Algonquian Studies," *Language,* 24 (1948), 117–131.

42. Morris Swadesh, "Salish Internal Relationships," *International Journal of American Linguistics,* 16 (1950), 157–167; "Diffusional Cumulation and Archaic Residue as Historical Explanations," *Southwestern Journal of Anthropology,* 7 (1951), 1–21.

43. R. Lees, "The Basis of Glottochronology," *Language,* 29 (1953), 113–127.

44. Dell Hymes, "Lexicostatistics So Far," *Current Anthropology,* 1 (1960), 3–44.

45. K. Bergsland and H. Vogt, "On the Validity of Glottochronology," *Current Anthropology,* 3 (1962), 115–153.

46. H. G. Lunt, "Discussion of Dyen (1964)," *Proceedings of the*

Ninth International Congress of Linguists, ed. H. G. Lunt (The Hague, 1964), pp. 247–252.

47. Morris Swadesh, "Toward Greater Accuracy in Lexicostatistic Dating," *International Journal of American Linguistics,* 21 (1955), 121–137; Martin Joos, "Glottochronology with Rentention-Rate Homogeneity," *Proceedings of the Ninth International Congress of Linguists,* ed. H. G. Lunt, p. 237; J. N. Van der Merwe, "New Mathematics for Glottochronology," *Current Anthropology,* 7 (1966), 485–500.

48. Rasmus K. Rask, *Undersögelse om det Gamle Nordiske eller Islandske Sprogs Oprindelse;* trans. quoted from T. Waterman, *Perspectives in Linguistics.*

49. Isidore Dyen, "The Lexicostatistical Classification of Malayo-Polynesian Languages," *Language,* 38 (1962), 38–46; "Lexicostatistically Determined Borrowing and Taboo," *Language,* 39 (1963), 60–66; "On the Validity of Comparative Lexicostatistics," in *Proceedings of the Ninth International Congress of Linguists,* ed. H. G. Lunt, pp. 238–247; "A Lexicostatistical Classification of the Austronesian Languages," *International Journal of American Linguistics,* Memoir 19, (1965).

50. F. v. Schlegel, *Über die Sprache und Weisheit der Indier: Ein Beitrag zur Begrundung der Alterthumskunde* (Heidelberg, 1808 p. 28), trans. quoted from Hanns Oertel, *Lectures on the Study of Language,* p. 36.

51. F. v. Schlegel, *ibid.,* p. 56.

52. *Ibid.,* p. 49.

53. A. v. Schlegel, "Observations sur la langue et la litérature provençales," in *Essais litteraires et historiques* (Bonn, 1842), pp. 211–340.

54. W. v. Humboldt, "Über das Entstehen der grammatischen Formen und ihren Einfluss auf die Ideenentwicklung," *Die sprachphilosophischen, Werke Wilhelm's von Humboldt,* ed. H. Steinthal (Berlin, 1884).

55. A. F. Pott, in *Jahrbücher der freien deutschen Akademie,* vol. I, 1848. Publication (and title) unavailable; see references in H. Steinthal, *Die Classification der Sprachen, dargestellt als die Entwickelung der Sprachidee* (Berlin, 1850), p. 7, and in O. Jespersen, "The Classification of Languages," *Selected Writings of Otto Jespersen* (London and Tokyo, n.d.), p. 698.

56. August Schleicher, *Sprachvergleichende Untersuchungen, Vol. I: Zur vergleichenden Sprachgeschichte* (Bonn, 1848).

57. Max Mueller, letter to Chevalier Bunsen, "On the Classification of the Turanian Languages," in *Outlines of the Philosophy of Universal History*, vol. I, by C. C. J. Bunsen (London, 1854), pp. 263–521.

58. *Ibid.*, p. 284.

59. Max Mueller, *Lectures on the Science of Language*, 2nd rev. ed. (New York, 1862).

60. William D. Whitney, *The Life and Growth of Language.*

61. P. S. DuPonceau, "Report of the Corresponding Secretary to the Committee, of His Progress in the Investigation Committed to Him, and of the General Character and Forms of the Languages of the American Indians," *Transactions of the American Philosophical Society*, 1 (1819), xvii–xlvi; *Mémoire sur le système grammatical des langues de quelques nations indiennes de l'Amérique du nord* (Paris, 1838).

62. Mary R. Haas, "Grammar or Lexicon? The American Indian Side of the Question from DuPonceau to Powell," paper read at the annual meeting of the Linguistic Society of America, December 1966.

63. William D. Whitney, *The Life and Growth of Language*, p. 238.

64. *Ibid.*

65. *Ibid.*

66. F. v. Schlegel, *Über die Sprache und Weisheit der Indier*, p. 49.

67. J. W. Powell, *Introduction to the Study of Indian Languages* (Washington, 1880), p. 70. Italics mine.

68. *Ibid.*, p. 74c.

69. William D. Whitney, *The Life and Growth of Language*, p. 261.

70. André Lefèvre, *Race and Language* (New York, 1894).

71. Otto Jespersen, *Progress in Language, With Special Reference to English* (London and New York, 1894); "The Classification of Languages," *Scientia*, 28 (1920); *Language: Its Nature, Development and Origin* (London, 1922); "Efficiency in Linguistic Change," *Historiskfilologiske Meddelelser*, 27 (1949).

72. Franz Boas, *The Mind of Primitive Man*, rev. ed. (New York, 1938), p. 194.

73. Edward Sapir, *Language: An Introduction to the Study of Speech* (New York, 1921).

74. *Ibid.*, p. 233. Italics mine.

75. Franz Boas, *The Mind of Primitive Man* (New York, 1911), p. 154.

76. Edward Sapir, *Language*, p. 233.

77. Franz Boas, "Introduction" to the *Handbook of American Indian Languages* (Washington, 1911), p. 63.

78. Edward Sapir, *Selected Writing of Edward Sapir in Language, Culture, and Personality*, ed. D. G. Mandelbaum (Berkeley and Los Angeles, 1949), p. 162. Italics mine.

79. Franz Boas, "Introduction" to the *Handbook of American Indian Languages*, p. 71. Italics mine.

80. *Ibid.*

81. Edward Sapir, *Selected Writings*, p. 153.

82. *Ibid.*, p. 162.

83. Franz Boas, "Introduction" to the *Handbook of American Indian Languages*, pp. 6–14; *The Mind of Primitive Man* (1911), pp. 124–139.

84. Franz Boas, "Introduction" to the *Handbook of American Indian Languages*, pp. 24–25; *The Mind of Primitive Man* (1911), pp. 142–143. Italics mine. The explanation of the intended meaning of "phonetic groups" is only in *The Mind of Primitive Man*.

85. Franz Boas, "Introduction" to the *Handbook of American Indian Languages*, p. 25; *The Mind of Primitive Man* (1911), p. 145. Italics mine.

86. *Ibid.*, p. 152.

87. Franz Boas, "On Alternating Sounds," *American Anthropologist*, 2 (1889), 47–53.

88. Franz Boas, *The Mind of Primitive Man* (1911), p. 154.

89. Edward Sapir, *Selected Writings*, p. 102. Italics mine.

90. Franz Boas, "Introduction" to the *Handbook of American Indian Languages*, p. 56.

91. Franz Boas, "The Classification of American Languages," *American Anthropologist*, n.s., 22 (1920), 367–376; "Classification of American Indian Languages," *Language*, 5 (1929), p. 1–7.

92. Franz Boas, "Introduction" to the *Handbook of American Indian Languages*, p. 63.

93. Edward Sapir, "Conceptual Categories in Primitive Languages," *Science*, 74 (1931), 578.

94. Edward Sapir, "Sound Patterns in Language," *Language*, 1 (1925), 37–51, reprinted in Edward Sapir, *Selected Writings*, pp. 33–45; "La Realité psychologique des phonemes," *Journal de Psychologie Normale et Pathologique*, 30 (1933), 247–265, reprinted as "The Psychological Reality of Phonemes" in Edward Sapir, *Selected Writings*, pp. 46–60.

95. B. L. Whorf, *Language, Thought, and Reality: Selected Writings of Benjamin Lee Whorf*, ed. John B. Carroll (Cambridge, Mass., 1956), 212–214.

96. *Ibid.*, p. 68.

97. *Ibid.*, p. 79.

98. *Ibid.*, p. 72.

99. L. Bloomfield, *Language* (New York, 1933), p. 139.

100. *Ibid.*, p. 141.

101. *Ibid.*, p. 162.

102. Noam Chomsky, *Cartesian Linguistics: A Chapter in the History of Rationalist Thought* (New York and London, 1966).

103. W. H. Goodenough, *Property, Kin, and Community on Truk* (New Haven, 1951); "Componential Analysis and the Study of Meaning," *Language*, 32 (1956), 195–216; H. C. Conklin, "Lexicographical Treatment of Folk Taxonomies," *Problems in Lexicography*, ed. F. W. Householder and S. Saporta (Bloomington, Ind., 1962); C. O. Frake, "The Diagnosis of Disease among the Subanun of Mindanao," *American Anthropologist*, 63 (1961), 113–132; "The Ethnographic Study of Cognitive Systems," *Anthropology and Human Behavior*, ed. T. Gladwin and W. C. Sturtevant (Washington, 1962).

104. Edward Sapir, *Language*, p. 234.

105. W. C. Sturtevant, "Studies in Ethnoscience," *Transcultural Studies in Cognition*, ed. A. K. Romney and R. G. Andrade, special publication of *American Anthropologist*, 66 (1964); B. N. Colby, "Ethnographic Semantics: A Preliminary Survey," *Current Anthropology*, 7 (1966), 3–32; Dell Hymes, "Directions in Ethnolinguistic Theory," *Transcultural Studies in Cognition*; E. A. Hammel, ed., *Formal Semantic Analysis*, special publication of *American Anthropologist*, 67 (1965).

106. U. Weinreich, "On the Semantic Structure of Language," *Universals of Language,* ed. J. N. Greenberg (Cambridge, Mass., 1963); "Explorations in Semantic Theory," *Current Trends in Linguistics, Vol III: Theoretical Foundations,* ed. T. A. Sebeok (The Hague, 1966); J. Katz and J. Fodor, "The Structure of a Semantic Theory," *Language,* 39 (1963), 170–210; S. Lamb, "The Semanic Approach to Structural Semantics," *Transcultural Studies in Cognition,* ed. A. K. Romney and R. G. D'Andrade; J. Lyons, *Structural Semantics* (Oxford, 1963); J. J. Katz, *The Philosophy of Language* (New York, 1966).

107. Stephen Ullmann, *The Principles of Semantics,* 2nd ed. (New York, 1963); N. C. W. Spence, "Linguistic Fields, Conceptual Systems and the Weltbild," *Transactions of the Philological Society,* 1961; Harold Basilius, "Neo-Humboldtian Ethnolinguistics," *Word,* 8 (1952), 95–105; Suzanne Öhman, "Theories of the 'Linguistic Field,'" *Word,* 9 (1953), 123–134; J. T. Waterman, "Benjamin Lee Whorf and Linguistic Field Theory," *Southwestern Journal of Anthropology,* 13 (1957), 201–211.

Index

Acheulian industry, 58

Adams, R. McC., his *The Evolution of Urban Society,* 50-51; 142

Agassiz, Louis, 15, 22, 124

Agricultural societies, 39, 40, 47, 84, 87-88, 91; rise of New World, 49-50, 86; and development of cities, 51

Alliance theory, 144. *See also* Kinship

American Academy of Arts and Sciences, 15

American Anthropological Association, 133-134

American Antiquarian Society, 15

American archaeology, 6, 29-53; Speculative Period, 29, 30-35, 57; Descriptive Period, 29, 35-40, 57; Descriptive-Historic Period, 29, 40-44, 57; Comparative-Historic Period, 29, 30, 44-53, 57. *See also* Archaeology; Prehistory

American Indians, *see* Indians, American

American Journal of Science, 76

American Museum of Natural History, 15, 129, 130; founded, 125

American Philosophical Society, 15

American School of Prehistoric Research, 14, 21

Ancient Monuments in the Mississippi Valley (Squier and Davis), 24

Andersson, J. Gunnar, 77

Anthropology, 119-121; five major phases of, 5-6; professionalization of, 121-127; early acceptance (1900-1930), 127-134; expansion of as science, 134-

144; new developments (1960's), 144-149; psychological, 147; political, 147; economic, 147; future research in, 148-149

"Anthropology Today," Wenner-Gren symposium, 141

Antiquity (journal), 73

Archaeological Institute of America, 15, 126

Archaeology, 16, 119, 132, 137, 141, 147; professionalization of, 36-37; and culture process, 46-51; new techniques, 72-74, 88-89; scientific aids to, 74-77. *See also* American archaeology; Prehistory, Old World

Archaic period, 42, 46

Arctic, 46, 47

Art, 92; Paleolithic, 77-78

Artifacts, 35, 52; cross-dating of, 75. *See also* Relics

Asiatic Mesolithic culture, 47, 48

Association pour l'Avancement des Sciences in Montauban, French, 78

Atwater, Caleb, 32, 33

Australopithecus, 103-104, 106

Aztecs, 125, 217

Bacon, Francis, 165

Bacon, Francis H., 69

Bandelier, A. F., 125

Bartram, William, 32

Basilius, Harold, 225

Bastian, Adolf, 122-123, 126

Beazeley, G. A., 73

Begouen, Comte Henri, 78

Behavior, evolution of, 97-98, 114-115; and social organization, 109-110; and man's use of space, 110-114